PERSPECTIVES ON EPIC

PERSPECTIVES ON EPIC

EDITED BY Frederick H. Candelaria

AND William C. Strange   Both, University of Oregon

ALLYN AND BACON, INC. • BOSTON, 1965

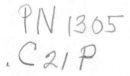
ALLYN AND BACON CASEBOOK SERIES

GENERAL EDITOR • LEONARD F. DEAN

PREFACE

Perhaps no anthology like this one has been attempted before because the epic is indeed a vast subject and the approaches to it varied. But the appeal, too, is vast and varied.

No other genre has the scope of epic, if we define epic and the epic spirit (as E. M. W. Tillyard does) to include certain novels and dramas such as *War and Peace* and Shakespeare's history plays. Even more strictly defined, the epic is *the* genre of the heroic age, and so succeeds better than any other form in evoking (and perhaps provoking) the heroic spirit in our unheroic age. There is also the appeal of literary problems posed by the many changes epic has undergone.

What is involved in the transformation of the oral (primary) epic into the literary (secondary) epic; of the heroic poem into the romance; of serious epics into mock epics; of the epic poem into the epic novel? Are works so diverse as *The Odyssey, The Divine Comedy,* and *The Wasteland; The Rape of the Lock, Joseph Andrews* and *Tom Jones, The Prelude,* and *War and Peace;* and Shakespeare's histories—all epics? Why was the epic so highly regarded in the Renaissance, an age so rich in other literary forms? Usually, epics are thought of as long poems, but is (as Poe asked) a long poem really possible? Is epic possible today?

The essays, chronologically arranged to correspond with the evolution of epic over the ages (historical and literary "periods"), and the exhibits, arranged to illustrate formal and other aspects of epic, are, respectively, secondary and primary materials that should be used with any of the several epics readily available in paperback books. The essays and exhibits will illuminate historical and critical questions that are raised in studying epics and other forms in introductory "types" courses, English literature survey courses, world literature panoramas, and advanced genre studies. The exhibits that comprise the second part of the book are primary materials especially useful for controlled research topics in teaching the research paper in freshman composition courses.

It is a pleasure to acknowledge the help and encouragement we received in preparing this book from Professor Leonard F. Dean, our general editor, the editoral staff of Allyn and Bacon, and especially Marilyn Triplett for her secretarial assistance.

Frederick Candelaria
William C. Strange

CONTENTS

PART ONE

✿

✿

ESSAYS

LITERATURE WITHOUT LETTERS*

Rhys Carpenter

The study of literature is an enterprise so vast that no one human mind can cope with it successfully. The multiplicity of languages, the centuries of time, are too formidable. Books and manuscripts, printed or written, recent, medieval, and ancient, make a total too great for a single lifetime's reading. And yet this terrifying array, stretching from the pyramid texts of Egypt down to the novels of our own day, derives from only a fraction of the years and a portion of the lands in which human literary activity has flourished—if we will admit the etymological contradiction that literature may exist without letters.

The craft of printing is only five hundred years old; European knowledge of paper dates back only a thousand years; the very art of writing has been known to most European peoples for less than two thousand years and nowhere, not even in China or Egypt or Mesopotamia, seems to be appreciably older than five thousand. A respectable antiquity, this last one! But how much older still are poetry and song and the craft of telling enthralling stories to attentive ears? Without benefit of writing, songs may be composed, sung, remembered, and sung again; adventures may be told, incidents, anecdotes, and marvelous happenings recounted; even poetry of great range and power and beauty may come into being and persist, nor die with the passing of its maker. Beside and beyond the known realm of written literature stretches interminably the almost unknown world of oral literature, whose merest fraction has been reduced to written or printed form.

Speech must be almost as old as humankind; song must be almost as old as speech; and poetry almost as old as song. Against this enormous vista, writing, on which our literary types depend, is almost a modernism. It is idle to ask how old is language, since no one, seemingly, yet knows securely the age of sentient loquent man; wherefore it is impossible to venture even a plausible guess at the antiquity of oral

* Rhys Carpenter, *Folk Tale, Fiction and Saga in the Homeric Epics* (Berkeley and Los Angeles: University of California Press, 1962), originally published as Vol. XX of the Sather Classical Lectures. Reprinted by permission.

literary forms. Yet is is fairly safe to say that, with the antiquity of writing nowhere transcending five thousand years, the literature of unwritten speech must outdate its written competitor and successor by many times its measure. Attic tragedy and history, Plato and the pre-Socratics, will then become milestones set only a little distance back along the road which leads to the shadowy unwritten beginnings of literature. What seems a giant stride back into the past from Ibsen to Aeschylos is but a step that could be repeated many times before we should come to man's primal discovery of the magic of assonances and cadences, when he began to use speech for something more than the mere grunted communication of his immediate want. But these other steps behind Aeschylos are steps into darkness where it is difficult to catch even a glimmer of a lost world.

Yet we are not, like the paleontologists, seeking for things utterly extinct. Out of this immeasurable past, oral literature still survives today, both in its own right in its own true oral forms as well as in written record of itself, preserved before it died out in the past. But it has suffered and diminished greatly, and in many lands where once it flourished it is all but extinct today, because literacy, the spreading use of writing, everywhere sooner or later destroys it.

Perhaps you remember the scene in Victor Hugo's *Notre-Dame* where a cleric makes the rather cryptic remark that the printed book will ultimately destroy the carven edifice of the cathedral wherein architecture and its attendant arts in the past had set the visual record of man's thoughts. "The book will kill the building," he insists; "this will kill that—*ceci tuera cela!*"

So it has been with the impact of writing on oral literature: *"ceci tuera cela!"* And human memory, which once perforce kept all human records, relinquished its powers to the newcomer and grew proportionately enfeebled with this cession of her strength. Most of us today can hardly credit the achievement of the *illiterati* who knew the Koran by heart or carried the entire Iliad and Odyssey in their minds. But nowadays whoever trusts his library and notebooks may no longer trust his remembrance. Only where memory cannot be displaced, as in the concert recitals of musicians or the operatic roles of singers, can we still observe its prodigious powers. But originally Mnemosyne was mother of *all* the Muses.

In the world of today, where the spread of literacy has remorselessly been destroying the oral literary forms and only the lowest cultural levels preserve their preliterate traditions, oral literature has had to take refuge with the peasant and with backward cultures. But there the strata which have escaped schooling will continue to foster it, and in all levels the children still too young to have acquired letters will be its eager audience. But the mature, the intelligent, the gifted of mankind will despise and neglect it and let it die. For this reason it has been able to survive only in such forms as the peasant or the immature mind likes, understands, and practices. Yet it has not always been so in the past; and it is not everywhere so, even today.

World over, the gradations of oral literature seem to be three: among fully literate nations like those of western Europe there is a prose form enshrining folk tales and *Märchen* of considerable variety; among partly literate peoples like those of eastern Europe there may also exist traditional verse forms, narrative ballads, often remembered through many generations and begetting imitative improvisations in like genre; while among wholly illiterate (but not therefore uncivilized) races there may flourish fully organized oral literature of unrestricted range and high artistic merit, such as has existed among Norse- and Celtic- and Greek-speaking peoples. It is in this latter environment that heroic epic properly belongs.

There is thus a sort of hierarchy of oral literature, with heroic epic near the highest and children's fairy tales near the lowest place; but there is a real and great difficulty in explaining how such a hierarchy is formed. If folk tale and fairy story are the last to resist the onset of literacy, shall we say that therefore these must merely be the hardest to kill, the toughest and stoutest of oral forms, able to outlive their more susceptible kindred? or shall we maintain that they more properly resemble a band of desperate survivors making their final stand in the only stronghold still uncaptured by the enemy, so that fugitives from all ranks may be found among them—from heroic epics, songs and ballads, myths and fables and adventure stories, all reduced to the lowly guise of *Märchen*? Are modern remnants of oral literature a historical residue of all that was great and good in the illiterate past? or—to change the metaphor—are they but a feeble growth of weeds in a poor man's garden from which all the statelier flowers have long since been taken?

Even if we grant that oral literature, as a genus of human artistic expression, may be a survival out of the immeasurable past before writing was invented, it does not thereby follow that its modern content, wherever it still survives, individually shares the antiquity of its kind. The date of any given piece of oral literature is the day on which it was last recited or on which it was reduced to writing. The true and proper date of those stories which the Brothers Grimm wrote down from the lips of unlettered reciters is the beginning of the nineteenth century. Most of them were uncontaminated by written literature, whose devices they ignore. In their form and pattern they often suggest great antiquity. Yet few of the stories, as they were actually told, can be oral documents handed down unaltered from a remote past, since they so often refer their surroundings to conditions recognizably recent. Manifestly, they have been retold to suit their narrator and audience. But how many times has this process of retelling already taken place? Some commentators, noting that stories of essentially the same content may be found dispersed over a huge area among races of very different speech, have concluded that such wide (even world-wide!) occurrence of comparable variants of a story is proof that once long ago, in a sort of primal Eden older than the Tower of Babel, there was told a primal story, an *Urmächen*, from which all the modern counterparts are descended, like the animals of today which pious belief claims for descendants of the weirdly assorted zoölogical household afloat in Noah's ark. The theological and the folklore creed are equally naïve. But it is easier to mock the dispersion theory than to find a satisfactory substitute for it. Let us grant that the range of story patterns is limited, and that more than one mind can think the same thought and construct the same story, or even that such tales, being reflections of universal wishes, hopes, and fears, must share the sameness of all human psychology. We shall still be left with a residue of inexplicable coincidences. Probably the solution is complex—almost as complex as the folklore material itself; and we shall have to be resigned to try every case on its individual merits. We shall therefore neither maintain that all the most familiar folk tales came originally from India or the Near East or from anywhere else, nor yet hold the extreme opposite view that like begets like, that any story can spring up anywhere at any time, and that the comparative study of folk tales is merely an exploration of the behavior of the human mind. We shall admit the possibility that there can be folk tales told today which have been told in strikingly similar form not merely centuries but thousands of years ago, since there is no good objection to such tenacity of oral memory and oral transmission. We shall admit the possibility that classical Greece was not the beginning of all Western literature, since behind its literature of reed pen and papyrus, unexplored and of vast extent, may have stretched an unwritten literature which lived by tongue and memory alone.

Milman Parry suffered the tragic and untimely death of those whom the old Homeric gods love, but not before he had completed and published his unanswerable and unassailable proof that Iliad and Odyssey belong to the class of oral literatures—composed in the mind and not on paper, retained in the memory and not in books, recited to audiences, heard and not read. In brief, Parry showed that Homeric verse does not work in formulas merely in order to be quaint, nor is it replete with repetitions through accident of style or contamination of text. It borrows and repeats so frequently because the very elements of speech out of which it is composed are not words but metrical phrases and complete poetical sentences. Where written literature with visual preciousness focuses the reader's attention on the individual adjective and turn of phrase, laying unceasing claim to novelty and variety, oral literature behaves like oral speech in general and recites the remarks of yesterday and yesteryear without being in the least abashed at its own uninventiveness. Only, unlike normal speech, this epic speech is metrical. For meter is mnemonic form as well as poet's privilege; and everday language must be converted and elevated to metrical language before the oral poet can traffic in it. Such metricized speech does not thereby become an individual possession which only its creator may use: it belongs, not to all men, but to all poets and reciters. It is no one's private property any more than ordinary prose speech is anyone's special preserve. It is merely another, although somewhat specialized, idiom of communication. Its practitioners, the oral poets, learn it as the native tongue of their calling. This metrical speech—like human speech in general—is created by many, used by many, and hence belongs to many. No wonder it resembles itself, reflects itself, and reduplicates itself! Once formed, it is stubbornly preserved. But like ordinary everyday speech it slowly alters to suit shifting taste and to match new topics.

Homeric hexameter fully displays these specific qualities of oral poetic speech. Its language is not that of any Greek dialect or any group of prose speakers, because it is a metrical creation markedly altering the vernacular and preserving its own traditional expressions even when it passed from an Aeolic to an Ionic environment. Many of its grammatical inflections are peculiarly its own, being devised to suit hexametrical patterns. So formed and so inherited, its phrases and expressions felt no shame in threadbare usage, but were content to serve without pride or preciosity as the current fabric of epic speech. When the Iliad in three different passages employs identical verses to describe how a warrior.

> set on his mighty head the well-made horsehair-crested
> helmet, whose plume dreadfully nodded down from above,

and the Odyssey uses these same verses to describe how Odysseus armed himself after he had exhausted his arrows against the cowering suitors, the identity proves or disproves nothing for the authorship of the poems. Whether the same or a different poet is speaking in any of the four instances, he has merely said the same thing in the same way because he has conveniently and fittingly expressed himself in the common language of his profession. The idiom of such a language does not reside in its individual words so much as in the large cohesive metrical units. Such use of a formulaic metric language need not reduce all poetical speech to the commonplace and the reiterative, even though this is its constant danger and may be its ultimate fate—whence much of the tediousness of the later Greek epic. Within and beside the stereotyped structure there will always be opportunity for originality of expression; and if this be felicitous or striking, it will impress itself enough to be remembered and thus to survive. In many of the most memorable passages in Homer it is not the matter or wording, but the application and effect, that are new. Thus, critics have often extolled the laconic grimness with which the poet of the Odyssey hangs the unfaithful handmaidens, who

> wriggled with their feet a little while, but not for very long.

Yet the poet's genius did not lie in the invention of so devastating a description of death by the noose but rather, having already likened the women to birds caught in a fowling net, in apprehending their further resemblance to fish struggling and expiring on the line. The phrase was already made and available; he merely used it with supreme aptness.

Or again, who having once read will ever forget the proud and cruel answer of Achilles to the wretched suppliant who has clasped his knees and begged for his life?—

> Die, friend, you too die! Why do you lament so? Patroklos died, who was a better man than you. And see you not what manner of man am I myself, how fair, how strong, I that had a hero for father and a goddess for my mother? Yet over me also hangs death, and the power of fate. A morning shall come, or an evening, or a midday, when some man shall take my life in battle with the casting of a spear or with an arrow from the bowstring.

I doubt if anyone except the scholar turning the pages of his concordance to Homer will suspect how much of that has also been used piecemeal here and there elsewhere in the poem.

The Greek epithet *rhapsode*, or "song-stitcher," admirably conveys the patchwork technique of the oral compositor, working with metrical rags and ribbons which he can sew together to make hexameters. Such a process, precisely because it dispenses with writing, could scarcely persevere without radical change if its author began to compose visually in script instead of by memory and ear. Under the eye's close scrutiny the *mot juste*, the unusual and original turn, would supplant the *mot poetique*, the merely traditional and metrically convenient epithet and phrase. The modern reader may be quick to suppose that written literature tends to length because there can be no such thing as fatigue in letters once set down, whereas oral literature should tend to brevity because every word of it must be remembered by a human brain. Yet quite the opposite is the case; for writing is slower and more arduous than speaking, and reading is a more toilsome accomplishment than reciting. So that, in defiance of what the thoughtless might imagine, early written literature (witness the earliest Greek elegiac and iambic poetry) tends to compactness and brevity, with sententious conciseness displacing colloquial loquacity, whereas mature oral epic, undismayed by what seems an impossible task to us moderns who have lost our memories through relying too much on letters, runs on like Odysseus in the Iliad, who "moved not his staff either forward or backward . . . but in a great voice uttered words more thickly than winter snowflakes."

For us of today, the Homeric poems constitute the very beginnings of Greek literature; actually, they could not possibly have occupied that position. Rather, they must have been very near the ending (as they certainly were the finest flowering) of a long antecedent tradition of oral poetry in Greece. Were we to insist that, as its name implies, all literature must be written with letters, then Hesiod and Archilochos would begin Greek literature; but Homer would *precede it*, as a survivor from an older and different genus.

HOMER*

C. M. Bowra

The origins of Greek literature are lost. The Greeks attributed the first flights of song to Orpheus and Linus and Musaeus, but even in antiquity nothing of their works was known, and their existence is open to question. For us Greek literature begins with the name of Homer and the two epics of the *Iliad* and the *Odyssey*. Unfortunately, for more than a hundred years such controversy has raged over these two poems that their place in history has been obscured and even their reputation undeservedly affected. Here it must suffice to say that the *Iliad* and the *Odyssey* were composed in the ninth or eighth century B.C., that their style, construction, and temper imply the existence of a single author, that there is no good reason to abandon an ancient and universally accepted tradition that his name was Homer and he came from the Greek coastland of Asia Minor. On the other hand, it is equally certain that Homer did not create epics out of nothing, that his work was the culmination of a long tradition of bardic poetry, that to this tradition he owed his stories, his language, his metre, many of his devices for making his work intelligible and attractive. He may have even embodied fragments of earlier poems, though he probably altered them in the process. Nor is the text, as we possess it, free from interpolations and linguistic changes. But the creative manner of a great poet reveals itself throughout, and the poems must be the work not of a school of poets but of a single man indebted to a rich tradition.

The *Iliad* and the *Odyssey* are heroic epics. They celebrate the great deeds of a generation which has passed from the earth and did what later men could not do. Their values are those of an age which judges everything by the standards of the heroic man who is equally notable in council and in war. These poems are the echo of events which shook the world, and like other heroic poetry they were composed in the aftermath of war and conquest. The conquerors are settling down in their new possessions, and in the growing civilization bards entertain their masters by the recitation of heroic doings. Homer is already far from

* C. M. Bowra, *Ancient Greek Literature* (New York: Oxford University Press, 1960), originally published in 1933. Reprinted by permission.

the war of which he sings, but he has appropriated the standards of the Heroic Age, and he is an authentic bard, trained in rhapsody and recitation. He composed for listeners, not for readers, and his art is the art which grew in the courts of the Greek conquerors and colonists of Ionia.

The Heroic Age of Greece was the mainspring of the epic tradition. It existed in the thirteenth and twelfth centuries B.C., when the confederated Greek tribes tried to establish new kingdoms in Asia Minor and Egypt. From historical·documents we know the anxiety they caused to the Pharaohs and the Hittite Kings, but their own poetic imagination crystallized these racial struggles into the story of the Siege of Troy, the rich fortress which guarded the passage from Europe to Asia over the Dardanelles. In the process many facts must have been distorted, but the epic poets kept the memory of efforts and achievements, even of failures, belonging to an age when men were still the sons of gods. To this tradition we owe the *Iliad*. It tells of the siege of Troy, and though its action falls into the last year of the ten years' siege and the actual capture lies outside its scope, it gives the main characters and issues of the Trojan War. Its action takes place mainly on the battlefield or in the camp; its chief characters are soldiers, and many of its excitements are military. Its broad plan succeeds in giving a picture of the Heroic Age at war, and the details of fighting are written for men who under-stand war and could take the fine points of a good fight. At a first reading the *Iliad* might seem to be a great picture of heroic warfare, so full is it of single combats and great attacks, so much space is given to the ebb and flow of armies on the battlefield. A hero has his crowded hour and gets wounded only to be succeeded by another hero. In this the *Iliad* resembles other martial epics, but its plot, though complicated, is really based on an original and important theme.

The *Iliad*, as Homer tells us, is the story of the wrath of Achilles. In this son of a sea-goddess, gifted with all that a man can ask, brave, beautiful, eloquent, but doomed to an early death, the Heroic Age found an ideal embodiment of itself. Even in the defects of his nobleness Achilles is the authentic hero. Therefore Homer took him for his story. But the context in which he placed him is not that which old stories had made familiar. In them Achilles must have been pre-eminently the warrior, who lost his friend Patroclus and revenged himself cruelly on his friend's slayer, Hector. The *Iliad* tells a different tale. The theme of "the wrath of Achilles" has been made into a tragic theme in which Achilles is the protagonist. His tragedy is that in spite of his half-divine gifts he makes the wrong use of his opportunities. He quarrels with his liege-lord, Agamemnon, over a captive girl, and right is on his side. But then he refuses to fight and lets his friends suffer loss and defeat. In their humiliation they ask for his help, and Agamemnon makes generous apologies. But Achilles persists in his refusal. He is now definitely in the wrong. He has broken the principle that a man must stand by his fellows in need. Worse follows. Patroclus asks to be allowed to help the defeated Achaeans. Achilles lets him go and lends his own armour. Patroclus is killed by Hector and the armour stripped from his body. Then Achilles takes the field, but his impulse is entirely desire for vengeance on Hector. Half-mad with anger and merciless to anyone who gets in his way he pursues Hector to death and then intends in defiance of all heroic codes to mutilate his body. In the old story the close came with this savage revenge, but Homer leads to a different conclusion. Hector's father, the old man Priam, comes to ransom the body from the slayer. When he sees the old suppliant "kissing the terrible man-slaying hands which had slain many of his sons," Achilles' heart is stirred to pity. He remembers his own father, and all traces of his passion disappear. He gives up the body; anger is purged in pity. Disaster has played its part, and Achilles is himself again.

This is the central theme of the *Iliad*, but round this Homer has set another story, that of the fall of Troy. And here too he has his ethical intention. Troy is besieged because Paris has abducted Menelaus' wife, Helen. In spite of entreaties from the Trojans he refuses to restore her, and Troy suffers in consequence. On Troy, as on Achilles, lies the curse of an infatuation sent by the gods. It is clear that Troy will fall and its fall will bring unreckonable miseries of death and enslavement. But because the Trojans too are heroes, they stand by Paris and pay for their loyalty. And in this tragedy, parallel to that of Achilles, Homer is careful to delineate the chief character. Hector is the ideal opponent and antithesis of Achilles. Born of ordinary human parentage he has the qualities which make a man instead of a hero. His very bravery is deliberate and inspired by love of his country. He has moments of doubt, even of fear. A devoted husband and father, the favourite son of his old parents, he is tied with human responsibilities as Achilles never is. Lovable and admirable, he fights magnificently because he must, but he never for long enjoys the sweet delight of battle. Over him too there hangs the shadow of death. The man is pitted against the demigod, and the man must perish. Hector seems to belong to an age later than that of the great heroes. He lacks their sublime self-confidence and their freedom from common claims. So in spite of his intimate appeal he is not so important as Achilles, but he is an adversary perfectly conceived for him.

These two themes, of Achilles and Troy, are set in a world of living men and women. Tradition must have provided Homer with the names and leading qualities of his characters, and perhaps to it he owed the epithets attached to them, "Agamemnon, king of men," "white-armed Helen," "Priam of the good ashen spear," "Nestor tamer of horses." But just as he took "swift-footed Achilles" and made him into a tragic hero, so Homer turned these creatures of saga into living beings. His characters fall into two groups admirably constructed and contrasted. The

Achaean life is that of the camp. Here are the High King, Agamemnon, impulsive and passionate, overburdened with responsibilities but capable of generous and brave actions, old Nestor, garrulous, wily and delightful, full of the garnered wisdom of three generations, the young Diomedes, who has been taught "ever to be the best and to surpass other men" and does not shrink from attacking the gods in battle, Odysseus, the embodiment of sense and stratagem. In Troy life is different. Hector has his supporters in the abductor Paris, who is not without charm and relics of physical courage, and in the young and chivalrous princes Sarpedon and Glaucus. But here the real masterpieces are in the old king, Priam, worn with disasters but courageously enduring though he knows that the worst is yet to come, his wife Hecuba, fiercer than her husband but lacking his real reserves of courage, the patient and pathetic Andromache, Hector's wife, and the radiant, tragic and beautiful Helen. She appears seldom, but we soon know her weariness and solitude, her hatred for her own beauty and for the goddess who gave it her. She is a fitting object for the deadly struggles which centre round her.

These different themes and characters are connected in a story of some complexity, varied with many episodes and often travelling far from Achilles. But they are held together by one thread—the effort which the Achaeans make when Achilles refuses to fight and its results, including the return of Achilles to the field. Naturally in such a poem there is much description of fighting, but Homer knows how to keep it lively. He will vary it with those similes which are the ancestors of all similes, short pictures drawn with great brilliance from the poet's own world. The great Ajax in obstinate retreat is like an ass strayed into a field and refusing to be beaten out of it; Paris running to battle is like a barley-fed stallion running to the pasturage of the mares; Apollo destroys the wall of the Achaean camp as a child destroys a sand castle he has built; the light shines on Achilles' head like the fire lit in a beleaguered city for neighbours to see and bring help. The scene too is always changing. From battle we are transported to the walls of Troy where Hector talks to his wife and tries to take up his child, who is frightened by the plumed helmet and only comforted when his father takes it off, or two opponents will stop fighting and tell delightful stories of ancestors who fought with monsters, or we are enchanted with the shield which Hephaestus makes for Achilles, inlaid with delicious pictures of peace and war.

Homer composed for recitation, and his narrative lacks the close cohesion of books written to be read slowly. He has to emphasize the important points and neglect the rest. Therefore his story seems loosely knit. He omits much that might give greater completeness, and once he has finished with an episode he dismisses it summarily, not troubling to tidy the loose threads of narrative. But these apparent carlessnesses are part of his technical skill. They help the rapid movement of his poem, and no epic travels at such a speed or gives such an impression of active and abundant life. The story is always the poet's first consideration and is never a peg for his philosophy. To this rapidity the conventions of style contribute. The stock lines and epithets make attention easier. But the real secret of the speed lies in the movement of the dactylic hexameter, a metre almost impossible in English, and in Homer's capacity for keeping to the point. His imaginative vision sees exactly what happens, and he reports it as an eye-witness in succinct and vivid words. There is no film between him and his characters, no distortion due to their belonging to the past. He is carried on by his story, and he carries us with him.

In achieving such results Homer is helped by his language. It is in a sense artificial. It was never spoken in ordinary life and takes liberties with rules. It is poetical speech, meant for themes more majestic than common life, full of synonyms and alternative forms, with a rich and adventurous vocabulary compounded from many sources. It is the work of many generations of poets, and its power is the greatest tribute to Homer's anonymous predecessors who perfected it. To them he must owe the beautiful recurring epithets, the "rosy-fingered" dawn, the "loudly-resounding" and the "wine-dark" sea, the "ambrosial" night, the "long-shadowing" spear. To them too he must owe some repeated phrases which have an air of great antiquity and seem to belong to a time when common things were dignified with peculiar titles, the "barrier of the teeth," the "holy might" of a man, the "yellow heads of horses." Yet in spite of archaisms this style seems always natural and appropriate. It is invariably lucid, and its richness serves to keep the subject at the proper level of heroic dignity.

For the *Iliad* is consistently heroic and derives its special power from its sense of human achievements. Homer maintains an outlook which is only possible for a man trained in the standards of the Heroic Age. Because true dignity belongs to man and cannot be lessened by comparison, even the gods must suffer. If Homer makes his men like gods, he makes his gods like men. They have moments of majesty, when Zeus nods and shakes Olympus, when Poseidon crosses the sea in three strides, when Apollo descends with the plague "like the night." But their action is not usually on this plane. Their life is like a holiday, the immortal counterpart of the feasting in a King's palace. So by a curious paradox Homer finds in them that element of comedy which he seldom finds in men. The war-god Ares is wounded and screams for pain; Hera tricks her husband with amorous wiles; the love-affairs of Zeus are catalogued with mock solemnity. These divine diversions are almost comic relief and belong to pure art. Homer's religion was not puritanical, and he could laugh at the gods. They are relieved from the anxieties of man, but they are also relieved from his moments of strife and splendour. In their world there is no heroism. There is no need to be solemn about them.

True dignity belongs to man, and he is a sufficient subject for poetry. This is the secret of Homer's outlook. He sees man occupied with great undertakings and menaced with an inevitable doom. In this lies the peculiar pathos of Achilles, and in the sense of the brief moment to be caught lies Homer's characteristic sublimity. When the old men "like crickets" discuss Helen and say "It is no matter for indignation that men should fight for such a woman; she is strangely like the immortal goddesses to look upon," they express Homer's own view. The war may bring unreckonable horrors, but its cause is strangely magnificent. When Hector's wife is full of forebodings, Hector has no soft comfort for her. He says "there will be a day when holy Ilium shall be destroyed, and Priam, and the people of Priam of the good ashen spear." But perhaps the most intimate passage is where Achilles, half-mad with the death of Patroclus, refuses to spare the life of Priam's young son, Lycaon: "But, friend, you too must die; why do you lament in this way? Even Patroclus died, who was a much better man than you. Do you not see what a man I am, beautiful and strong? I am the son of a noble father, and a goddess was the mother who gave me birth; but even over me hangs death and powerful doom. There will be a dawn or a sunset or a midday when some man shall take away my life from me in war, shooting me with a spear or with an arrow from the bow-string."

When Homer composed the *Odyssey*, he must have felt that he could not repeat the tragic effects of the *Iliad*. The *Odyssey* is a story of adventure and its roots lie not in heroic lays but in immemorial folk-tales and popular stories. It tells of a man who after many troubles and wanderings comes home to find his wife besieged with suitors and kills them. This ancient theme is built into an epic of rich complexity by the incorporation of other stories equally ancient and by a plot of great ingenuity and human interest. The story is less diffuse than that of the *Iliad* and there is a greater economy in the structure. The main plan is simple and masterly. The first section tells of Odysseus' home in Ithaca ten years after the capture of Troy. The pathetic but not uncalculating Penelope is uncertain and unwilling to decide whether her absent husband is dead or not. There is some comedy in Homer's treatment of her, but there is also pathos and sympathy for her isolation and perplexity. The suitors who invade her home and devour her wealth are a study in vulgarity, far removed from the heroes of the *Iliad*. In them heroic dignity has given place to self-satisfaction and self-seeking. Their admiration of Penelope is adventitious and perfunctory. What they want is her wealth and the position it brings. They have their personalities and separate traits, but they are all alike contemptible, and Homer is careful to keep us from feeling any sympathy for them.

The chief personality of this section is Odysseus' son, Telemachus. He is on the verge of manhood, shy and sensitive, but the shame he feels at the suitors' treatment of his home prompts him to action, and he risks his life in a voyage to find news of his father. In the course of this we meet some old friends from the *Iliad*, and it is plain that the same hand which created Nestor and Helen is still at work. But the real purpose of the voyage is to create our need for Odysseus. His absence is continually remarked, and we are made to feel a great curiosity about him, to ask where he is, and that is why Homer took such pains to make us feel his absence.

The second section concerns Odysseus himself from the fall of Troy to his home-coming. It is a masterpiece of story-telling and has been the despair of all its imitators. The construction is partly narrative by the poet, partly a recital by Odysseus himself. By this device we start where we left Telemachus but are taken right back to earlier events. Incidentally Odysseus is made more intimate by having to speak for himself. We see the reckless spirit which carries him into desperate straits and the wits which get him out of them. The poet passes no judgment on him, but plainly he finds Odysseus an ideal of manhood, courteous, courageous, princely, ready for any mishap but pursuing steadfastly his determination to get home and see "the smoke leaping up from his dear native shore."

In this section Homer has retold some ancient stories of fabulous monsters and adventures in uncharted seas. Versions of these stories may be found in folk-lore from Polynesia to Scandinavia, and their antiquity is past calculation. The one-eyed monster tricked and blinded by a stranger calling himself "No Man," the winds let out of a bag to carry a ship all over the sea, the ogress "big as a mountain" who eats sailors, the enchantress who transforms men into beasts, the drug which makes them forget their home, the moving islands and colliding rocks, all these may be paralleled outside Greece. They existed before Homer and would have survived if he had never lived. But Homer's peculiar art is to exalt the fancies of folk-lore into poetry. The primitive versions are concerned largely with animals, with the crafty fox and the jumping hare, but Homer applies them to men. Even the man-eating one-eyed ogre, Polyphemus, has some of the clumsy and bestial pathos of an aboriginal savage. His gluttony and drunkenness, his clumsy jokes, his affection for his ram, make him intelligible and not entirely unsympathetic. And the witches Circe and Calypso, the "Hawk" and the "Concealer," despite their magic and their desert islands, are delightfully human in their admiration and affection for Odysseus.

In one or two places the preservation of ancient stories in other countries shows the quality of Homer's art. An Egyptian story of 2000 B.C. tells of a hero who is wrecked and after floating on a log of wood is washed up on an island, where he sleeps long from exhaustion. He wakes to meet a beautiful serpent who gives him royal entertainment and sends him away in a ship loaded with gifts. In outline this resembles Odysseus' adventures in Phaeacia, but instead of the serpent we have the enchanting figure of Nausicaa, the King's daughter, who when she is washing clothes on the beach meets the sea-soiled and naked Odysseus and with perfect simplicity and self-possession clothes him and sends him to her parents. From them Odysseus receives boundless hospitality, and Phaeacia is a country where everyone is rich and happy. But even in this Never Never Land Homer creates a real world. The King and Queen have their human side, their anxiety to impress the distinguished stranger, their consciousness that they are the only people in the world who count. To them Odysseus tells his adventures, and this stirring tale of endurance is the proper contrast to their idle, agreeable, and sheltered lives.

Another ancient story is that of the hero who crosses the Ocean and calls up the ghosts of the dead. Connected with the name of Gilgamesh it was familiar in Babylonia and Assyria. Homer too takes Odysseus across the Ocean. He digs a trench and fills it with blood, and the ghosts come up to drink, for only so can they regain for a little their lost vitality. In this remote scene Homer provides something more than necromancy. When they have drunk of the blood, the shades speak. Among them is Odysseus' mother who has died in his absence and of whose death he has not heard. He questions her about it, and she answers: "Neither in my halls did the Far-Seeing Shooter of Arrows come on me and kill me with gentle shafts, nor did any disease attack me, such as most often with hateful corruption robs the life from the limbs, but desire for thee and thy ways, glorious Odysseus, and thy gentleness of heart took away my honey-sweet life." Odysseus tries to embrace her but she slips away "like a shadow or a dream." The old theme of a strange adventure is made intimately human and pathetic.

The second section closes with Odysseus' return to Ithaca on the enchanted ship of the Phaeacians, and the rest of the poem is concerned with his adventures at home and their culmination in the slaughter of the suitors. Here Homer returns to the manner of the first section. Events arc told on a full scale with free play for character and conversation. Odysseus is revealed in turn to his son, his old nurse, his swineherd, his wife and his father. Recognitions delighted the Greeks, and Homer contrives his with ingenuity and variety. More touching than any is the scene where the old dog, Argus, lying in the dung-heap full of ticks, old and neglected, recognizes his master. He wags his tail and droops his ears, but cannot even crawl up to him, and dies after Odysseus has seen him. Through this series of encounters Homer brings Odysseus to his revenge on the suitors. The speed of the narrative increases, and the note of benevolent comedy yields to something more sinister. The old theme of revenge takes command; there are portents in the sky, and the seer, Theoclymenus, proclaims them: "Ah! wretched men, what evil is this you suffer? In night are your heads wrapped, and your faces, and your knees below, and lamentation is kindled, and your cheeks are wet with tears. The walls drip with blood, and the fair interspaces; the fore-court is full of ghosts, and full the court also, of ghosts sped to Erebus and the gloom below. The sun is destroyed out of the sky, and an evil mist is spread over all." Methodically and coldly Odysseus proceeds to his revenge. His triumph is due to his bowmanship, and he shoots down the suitors with unerring aim. The details of the killing show that good shooting was appreciated by Homer, but there is also a fierce delight in the punishment of men "who honoured no one among mortal men, either good or bad, who came unto them."

The slaughter done, we might expect the *Odyssey* to come to a close, but the Greeks liked to end in quiet ease and dignity, and the stray threads of the plot had to be gathered together. Therefore the poem continues until Odysseus has buried the suitors and made himself known to his wife and father. All that is natural enough, but more interesting is the scene where the ghosts of the suitors gather beyond the stream of Ocean and talk with the great heroes of the *Iliad*, and especially with the murdered Agamemnon. Here Homer points his moral and unites the *Iliad* to the *Odyssey*. The array of great dead is in strong contrast to the suitors, men of meaner lineage and unheroic behaviour, and we realize that Odysseus and Penelope belong to the nobler company and that this time nobility has triumphed.

Between the *Iliad* and the *Odyssey* there is a noticeable difference of temper. The *Iliad* celebrates heroic strength, but the *Odyssey* celebrates heroic wit and cunning. Much of Odysseus' triumph is due to his being cleverer than his adversaries. In his task he is aided and abetted by Athena, whose tenderness for him is delightfully unashamed. She admires him because he has all the qualities she likes most in herself. She is not above praising trickery and dishonesty, though her praise is not without irony. Odysseus triumphs over a meaner world because he is in every way a better man than those who try to dispossess him. But it is hard to feel that in the *Odyssey* Homer has kept all his old confidence in life. The high heroic world is menaced by upstarts who lack the heroic virtues and think they can reap rich rewards without qualification of effort. The slaughter of the suitors seems the last fling of the heroic generation before it went down to oblivion. And perhaps this note of despair, implicit and modified though it is, accounts for the great praise given to Odysseus' wits. Wits win their greatest renown when other nobler qualities have failed, and Odysseus comes into his own when Agamemnon and Achilles are dead. They perished and Odysseus survived, because he was cleverer than they were, and therefore Homer makes him his hero.

An ancient critic compares Homer in the *Odyssey* to the setting sun, "whose greatness remains without violence," and there is truth in the words. If we miss the abundant vitality of the *Iliad*, we are recompensed with greater intimacy and fuller detail. The chief characters are drawn with more fullness than any in the *Iliad* except Hector, and the whole of life on Ithaca is revealed from the swine-herd sleeping among his pigs to the maids flirting with the suitors at the palace, from the secret store-room of Penelope to the busy life at the well or the silent cave to which the gods have their own entrance. In this world where the sea is never out of sight or hearing, where the goats pasture among the rocks and the crops are grown in hollows on the hill-side, Homer places his drama, and from it he fills the interstices of his story. It is a small world where everyone is known and a stranger is a great event, where the great and the humble speak on equal terms, and the King's father works in the orchard with gloves to keep off the thorns. All takes place on misty islands on the edge of the Greek world, far from the plains of Troy or the rich palaces of the Peloponnese. The isolated members of a royal house are almost alone in their exposure to danger and dishonour. They fight their battles unaided, and their triumph is that of their inherited nobleness.

Even if we allow for many differences between the *Iliad* and the *Odyssey*, the resemblances are more numerous and striking. In both there is the same generous understanding of humanity, the same pleasure in the good things of life, in eating and drinking, in wealth and courtesy and hospitality, in skill at shooting or ship-building, in the numerous details of pastoral life, in cows, sheep and pigs, finally in all the natural sights of the Greek world, in the sea-birds diving or perching on rafters, in the rise and fall of the wind, in the return of evening and morning, in the sun and the sea and the sky. If Homer was blind, and the tradition is but poorly founded, he remembered well what he once saw. Few poets have the gift of conveying visible things so clearly as he can. In the *Odyssey* he gives freer play to this gift than in the *Iliad* and writes of harbours safe behind cliffs, of gardens where fruit never fails and caves clothed with creeping vines. He had good ears too, and his verse repeats the scudding of water under a ship, the bleat of ewes in their stalls, the wash of waves on rocks, the bumping of a stone downhill.

But all this is only the background for his great characters. Out of their actions he made his poetry, and though he was capable of lyrical sweetness, he kept to his special art and made the chief interest of his epics what is done and the people who do it. His great effects are of emotion expressed in action, and he secures his object through his characters without ever obtruding his own judgments on life or on them. So in the end he remains impersonal. We know his tastes, what men he liked, what he noticed in the world, but of what he thought, what judgments he passed, what he hoped or feared for his time or his art, he says not a word. The first poet of Europe keeps company with Shakespeare in that his works have been denied to him because he excluded his own name and opinions from publicity and fame. But as a poet we know him. He laid the foundations of Greek literature, and the Greeks turned to him continually for inspiration and example. He was the father of both comedy and tragedy, and though his epic manner could never be successfully reproduced, other poets learned from it how to shape their material and to manage their language. From him too they learned that economy in presenting experience which keeps us wondering that so much can be said in so few words. What he almost alone possesses, what none of his successors in epic has shared, is his wide range of creation. His world was circumscribed by the knowledge of his age, but he packed it with living men and women and fashioned from saga and folk-story characters and events as vivid to-day as when he brought them into existence.

TRAGEDY VERSUS EPIC*

Aristotle

The question may be raised whether the Epic or Tragic mode of imitation is the higher. If the more refined art is the higher, and the more refined in every case is that which appeals to the better sort of audience, the art which imitates anything and everything is manifestly most unrefined. The audience is supposed to be too dull to comprehend unless something of their own is thrown in by the performers, who therefore indulge in restless movements. Bad fluteplayers twist and twirl, if they have to represent "the quoit-throw," or hustle the coryphaeus when they perform the "Scylla." 2. Tragedy, it is said, has this same defect. We may compare the opinion that the older actors entertained of their successors. Mynniscus used to call Callippides "ape" on account of the extravagance of his action, and the same view was held of Pindarus. Tragic art, then, as a whole, stands to Epic in the same relation as the younger to the elder actors. So we are told that Epic poetry is addressed to a cultivated audience, who do not need gesture; Tragedy, to an inferior public. 3. Being then unrefined, it is evidently the lower of the two.

Now, in the first place, this censure attaches not to the poetic but to the histrionic art; for gesticulation may be equally overdone in epic recitation, as by Sosistratus, or in lyrical competition, as by Mnasitheus the Opuntian. Next, all action is not to be condemned—any more than all dancing—but only that of bad performers. Such was the fault found in Callippides, as also in others of our own day, who are censured for representing degraded women. Again, Tragedy like Epic poetry produces its effect even without action; it reveals its power by mere reading. If, then, in all other respects it is superior, this fault, we say, is not inherent in it.

4. And superior it is, because it has all the epic elements—it may even use the epic metre—with the music and spectacular effects as important accessories; and these produce the most vivid of pleasures. Further, it has vividness of impression in reading as well as in represen-

* Aristotle, "Chapter 26," *The Poetics*, trans., S. H. Butcher, 4th rev. ed. (London: Macmillan & Co., 1932). Originally published in 1911. Reprinted by permission.

tation. 5. Moreover, the art attains its end within narrower limits; for the concentrated effect is more pleasurable than one which is spread over a long time and so diluted. What, for example, would be the effect of the Oedipus of Sophocles, if it were cast into a form as long as the Iliad? 6. Once more, the Epic imitation has less unity; as is shown by this, that any Epic poem will furnish subjects for several tragedies. Thus if the story adopted by the poet has a strict unity, it must either be concisely told and appear truncated; or, if it conform to the Epic canon of length, it must seem weak and watery. <Such length implies some loss of unity,> if, I mean, the poem is constructed out of several actions, like the Iliad and the Odyssey, which have many such parts, each with a certain magnitude of its own. Yet these poems are as perfect as possible in structure; each is, in the highest degree attainable, an imitation of a single action.

7. If, then, Tragedy is superior to Epic poetry in all these respects, and, moreover, fulfils its specific function better as an art—for each art ought to produce, not any chance pleasure, but the pleasure proper to it, as already stated—it plainly follows that Tragedy is the higher art, as attaining its end more perfectly.

8. Thus much may suffice concerning Tragic and Epic poetry in general; their several kinds and parts, with the number of each and their differences; the causes that make a poem good or bad; the objections of the critics and the answers to these objections.

ENTER THE ROMANTIC ROMAN: VIRGIL*

Edith Hamilton

A great literary gossip of the second century A.D. whose work has come down to us in many volumes and whose name was Aulus Gellius has recorded a comparison he once heard a literary friend of his make between Pindar's and Virgil's description of Aetna in eruption. The Greek poet writes: "In the darkness of the night the red flame whirls rocks with a roar far down to the sea. And high aloft are sent fearful fountains of fire." Virgil says: "Skyward are sent balls of flame that lick the stars and ever and again rocks are spewed forth, the torn entrails of the mountains, and molten crags are hurled groaning to heaven." "Pindar," the critic pointed out to his friend, "describes what actually happened and what he saw with his own eyes, but Virgil's balls of flame that lick the stars' is a useless and foolish elaboration, and when he says crags are molten and groan and are hurled to heaven, this is such an account as Pindar never wrote and is monstrous." That is a comparison between a classic and a romantic description. Pindar was using his eyes, Virgil his imagination. The man who compared them was a classicist who, of course, detested romantic exaggeration, and could not see the grandeur that we see in Virgil's "flame that licks the stars."

The romantic artist must not be judged by the canon of strict accuracy. He will not be bound by fact, "the world being inferior to the soul," as Bacon says, "by reason whereof there is a more ample greatness, a more exact goodness, and a more absolute variety, than can be found in the nature of things." To the classicist the nature of things is the truth and he desires only to see clearly what it is. The romanticist is the adventurer drawn on by the new and the strange where to him truth is to be found. The classic writer depends upon reason no less than upon imagination. To the romantic writer imagination can transcend the narrow limits of experience and move on unhampered by it to what eye hath not seen nor ear heard.

* Reprinted from *The Roman Way* by Edith Hamilton by permission of W. W. Norton & Company, Inc. Copyright 1932 by W. W. Norton & Company, Inc. Copyright renewed 1960 by Edith Hamilton. Norton Library Edition published January, 1964.

The *Aeneid* from first to last is pure romance and Virgil, Rome's greatest poet, is one of the world's greatest romanticists.

He was a few years older than Horace who loved him and wrote of him with tender admiration. Everyone seems to have felt like that about him. The allusions to him in Latin literature show a feeling far beyond that for any other man of letters, and in later days it is safe to say that of all poets, of all writers, indeed, he has been the most loved and praised. He was the only ancient author, either Greek or Roman, to make his way into the Christian church. There was a legend, often repeated and embodied in a hymn, that St. Paul had visited his grave and dropped a tear upon it. Again and again his name was introduced into a ritual of the church as one of the prophets, because in an early poem he wrote of a child about to be born who would bring back the golden age and the reign of peace, interpreted by the Christians as meaning the birth of Christ. So all his poems became in some sort sanctified. The monasteries most hostile to pagan learning could allow copies of them, and pious Christians felt it no sin to use him for looking into the future by opening the *Aeneid* and reading the first line their eyes happened to light upon. His transformation into a magician was the next step, and as such the polished, suave man of letters figured strangely during the Middle Ages. To Dante he was "the poet," the one to conduct him through Hell and Purgatory, and "my master and my author, he who taught me the good style that did me honor." And from his death on to the present, from Juvenal who—early in the second century—deplored the schoolmaster's hardships in having to listen to "the same daily fare always repeated from the soot-blackened Virgil," up to the last June before the College Board examinations, the generations of school children have owed part of their training to him. In our western world the Bible alone has had a wider influence. From this point of view he is more important that the poets of Greece. For seventeen or eighteen hundred years, he was the master of literature to all the western nations.

The romantic spirit took root and spread through Europe; the classic spirit departed. So much is fact. How far the great Latin romantics were responsible for the change is one of the matters not susceptible of proof. It is impossible to say what would have happened if Virgil and Livy and their greatly inferior, but very influential follower, Seneca, had not lived. In the immense German forests, in the soft sea-airs of Ireland, there were no sharp, clear outlines as in Greece. Luminous mists made dim distances where the imagination was free to see what it chose. Also as the church grew in power, side by side with the intellectualizing effort of dogmatic theology, eastern mysticism worked, with its absolute conviction of "a more ample greatness, a more exact goodness than can be found in the nature of things." There was much apart from Roman literature that pointed to romanticism. But, at the least, it may be said with certainty that Virgil and Livy inaugurated the new movement of the spirit the world was ready for. Classicism had grown thinner and dryer from the beginning of the fourth century B.C. on. It became precious, pedantic, all polished surface. Learning and style were the combination out of which to make poetry. This tendency is the evil genius of the classic spirit and has killed it many a time since the polite and erudite and cultivated society of Alexandria dealt it the blow which by the time Virgil appeared had been fatal to it.

"A talent is formed in stillness," said Goethe, "a character in the stream of the world." That is the romantic view; the Greeks of the great age would have violently disagreed. The stream of the world was to them precisely the place to develop the artist, the classical artist, whose eyes are ever turned upon life. But it is not the place to develop the imagination. The romantic artist withdraws from the busy haunts of men to some fair and tranquil retreat, in Sicilian meadows, or by the deep blue sea of the south, or on the hillslope of an English lake, where he may see and tell of things invisible to mortal sight. Alone of the Augustan poets Virgil had no love for life in Rome. During all the years that he wrote he lived in the country, near the Bay of Naples. Even Augustus, who cared much for him and recognized early his genius, was unable to persuade him to do more than make brief visits to the capital.

Very little is known about him. His home was near Mantua and he lost it as Horace did his after the republican cause was defeated. In Naples they called him "the maiden," for his purity of life, some said, others, for his gentleness, and it may be both had a share in the nickname. He went once to Greece and Horace wrote a poem to the ship that carried so precious a burden. One account is that he died on the way home, another, that this happened after a second voyage. Our gossip, Aulus Gellius, tells at length how on his death bed he begged his friends to burn the Aeneid, "because," Gellius says, "those parts which he left perfected and polished enjoy the highest praise for poetical beauty, but those which he was unable to revise because he was overtaken by death are not worthy of the taste of the most elegant of poets." Augustus is said to have prevented this last wish from being fulfilled. The point of the story is, of course, the intense desire it shows on Virgil's part for perfected finish, and this is borne out by the length of time he spent on each piece of writing—eleven years given to the Aeneid alone.

A romantic subject may be treated classically and a classic subject romantically. The beauty of a Greek god is human, realized by the artist from the living men he had seen; it is what a romantic subject will become under classic treatment. The romance has suffered: the statue is a god merely because it is so labelled. The strange beauty of a Hindoo god, like nothing ever seen on earth, is completely romantic. The Hindoo artist's imagination has conceived something beyond or, at the least, apart from, humanity. The same distinction emerges from a comparison between the romantic Aeneid and the classic Iliad. The Iliad has as romantic a subject as the *Aeneid*, as romantic, indeed, as there could be: battles where heroes and gods fight for a marvelously beautiful woman, and conclaves held in silver Olympus where deities watch the contest and give victory to this side or that. But when Homer's method of treatment is compared with Virgil's the difference between classic romanticism and the purely romantic is instantly perceived.

In the *Iliad*, Achilles has lost his armor, and his goddess-mother goes to the fire-god to beg a new set from him. She finds him "in his halls wrought of brass by his own hand, sweating and toiling and with busy hand plying the bellows. He was fashioning a score of tripods, all placed on wheels of gold that they might roll in and back, a marvel to behold. Not yet was added the neat handles, for which the god was forging rivets busily." This description of a god, like the Greek statue, is a classic treatment of a romantic theme which does damage to the romance. The classic artist's home is the earth; if he ascends to heaven, heaven takes on the look of earth. But when Aeneas loses his armor and his mother goes to Vulcan for the same purpose there is nothing of earth in the scene: "An island towering with fiery mountains; beneath thunders a cavern blasted out by the Cyclops' forges; the sound of mighty blows echo on anvils; molten metal hisses; fires dart from the great jaws of the furnace. Hither the lord of fire descends from heaven's height. There in the mighty cave the Cyclops were forging"—not smoothly rolling tripods fitted with neat handles, but "the thunderbolt, one of those many which the great Father showers down on earth. Three spokes of frozen rain, three of watery cloud, had they put together, three of ruddy flame and the winged wind of the south; and now they blend the awful flash and the noise and the terror and the fury of the untiring lightning flame." That is what your true romantic can do with the fearful fire-god and the forges of the Cyclops. Thunderbolts, every reader must feel, are what ought to be produced by such means.

If it is objected that the pictures of the supernatural in the *Iliad* are not classic, but only primitive, the truth is that the realism so strikingly marked in Homer is essentially the same as that which stamps the whole of Greek art. It is not a mere matter of childish details. His Olympians are human just as the Hermes and the Venus of Milo are.

When the Old Testament writer says that the Lord God was walking in the cool of the evening, he too, like Homer, is doing all that a classicist can do with such a subject: he makes it delightful, quaint and charming. But the description in the Book of Revelation, "And I saw a great white throne and him that sat on it, from whose face the earth and the heaven fled away and there was found no place for them," is the work of a lofty romantic imagination.

To us romance means chiefly the passion of love. The Greeks, Plato excepted, did not think much of that as a subject for literature. They practically ignored it. Even Greek tragedy has very little to do with it.

The romantic lover, we know, is allied to the lunatic, and the Greeks had a complete prepossession in favor of sanity. To be sure, the *Iliad* centres in Helen, but Homer's treatment of the loveliest woman of the world is soberly matter-of-fact. When Paris is about to be killed by Menelaus, Aphrodite saves him and carries him away to Troy and his own house. Then she goes to find Helen and bring her to him. Helen is sullen and unwilling. She bids the goddess if she loves him so much, to serve him herself, "and he may take thee for his wife—or his handmaid. I will never go to share his couch." But under Aphrodite's threats she does go and speaks to Paris scornfully, with averted eyes: "Thou hast left the battle. Would thou hadst perished by the mighty hand of him who was my husband. Once thou didst boast to be his peer. Then up—defy him. Yet I counsel thee not—for fear he smite thee and thou be slain." Paris takes all this with the serenity of a man who knows he is going to have what he wants no matter how his wife talks. Menelaus is victor at the moment, he tells her, but he may yet vanquish him in turn. "But now is the time for love. Never before have I felt such sweetness of desire. He spake and went to his fair couch and the lady followed him." There could be nothing less romantic. Angry, scolding, reluctant Helen, and Paris completely indifferent to all save one thing.

Virgil could do a great love story. Aeneas and Dido are not only the hero and heroine of our very first romance, they are great lovers, too, the woman the greater, as through the ages the poets have loved to portray her. She "is pierced by love's cruel shaft, feeding the wound with her life-blood and wasting under a hidden fire"; if she is with him "she begins to speak and stops midway in the utterance"; he speaks and "she hangs upon his lips." When the night comes and the banquet hall is empty, she steals there from her bed to find the couch he had lain on and stretch herself upon it. "Him far away she sees and hears, herself far away."

The episode of the hunting party is ushered in with all the trappings of romance. Before the palace door "Dido's charger splendid in purple and gold champs his foaming bit." The queen "comes forth with a great company attending her. Her cloak was purple bordered with embroidery; her quiver of gold, her hair knotted up with gold, her purple dress was fastened with a golden clasp." A hero's beauty in romance is quite as important as a heroine's, and when Aeneas joins her he is "like Apollo as he leaves his wintry Lycia and visits Delos, his mother-isle; his flowing hair restrained by a wreath of soft leaves and entwined with gold; his arrows ring upon his shoulders. Even so swift came Aeneas, such the beauty that shone forth from his peerless look and mien." Their union, when the hunt is broken up by the storm, takes place in surroundings perfectly fitted to two such personages, a Gustave Doré cavern lit by lightning flashes and echoing the roll of thunder and the cry of the mountain nymphs.

Virgil's attitude at this point in the story, the Roman attitude, was to have a far-reaching influence. Dido has made the fatal slip: her good name is lost; she has fallen from her high estate. Not so Aeneas; the matter is merely incidental to him. His good name is not affected at all. Jupiter sends down the messenger god to bid him remember his high charge to found the Roman race, and he makes ready to sail with little more distress than at the difficulty of how to break the news to her: "What first beginning can he make?" But for her, of course, everything is over. She pleads with him for a moment in beautiful, tender words: "Flying, and from me? By these tears and by your plighted hand—since I myself have left my wretched self nothing else to plead—by our union, by marriage-rites yet unfulfilled, if in anything I have deserved well of you, if anything of mine was ever sweet to you"—but the gods have spoken and Aeneas must go, and all that is left for Dido and her tarnished fair fame is death, the only refuge in such straits for the romantic heroine through all the centuries since.

Here is a great change from Homer and his treatment of Helen. A long way has been travelled on the long road of woman's destiny. In the *Iliad*, Helen is not blamed at all. What could a woman do but go with whatever man was at hand to carry her off? All the blame is put upon Paris. In the *Odyssey*, when Telemachus goes to Menelaus' palace to ask news of his father, Helen comes down into the great hall, lovely and serene. A handmaid places a well-wrought chair for her; another brings her silver work-basket, and Helen sits and works and talks tranquilly of ruined Troy and the men gaze adoringly. Homer is logical: a woman was helpless in those days; the fault could not be hers. But Roman women were not like that ever; they were responsible human beings, a force to be reckoned with; Dido clearly did not have to yield to Aeneas. Then, by a curious shifting of the balance, all the blame was put upon her. Aeneas got none of it. This was the Roman point of view, in line with all the early stories of Lucretia and Virginia and the like, and embodied in Virgil's poem it went over the whole western world, never even challenged until almost the end of the nineteenth century. Trollope held it as firmly as Virgil. When lovely woman stooped to folly, her only refuge was to die, while the man in the case did just as Aeneas did, married somebody else.

The completely romantic view of woman, as what Havelock Ellis called "a silly angel," is only dimly foreshadowed by Virgil. It could never have found a real footing in Rome. Dido is the Roman matron, remembering for her consolation as she dies that she has built a splendid city and avenged a brother's death. But the foundation for the later development was laid, and the long line of lovely, innocent, trusting women, betrayed to their undoing, who for hundreds of years took possession of romance, goes directly back to the *Aeneid*.

There is nothing more romantic than heroism and great deeds in battle and a glorious death. They are all ideas Greek literature fights shy of. The *Iliad* is a poem of battles but there is very little talk about glory of any kind, and none at all about the glory of a noble death. Homer's heroes all know that there is a time for heroism and a time not. When a mightier warrior faces them they retreat, even if unwillingly, "for this sore grief enters my heart, Hector some day shall boast that I fled before his face," but they never lose the common-sense point of view that "there is no shame in fleeing from ruin, yea, even in the night. Better he fares who flees from trouble than he that is overtaken." A matter-of-fact atmosphere pervades the ringing plains of windy Troy. When Ajax dares to fight with Hector and withstand him, his reward at close of day is substantial: "And wide-ruling Agamemnon gave to Ajax slices of the full length of the [roasted] ox's back for his honor." Homeric heroes do a great deal of eating and drinking and cooking, too; there are receipts given, how to make a pleasant drink from grated cheese and wine and barley, what relishes go best with wine, and so on. The things of daily life play quite as prominent a part as valorous deeds do and "the joy of battle."

All this is completely unlike the *Aeneid*. The heroes there are not human beings, but bigger, stronger, grander. Hector in the *Iliad* advancing to battle is "like a stalled horse, full fed at the manger, when he breaks his tether and speeds exultingly over the plain," or—the extreme of romantic description in the poem—"all in bronze shone Hector even as the lightning of Father Zeus." But Aeneas in the same case is "vast as Mount Athos or Mount Eryx, vast as Father Apennine himself when he shakes his mighty oaks and lifts his snow-topped peak to the sky," or "like Ægaeon who, fable tells, had a hundred arms and a hundred hands and flashed fire through fifty mouths from the depths of fifty bosoms, thundering on fifty strong shields and drawing fifty sharp swords—even so Aeneas slakes his victorious fury the whole field over."

No one in the *Aeneid*, except Dido alone, ever comes down to earth. The heroes never are afraid. They fight for glory only and in its pursuit they are as disdainful of death as the knights of the Round Table or Charlemagne's paladins. "The combatants rush on glorious death through a storm of wounds" over and over again. They pray for death and they go willingly to meet it. "Death I fear not," a wounded warrior cries advancing upon Aeneas, "I come to die." "Have compassion upon me," another hero, defeated, prays. "Dash me on reef, on rock, that none may know my shame." Aeneas bitterly regrets that he did not die when Troy fell:

> Ye Troyan ashes and dear shades of mine,
> I call you witness, that at your last fall
> I fled no stroke of any Greekish sword,
> And if the fates would I had fallen in fight,
> That by my hand I did deserve it well.

But Homer's heroes never want to die. Death is the worst of ills. "Then Hector knew the truth in his heart and he spoke and said, Aye, now verily is evil death come very nigh me nor is there way of escape. He ended and the dark shadow of death came down and his soul flew forth and was gone to the house of Hades, wailing h's fate, leaving fair youth and vigor."

Nowhere, indeed, is the distinction between the classicist and the romanticist seen more clearly than in the way they regard death. On the whole, in Latin literature death is desirable. Even to Horace, the most classic in spirit of all Roman writers, it is "sweet and seemly to die for one's country." English poetry has the same tendency in a notable degree, "Eloquent, just and mighty death," "Dear, beauteous death, the jewel of the just"—there are endless examples. It is the romantic view: the lure to the spirit of the mystery life cannot solve, the sense of all that the unknown may hold, the thrill of the final great adventure. But to the classicist death is always evil unalloyed. Homer's heroes speak in that respect for all Greece. His familiar line that it is better to be a serf on earth than to rule over the dead gives the Greek point of view.

Quotations to decorate soldiers' monuments are found by the score in Latin, but not in Greek. Greek heroism wears an air of soberness always. It is never exultant. The epitaphs the Greeks set on their own soldiers' monuments do not praise heroic death or speak of glory. In all their literature they talk very little of either. They saw too clearly the agony they are rooted in. The Roman boy's thrusting his hand into the fire was beyond question magnificent, a superb gesture of defiance, but I believe a Greek would have been hard put to it to understand it. The Greeks had no gestures. Aeneas, when the great storm comes upon him, lifts his hands to heaven and cries aloud, "Oh, thrice and four times blessed, those who died beneath the walls of Troy." The words are taken from the *Odyssey,* but spoken so differently. Odysseus huddled in the bottom of the boat says them wretchedly to himself. It is impossible to imagine the Greek hero declaiming them to the winds and waves, but it is completely in keeping with the Latin. All the talk in the *Aeneid* is grand. To Virgil, the romantic, the ordinary had no place in an epic. But the classic Homer thought otherwise.

The real subject of the *Aeneid* is not Aeneas, as the real subject of of the *Iliad* is the wrath of Achilles; it is Rome and the glories of her empire, seen as the romanticist sees the great past. The first title given it was *The Deeds of the Roman People.* Aeneas is important because he carries Rome's destiny; he is to be her founder by the high decrees of fate. Repeatedly in the poem the names of the men who made Rome are rehearsed, glowing history in noble poetry: "Love of country shall conquer and the unmeasured thirst for glory. Look—the Decii and the Drusi and Torquatus with his pitiless ax, and Camillus bringing home the standards saved. What tongue would leave you unpraised, great Cato, or you, great Cossus, or pass over in silence the race of the Gracchi or the two Scipios, twin thunderbolts of war, Africa's ruin, or Fabricius mighty in his poverty, or you, Serranus, sowing your own ploughed field? Others, I doubt not, will mold better the breathing bronze to lifelike softness and from marble draw forth living faces. They will plead better at the bar, and mark out the courses of the sky with their rod and tell of the rising stars. Do you, Roman, remember to rule nations with power supreme. Your art shall be this, to impose the custom of peace, to spare the humbled and war down the proud."

HEROIC SONG: SIEGFRIED*

Jan de Vries

It is impossible within the narrow scope of this book to discuss all the products of Germanic epic poetry. Much will therefore have to be left out. But the *Nibelungenlied,* the crown and glory of the Germanic epic, deserves a final brief discussion. When, at the end of the eighteenth century, it was edited from a recently discovered manuscript by the Swiss Myller, Frederic the Great wrote to him, on 22 February 1784, that this miserable trash was not worth a shot of powder. One need not take a general's comparison of a literary work with gunshot too seriously, but the remarkable fact remains that a venerable relic of old national poetry met with so little response when it appeared in the age of classicism. And we can even understand Goethe saying: 'I have feasted at the Homeric as well as the Nibelungen table, but nothing is more in accordance with my character than the breadth and depth of ever-living nature, the works of the Greek poets and sculptors.' The age of Romanticism took a different view. In the years round about 1812 when Jakob Grimm discovered the manuscript of the *Lay of Hildebrand,* one surprise followed another. In 1815 *Beowulf* became known; in 1820 *Kudrun;* in 1830 the Old Saxon *Heliand.* A whole world opened up—a world which had lain buried in monastic libraries from the Middle Ages onwards.

At the beginning of this chapter we glanced at the prehistory of the *Nibelungenlied.* It reaches far back into the past. A whole chain of poems, which came into being and were lost again in the course of the centuries, link the Austrian epic from the beginning of the thirteenth century with its underlying facts, which belong to the time of Attila. It is outside our scope to unravel the mysterious development of this tradition; we shall here try only to determine the nature of the *Nibelungenlied* itself. It corresponds to *Beowulf* in that it consists of two parts which originally did not belong together. It surpasses *Beowulf* in that these parts are closely linked together. For, although the legend of Siegfried is entirely independent, and although the Frankish hero

---

* Jan de Vries, *Heroic Song and Heroic Legend,* trans., B. J. Timmer (London: Oxford University Press, 1963). Reprinted by permission.

had nothing to do with the fall of the Burgundian kings, the epic describes how the death of Siegfried brought the Burgundian catastrophe in its train. This has no connexion at all with real history. It is purely poetic creation that sees or makes connexions where they do not exist in reality.

There are even sharper contrasts between the two parts of the German epic. The second part contains an at times breathtaking account of a genuine heroic story. The fight that breaks out at the banquet given by Etzel to his Burgundian brothers-in-law on their arrival, then the siege of the heroes in the hall that is set alight over their heads, the duels, the figures of Hagen and Rüedeger—all this to a large extent still has the ring of the old heroic legend. But the first part is entirely different. Banquets and journeys by messengers are described in easy-going prolixity, details of dress and armour hardly hold our attention for stanzas on end, especially as the poet seems to be concerned only with displaying royal pomp and splendour. At times the action does not seem to progress. The way in which Siegfried woos the beautiful daughter of the king, Kriemhild, betrays a noble nature such as one naturally encounters at the court of the Staufen, but which does not in the least accord with the crude milieu of fifth-century Worms. Let us be honest: when we come to the second part, we feel something like relief. Our flagging interest is revived again, for now the action gathers speed, tense scenes follow one another, and the events are full of breathtaking tragedy. The story of Siegfried, which ends so dramatically, is told as a charming idyll. We are astonished that the poet pushes the colourful scenes that were actually there—the story of Siegfried's youth with its dragon-fight and the winning of the hoard, the freeing of the maiden, the fight with the dwarf Alberich—entirely into the background, in order to describe with exhausting diffuseness tournaments and hunting scenes instead.

This is no longer a genuine heroic legend. It reminds us rather of the courtly romance which came to Germany from the France of Chrétien de Troyes in the twelfth century. There we find the picture of the cultured and knightly aristocracy with all the *courtoisie* and luxury of France under Philippe-Auguste, with their psychological interest in *amour courtois*, the service which the knight renders to his chosen one, the courtly tournament, and the richness of dress and banquet. There can be no doubt that the poet of the *Nibelungenlied* was familiar with the *roman courtois*; he wanted to imitate its elegant refinement at the Viennese court. One is, indeed, almost inclined to assume that in this case, too, a foreign example showed the Germanic heroic song the way to an extensive and colourful epic, even if it is not Virgil here, but Chrétien de Troyes. The *Nibelungenlied* is like a good hunk of boar's meat smothered in a delicious sauce from the French kitchen.

Two kinds of material, two styles, two ages, clash violently in the *Nibelungenlied*. Was it the poet's lack of ability, or was it perhaps a well-considered plan? Was the granite of the Burgundian heroic legend too much for him, and did he want to transform the undoubtedly more romantic and fairy-tale material of Siegfried's life into a knightly romance of the day with all the refinements of a then modern art? For the *Nibelungenlied* actually has no inner unity. It is astonishing that the same poet who could recount the fall of the Burgundians with all the starkness of an old heroic legend, should be so weak and soft at the beginning of his epic.

It would be too easy to consider this peculiarity in a work of art like the *Nibelungenlied* merely as a failing of the poet. Perhaps he meant it to be like that, and even if we regret that he arranged his work in this way, it is still our duty to try to understand his intentions. The almost brazen contrast between the heroism of the fifth century and the courtly life of the thirteenth cannot have escaped the poet. If he did not avoid this, or at least did not soften it, then he must have wished it thus. It is possible that he composed his poem in such a way that the charm of the beginning gradually darkens to the harshness of the tragic ending, and that he wanted to represent the death of the radiant Siegfried as such a gross injustice that Kriemhild's inhuman revenge is the only acceptable redemption for it. What a contrast it is: Gunther and Hagen at their happy knightly court at Worms and their bitter fight in the burning hall of Etzel. It is, of course, not known how much he took over from his predecessors, but the scene in which Gunther and Hagen keep guard after their arrival is magnificently drawn, and I, for one, would like to take this as the work of the last poet. The two heroes are seated on the bench in front of the hall where the Burgundians are sleeping. The moon is shining in a cloudy sky. Light and dark alternate. Kriemhild emerges from Etzel's palace with some of her faithful attendants, to find out whether she can take the Burgundians by surprise in their sleep. But she finds them watchful, and they see her too. Hagen has Siegfried's sword on his lap. He draws it half-way out of its sheath. The moonlight glitters on the white blade. Kriemhild sees it, and turns back into the stronghold.

That is all. What the woman must have felt, what hot thoughts of revenge must have welled up in her heart at the sight of that sword in the hands of the man who had killed Siegfried, the poet makes no attempt to describe. The situation speaks for itself. It is not the worst artists who sometimes conceal what is most important. For by doing precisely this, they create a picture which rises spontaneously and with an immediate sharp clarity in the reader's mind.

Two worlds, then, are seen beside, if not opposite, each other. One of Worms and Etzel's stronghold in the sphere of the Migration period; the second of about the year 1200. But there is more: there is

Brünhild's Isenstein, situated far in the North, a mythical realm that seems to belong to the remotest past. Three worlds, therefore, which are continually overlapping, and, by doing so, shed all the more light on one another. Or perhaps more correctly, three worlds that are entirely cut off from one another and are placed beside one another without any connexion, but with characters continually moving to and fro between these completely incongruous spaces. Do they feel that they do not belong there? Do their souls not suffer harm when suddenly they pass from one space into the other?

Siegfried, the hero of the dragon-fight and the liberation of the maiden, undoubtedly belongs to the highly archaic sphere of mythical, prehistoric times. How can he presently appear as a perfect and courtly knight at the medievel court of Worms without belying part of himself? The king of that same Worms, however, goes to Isenstein in search of adventure, and there loses his way in the world of the amazon Brünhild. He who adapts himself in such a way must belie his nature. And indeed both perish from this antithesis. Siegfried does not fit in in the Worms of Gunther, where he falls victim to women's intrigues; Gunther has brought back from the mythical Isenstein a wife who is not suited to him and who will be his ruin.

The characters move between two worlds of reality and semblance. What is Siegfried the strong hero doing at the highly civilized court of Worms? How dare the weak Gunther set his heart on the strong Brünhild? The two marriages celebrated with so much outward splendour are suitable in a certain sense, for Siegfried and Kriemhild are well matched in manly strength and female beauty as in every heroic legend. Gunther and Brünhild are a typical royal pair, both borne up by the grandeur of royal majesty. Yet both marriages are based on an inner falseness, because the partners have come together from such different worlds. Siegfried's role as Gunther's retainer is false: the hero belies his own nature when he puts his services at the disposal of the weak Gunther. This falseness ruins him, and it is precisely this false servitude which Brünhild will emphasize so as to raise herself above Kriemhild. The king, who has only a semblance of power, wants to show himself in the role of hero, and is so bold as to desire to marry a woman like Brünhild. How miserably he plays that role! Weakness always has deceit as an ally. Like a true maiden from fairy-tales, Brünhild has made the winning of herself dependent upon tasks which will reveal to her the courage and the strength of her future husband. Gunther is not equal to these, and he has to ask Siegfried to perform the trials of strength in his place. And Siegfried undertakes this unworthy deceitful role; invisible through his *Tarnkappe,* he takes Gunther's place.

Here, then, lie the actual roots of the tragedy of the Nibelungs. The quarrel of the women threatens to lead to the discovery of this deceit. So Gunther must at all costs see to it that the truth will never come out. Yet he cannot prevent himself from losing the nimbus of heroic strength in the eyes of Brünhild. The daily association with this weakling has revealed to her that he is not the husband she had dreamed of. One word from Siegfried is sufficient to dispel the semblance of heroism that he had gained by his deceit in Isenstein. At any moment Siegfried, the man of the real world, can destroy Gunther's world of semblance. That everlasting menace is unbearable: Siegfried will have to be removed. With diabolical cunning a hunting party is planned, at which Hagen gets the opportunity to kill Siegfried.

With the hero's death the world of mythical prehistoric times has come to an end. It is only natural therefore that Brünhild, who belonged to the same sphere, should also disappear completely from the scene: it is as if she has returned to Isenstein. But now the struggle is between Kriemhild and her brothers. Ostensibly the issue is the revenge that will have to be taken for Siegfried, but, in reality, the struggle for power whose symbol is the Nibelung hoard lies behind it. This hoard, for which the people of this courtly world of semblance fight and which will ruin them pitiably, is also mythical. The *motif* of the hoard is very old: it appears much more openly in the *Edda* songs. But whereas in the North the treasure is a symbol of royal power, for which real heroic figures fight bitterly, in the *Nibelungenlied* it is only shadows of power that try to win it. For what is Kriemhild without Siegfried? And similarly, what is Gunther, the king of semblance, without his retainer? The lack of power in both originates from the murder of Siegfried. His shadow falls over the whole final part of the epic.[1]

The poet of the *Nibelungenlied*, then, did not merely want to repeat an old legend. He was posing a problem that was acute in his own day. By placing the Siegfried of unbroken, mythical, prehistoric times in the world of semblance that represented the Worms of about 1200, he has pronounced judgment on the latter. There can be no doubt that to him the world of Siegfried meant an ideal of inner genuineness and solidity. Heroes of the old days perish when they lose their way in the false pretence of courtly life. But why, then, bring back once more to the court of the Staufen that old heroic material from the centuries of the Migration? Is it merely the nostalgia of an over-refined age for the strong primitive life of old? Is it the same nostalgia which was to make Western European man in the eighteenth century dream of an unspoilt natural savage, who is inwardly more genuine and civilized than he himself? Certainly this was partly so, for in the course of the thirteenth century the great epic poems sprang up like mushrooms: *Kudrum*, the poems of Ortnit and Wolfdietrich, and many others from

---

[1] For this view I refer to the essay by W. J. Schröder, 'Das Nibelungenlied', in *Paul und Braunes Beiträge* lxxvi, Halle 1954, pp. 56–143.

the cycle of Dietrich of Bern. It is a renaissance of the old heroic epic, such as France had witnessed a century before; a slow-motion film, as it were, now shown in South-East Germany. But let us remember that such a revival of an old tradition is not merely a matter of fashion, it springs from the very real needs of such a period. Did thirteenth-century Germany want to pull itself up by these old heroic figures? Did the poet of the *Nibelungenlied* wish to point the way?

He certainly had more in mind than merely to make a new song of old and, at the time, surely well-worn material. His devastating criticism of the world of pretence at Worms is really aimed directly at Vienna, where Etzel is in residence and the fall of the Burgundians takes place. With the posing of the problem of nature and civilization, doubts also arise about the value of civilization (in Rousseau at the end of the eighteenth century no less than in the poet at the end of the twelfth). Schröder goes so far as to suppose that this antithesis, which here appears in the modern dress of the thirteenth century, is really only a repetition of what had happened much earlier in the kingdom of the Merovingians: the old kings of this family had relied on power only and created the Frankish kingdom, the younger Merovingians lacked this power and appealed to authority. If this is so, then the poet of the thirteenth century brought this antithesis to light again out of the old legend, which certainly no longer showed it openly, with admirable flair. Moreover, he made it subservient to the posing of the problem of his own time. We need only think of the years in which the epic was written, the reign of Philip of Swabia. The struggle between Guelphs and Ghibellines had flared up again in all its violence. Although officially elected in 1201, Philip still had to contest his real power against the Guelph Otto IV of Brunswick, the son of Henry the Lion. The coronation could not take place in Aachen till 1205. In 1206 Otto's army was definitely defeated.

One wonders if the murder of the emperor in Bamberg in 1208 is reflected in the epic. At any rate, it was the aftermath of a struggle which revealed only too clearly how inwardly weak the Holy Roman Empire had become. Philip of Swabia is depicted as a mild and pious man who strove to make his court the centre of civilization; another Gunther of Worms, therefore, placed in a time that was hard and ruthless. Could the *Nibelungenlied* have been a warning to the emperor, or a covert criticism of him? Possibly both. Here the poet held up a mirror to his time, i.e. to the rulers of his time, in which they could recognize themselves. What did they want? To be Siegfried or Gunther? But these are mere conjectures that will never be proved. Suffice it to stress that this poem did not originate by accident, but that the time cried out for it and found the poet who was able to illustrate the essential problems of the period.

Let us return to literary considerations. For, granting that the *Nibelungenlied* as it has come down was prompted by the needs of its time, can it be called a masterpiece? Can we be allowed to consider this culmination of Germanic epic tradition a sound and successful work? Frankly, we hesitate to place it beside the *Iliad*; perhaps the *Song of Roland*, too, has to be put above the German epic. Aesthetically it is an almost insuperable drawback that neither inwardly nor outwardly does the epic possess a real unity. The poet may have purposely placed two worlds in sharp opposition to each other, but has he managed to solve the antithesis in a higher unity? In this he does not seem to have been quite successful. In reading it, we regret the many weak places and consider many an *aventiure* as a stopgap. The preamble to the action proper is too long; the transition from the first to the second part is too flat. But we should not forget that what is indifferent to us—the long drawn-out scenes of banquets and tournaments—enchanted the Middle Ages. It is not the poet who should be blamed for this, but we ourselves. How many people do really feel, in the endless descriptions of daily life to which the realistic novel treats us, something of the charm of seeing that small world, in which we feel ourselves at home, illuminated in a poetic lustre? That is what makes us feel how beautiful life really is, though we so often live in a humdrum way. But what one can enjoy in the present day fades when one reads about it in a poem of far-off days. It does not live for us. We experience at best a second-hand enjoyment of the beautiful splendour that is gone beyond recall. It is precisely these descriptions of the details of milieu which date a work of art most quickly and irrevocably. Therefore we are only satisfied when we come to the parts of the *Nibelungenlied* that are full of fierce action; to the overheated tension at Etzel's court. But then we are richly rewarded for our severely taxed patience. From the crossing of the Danube to the deaths of Gunther and Hagen, what a tremendous succession of really stirring moments!

In this second part the poet undoubtedly rises to the height of his powers. It may be said that he is borne along by a long tradition, which in some places he follows so faithfully than an Old Norse heroic song is discernible behind it. In other places, it is an insignificant detail of description that turns out to have a truly symbolic meaning. The graphic description of the crossing of the Danube reveals with what impetuous strength Hagen is rowing:

> To turn the boat he held the oar in the water,
> Until the strong oar broke in his hand.
> He wanted to go to his comrades on the shore,
> To mend the damage, he bound the pieces together.

More forcibly it is said in the second *Lay of Atli:*

> Full stoutly they rowed,   and the keel clove asunder,
> Their backs strained at the oars   and their strength was fierce;
> The oar-loops were burst,   the thole-pins were broken
> Nor the ship made they fast,   ere from her they fared.

That violent strength, which breaks the oars, is the expression of the grimness of the heroes when they realize that they will not come back from their journey to the land of the Huns. Yet they refuse to shun the danger and return. What a perspective of tradition opens up here! On the one hand this little scene found its way into a lay said to have been made in Greenland, on the other it found its way, so many centuries later, into the Austrian epic. Neither time nor space have been able to obliterate the deep notches in the epic woodcarving.

Yet it would not be right to praise the poet of the *Nibelungenlied* for preserving so magnificently what was old and, at the same time, to blame him for sometimes failing in his own additions. If the character of Rüedeger is his own creation, which I would gladly believe, it proves his mastery. And if he took it over from a predecessor, he still put something of his soul into it. When the Burgundians enter Bavaria they know from the prophecy of the mermaids in the Danube that they are heading for their downfall. The air is heavy with disaster. They arrive at Bechelaeren and are received by the margrave Rüedeger, and suddenly the gentle sun of idyll shines through the stormy clouds. What a cordial and carefree reception, crowned by the engagement of Giselher to the margrave's daughter! What perspectives of happiness are opening up! We think that this tender happiness will not be broken: will the heroes return from Vienna safe and sound? The reception in Vienna is full of pomp and splendour. But Kriemhild is brooding on revenge. When the battle for the hall, where the Burgundians have ultimately entrenched themselves, is raging, Etzel summons his retainers, one after the other, to throw themselves into the fight with Gunther and his men. Finally Rüedeger's turn comes. He appeals to the recent ties of kinship with the Burgundian princes, but in vain: Etzel reminds him of the other and much stronger ties that bind the retainer to his lord. Rüedeger has the same inner conflict as Hagen in the *Waltharius*. In both cases the retainers' oath turns the scale. Uneasy in mind, Rüedeger proceeds to the entrance of the hall. The Burgundians see him coming and can only suppose that he comes to offer peace. How dreadful it is for the margrave to have to say that he has come to fight against them. It shows the poet's exquisite tact that he has not made him fall in a duel with Giselher, but with his brother Gernot with the sword that Rüedeger himself had given him.

Such a scene reveals the true poet. In him the feeling for the old heroic poetry had indeed not been extinguished, for he could sympathize with the old heroes, even though he was enough of a modern man to turn the inexorable pathos into an inhuman cruelty which almost mars the end of the poem. Inner uncertainty of later generations towards the ideals of the old heroic days often reveals itself through an exaggeration in two directions: either in that of a weak sentimentality or in that of pushing the stark tragedy to extremes.

The poet of the *Nibelungenlied* was compelled to his creation by an inner urge of vocation. How else could he, in the century of the playful love-song and of Celtic romanticism, have blown so resolutely on the Nibelung bugle? Were people still willing to listen to such fierce sounds at that time? Was there still an interest in those far-off legends? But every truly great poet is both an end and a beginning. This is that last poem that celebrates the story of Siegfried and the Burgundians, but at the same time, as we have already seen, it stands at the beginning of a short, flourishing period of German literature in which the old legends, in rejuvenated form, were once more to enchant large circles of attentive listeners.

THE DARK AGES: *BEOWULF**

Gilbert Highet

Of all the great modern European languages, English has by far the largest and most important early literature. During the Dark Ages of history, between the fall of Rome and, say, the year 1000, there must have been some vernacular poetry in France, in Italy, in Russia, in Spain, and elsewhere—although it is unlikely that there was much more than songs and ballads in local dialects. But virtually none of it has survived: it may never have been written down. In German there is nothing but two or three fragments of war-poems; two poetic paraphrases of the Gospel story, with a section of a poem on Genesis and a short description of Doomsday; and several of Notker's philosophical and biblical translations. In the peripheral lands—Iceland, Ireland, Norway, Wales—there were growing up interesting collections of sagas and romances, mythical, gnomic, and occasionally elegiac poems; and in popular Greek some ballads and heroic tales have survived. Of course Latin books were being written in a continuous international tradition, while the Byzantine scholars continued, often with remarkable freshness, to compose in the forms of classical Greek literature. But scarcely anything else has survived in the language of the people out of so many centuries.

However, long before 1000, a rich, varied, original, and lively national literature was being created in England. It began soon after the western Roman empire fell; and it developed, in spite of frightful difficulties, during the dismal years known as the Dark Ages, when western European civilization was fighting its way up from barbarism once again.

ANGLO-SAXON POETRY

The most important poem in old English literature is an epic called *Beowulf*. It deals with two heroic exploits in the life of a warrior chief, but also covers his youth, his accession to the throne, his kingship, and his death. Beowulf is his name, and he is called prince of the Geatas.

* Gilbert Highet, *The Classical Tradition* (New York: Oxford University Press, 1949). Reprinted by permission.

This tribe is believed to have lived in Götaland, which is still the name of southern Sweden; and one of the battles in which the poem says he fought is known to have occurred about the year A.D. 520.[1] The chief tribes mentioned are the Angles, the Swedes, the Franks, the Danes, and the Geatas themselves. The material of the poem was therefore brought over from the Baltic area by some of the fierce war-bands who invaded Britain after the Romans left it.

Its chief interest is that it shows us an earlier stage of development in European civilization than any other comparable document, Greek and Roman books included. Compare it with Homer. The type of life described, a disorganized world of tribal states, raiding-parties, and gallant chiefs, is pretty much the same. Beowulf himself would have been welcomed in the camp of the Achaeans outside Troy, and would have won the swimming prize at Patroclus' funeral games. But there are important differences:

(a) In *Beowulf*, the conflict is between man and the sub-human. Beowulf's chief enemy Grendel is a giant cannibal living in a cave. (Apart from Grendel's terrific size, he is not necessarily a mere fable. As late as the seventeenth century there are reports from outlying parts of Europe of cannibal families inhabiting caves not unlike Grendel's. The most famous case is Sawney Bean, in southern Scotland.) The other opponent of Beowulf is a firedrake, a flame-spitting dragon guarding a treasure. So the story represents the long fight between brave tribal warriors on one side and, on the other, the fierce animals of the wilderness and the bestial cave-beings who live outside the world of men and hate it.[2] But in the *Iliad* the war is between raiding tribesmen from a Greece which, though primitive, is not empty of towns and commerce, and the rich civilized Asiatic city of Troy, with rich and civilized allies like Memnon. There is no prolonged conflict between men and animal monsters in Homer. (Bellerophon was forced to fight against a lion-goat-snake monster, the Chimera, which breathed fire; but that incident takes

---

[1] See R. W. Chambers, *Beowulf* (Cambridge, 1932²), 3, with his quotation from Gregory of Tours, *Hist. Franc.* 110; H. M. Chadwick, in *The Cambridge History of English Literature* (ed. A. W. Ward and A. R. Waller, Cambridge, 1920), 1. 3; C. W. Kennedy, *The Earliest English Poetry* (New York, 1943), 54 and 78 f.; and W. W. Lawrence, *Beowulf and Epic Tradition* (Cambridge, Mass., 1930), c. 2. On the Geatas in particular see the discussions in Chambers, 2–12 and 333–45.

[2] Bodvar Biarki, who may have been the prototype of Beowulf, won fame by killing a monstrous great bear. Another view is that Beowulf himself was the son of a bear, a bear-like spirit: hence his riddling name, 'bee-wolf', since the bear is death to bees. If this is true, he reaches even farther back in history, to the point where man is just emerging from the animal world. See Chambers (cited in n. I), 365 f., and Rhys Carpenter, *Folk tale, Fiction, and Saga in the Homeric Epics* (Sather Classical Lectures, 20, Berkeley, Cal., 1946).

only five lines to narrate.[3] The chief Homeric parallels to this aspect of *Beowulf* are to be found in the *Odyssey*, where they are located in wild regions far outside the Greek world: Grendel's nearest kinsmen are the Cyclopes of the Sicilian mountains, or the man-eating Laestrygones in the land of the midnight sun.) Compared with Homer, Beowulf's adventures take place, not in the morning light of civilization, but in the twilight gloom of that huge, lonely, anti-human world, the forest primeval, the world so beautifully and horribly evoked by Wagner in *The Ring of the Nibelungs*; or that of the weird Finnish *Kalevala*, which is ennobled in the music of Sibelius.

(b) The world of *Beowulf* is narrower and simpler than that of Homer. Men's memories are very short. Their geographical range is small: north central Europe, bounded by pathless forest and serpent-haunted sea, with no trace of Slavs or Romans beyond. Within this frontier their settlements are lonely, scattered, and ill organized. When new champions face each other in the *Iliad*, or when Odysseus makes a new landfall in the *Odyssey*, there is usually a polite but clear exchange of information which shoots rays of light into the surrounding darkness. We hear of great cities in the distance and great heroes in the past. The result is that the epics gradually build up a rich collection of historical and geographical knowledge, rather like the books of Judges and Samuel in the Bible. But *Beowulf* contains far less such information, because its characters and composers knew far less of the past and of the world around. Any three thousand lines of *Iliad* or *Odyssey* take us into a wider, more populous, more highly explored and interdependent world than all the 3,183 lines of *Beowulf*; and the customs, weapons, stratagems, arts, and personalities of Homer are vastly more complex than those of the Saxon epic.

(c) Artistically, *Beowulf* is a rude and comparatively unskilled poem. Epic poetry is, like tragedy, a highly developed literary growth. Its wild ancestors still exist in many countries. They are short poems describing single deeds of heroic energy or suffering: the ballads of the Scottish borders, the songs about Marko Kraljević and other Serbian chiefs, the fine Anglo-Saxon fragment, *Maldon*, about a battle against the invading Danes. Sometimes these are roughly linked together, to make a cycle or a chronicle telling of many great exploits performed in one war, or under one dynasty, or by one group of strong men.[4] But

---

[3] *Iliad*, 6, 179–83.
[4] For the sake of brevity the account in the text has been simplified. Strictly we should distinguish between different types of short heroic poems, since it is probable that only formal lays, and not songs and ballads of heroism, grew into the full stature of epic. See C. M. Bowra, *Tradition and Design in the Iliad* (Oxford, 1930), c. 2, and A. J. Toynbee, *A Study of History* (Oxford, 1939), 5. 296 f.

still these do not make an epic. All the adventures of Hercules, or King David, or King Arthur and his knights, will form a interesting story, but they will not have the artistic impact of a real epic. An epic is made by a single poet (or perhaps a closely linked succession, a family of poets) who relates one great heroic adventure in detail, connecting it with as much historical, geographical, and spiritual background as will make it something much more deeply significant than any isolated incident, however remarkable, and causing it to embody a profound moral truth.

Now, most of the heroic poetry in the world belongs to the first stage of this development. It tells the story of Sir Patrick Spens, or the battle of Otterburn, and then stops. There is an Anglo-Saxon poem like this, called *Finnsburh*, which we can also find built into *Beowulf* in a different shape, like the little chapel which later architects have worked into a large and complex church.[5] The Icelandic sagas correspond to the second stage, the long chronicle—although a few, like *Njala*, have the nobility of true epic. *Beowulf* is a dogged, though unskilled, attempt to reach the third stage, and to make a poem combining unity and variety, heroic action and spiritual meaning. Here is its skeleton:

100–1,062 Beowulf fights the giant Grendel;
1,233–1,921 Beowulf fights Gendel's mother;
2,211–3,183 Beowulf fights the fiery dragon, and dies.

So the poem is mostly occupied by relating two (or at most three) heroic adventures, which are essentially similar, not to say repetitious. Two happen in a distant country and the third at the end of Beowulf's long life; while his accession to the throne and his fifty years' reign are passed over in less than 150 lines.[6] The other episodes, evoking the past,[7] comparing Beowulf with earlier heroes,[8] and foretelling the gloomy future,[9] were designed to coordinate these adventures into a single multidimensional structure; but the builder could scarcely plan well enough. It would have been astonishing if the age which made only the most primitive churches and castles and codes of law could have produced poets with the power to conceive a large and subtle plan and to impose it on the rough recalcitrant material and half-barbarous audiences with which they had to deal. The style and language of the poem, in comparison with the greater epics of Greece and Rome, are limited in range, sometimes painfully harsh and difficult; yet, even if awkward,

[5] *Beowulf*, 1063–1159.
[6] *Beowulf*, 2200–10, 2397–509.
[7] *Beowulf*, 1–52, the funeral of that mysterious monarch Scyld Scefing.
[8] *Beowulf*, 853–1159.
[9] *Beowulf*, 2892–3075.

they are tremendously bold and powerful, like the hero of whom they tell.[10]

There is apparently no direct classical influence on *Beowulf* and the other Anglo-Saxon secular poems.[11] They belong to a different world

[10] This judgment depends partly upon taste, but partly too on objective facts. Homer, for instance, has proportionately a much wider vocabulary, many more types of sentence-structure, far subtler varieties of metre, and a more delicate sense of language than the author of *Beowulf*, without being less powerful in scenes of conflict. No doubt this is because there was a longer tradition of composition behind him, and a larger range of dialects and poetic styles from which he made his language (see pp. 481–2). But it is quite wrong to believe that one cannot praise *Beowulf* if one admires the *Iliad*. *Beowulf* contains much fine and memorable poetry, and has often been unfairly criticized: for example by Taine, who writes:

'On ne peut traduire ces idées fichées en travers, qui déconcertent toute l'économie de notre style moderne. Souvent on ne les entend pas; les articles, les particules, tous les moyens d'éclaircir la pensée, de marquer les attaches des termes, d'assembler les idées en un corps régulier, tous les artifices de la raison et de la logique sont supprimés. La passion mugit ici comme une énorme bête informe, et puis c'est tout.' (*Histoire de la littérature anglaise*, Paris, 1905[12], 1. 5.)

The critics have recently been criticized by Mr. J. R. Hulbert, '*Beowulf* and the Classical Epic' (*Modern Philology*, 44 (1946–7), 2. 65–75). He defends the plan of the poem—packed as it is with digressions sometimes obscurely told and abruptly introduced—by suggesting that the poet was using the allusive, associative method of such sophisticated writers as Browning and Conrad. This is possible, but, considering the simplicity of Old English society and thought, scarcely probable. Mr. Hulbert is right in saying that the style of *Beowulf* is strong and impressive, but he has been misled by Matthew Arnold into thinking that Homer's style is 'prosaic'. In fact, it is as rich, strong, and poetic in both simplicity and elaboration as that of Shakespeare's tragedies. (On this point also see p. 481 f.) The truth is that *Beowulf*, like the life it describes, belongs to a more primitive stage of history than Homer. Judging from their fragments, the early epics of the fighting Romans, such as Naevius' *Punic War*, must have looked a little like *Beowulf* Naevius' poem is lost, but *Beowulf* has been miraculously preserved, like the shields and helmets and drinking-horns which are still found in the Scandinavian peat-bogs, to be treasured both as rare historical relics and as true works of art.

[11] In recent years there have been several studies of possible classical influence on *Beowulf*, and in particular of the supposed influence of Vergil. The following are the main arguments:

(a) We could scarcely 'explain the existence of such a broadly constructed epic poem without the model of Vergil' (F. Klaeber, 'Aeneis und Beowulf', in *Archiv fur das Studium der neueren Sprachen und Literaturen*, n.s. 26 (1911), 40 f. and 339 f.). This means that no Anglo-Saxon poet was capable of conceiving a large-scale poem from his own imagination and from the earlier heroic Anglo-Saxon poems he had learnt in his youth. That is an assumption which by its nature cannot be proved, and is improbable. Large heroic poems have been composed in a number of countries outside any possible Vergilian influence (we shall soon be dealing with The Song of Roland, whose author or authors obviously knew no Latin), and the Anglo-Saxon poets have no lack of originality and boldness. What they did lack was the finer taster which would have allowed the composer of *Beowulf* to con-

Footnote 11, continued:
struct his epic more graciously and richly and symmetrically. If he had really known the *Aeneid, Beowulf* would have been better built. In addition, as Klaeber himself admits, there is hardly anything in common between the general plan of Beowulf.

(b) A number of incidents in the *Aeneid* and in *Beowulf* are similar. (Klaeber gives a list; there are others in T. B. Haber, *A Comparison of the 'Aeneid' and the 'Beowulf'*, Princeton, 1931.) Some of these parallels are ludicrously far-fetched: for instance,

⌡Beowulf lands in Denmark and is interrogated by coastguards.
⌠Aeneas lands in Libya and is interrogated by his mother Venus in disguise.

Others are genuine resemblances, as when both heroes tell of their past exploits, at a royal banquet. These resemblances, however, prove not that one poet copied the other, but that the scenes and customs they described were similar: which we know to be true. In order to show that *Beowulf* copied the *Aeneid* in describing a hero's feast or funeral we should have to prove that the Anglo-Saxons had no such customs of their own. But we know that they, and their predecessors in Europe, had a culture very similar to that of the Homeric Greeks and Trojans. (See H. M. Chadwick, *The Heroic Age*, cc. 15–19.) It is therefore more probable that the author of *Beowulf* described customs practised or known through tradition among his own people than that he borrowed from an account in a book written in an alien language and a different language and a different national tradition.

(c) Some of the descriptions of nature in the *Aeneid* and *Beowulf* are similar. (Thus, C. W. Kennedy, *The Earliest English Poetry*, 92–7, suggests that the description of the haunted tarn where Grendel lives, *Beowulf*, 1337–76, is imitated from Vergil's *Aeneid*, 7. 563–71.) It is possible that the poet of *Beowulf* copied such descriptions from Vergil, but it is highly improbable. First, because there was a much larger and handier reservoir of poetic description on which he could draw: the existing Old English poetry, which must have been far greater in volume than the few fragments which have survived to modern times. Mr. Kennedy himself points out on pp. 180–2 how the poet of *Exodus* inserted incongruous conventional descriptions of battle and blood-stained water into his account of Pharaoh pursuing the Hebrews into the Red Sea; and Mr. Rhys Carpenter, in *Folk tale, Fiction, and Saga in the Homeric Epics*, 6–9, reminds us how full a collection of stereotyped descriptions and phrases oral poets possess and transmit. Then, secondly, the Anglo-Saxon poets, if they did not use traditional descriptions in their own tongue, were well able to evoke the scenery of the gloomy north without borrowing details from an Italian poet. The splendid descriptions of the sea in many Old English poems, and the fine elegiac account of Roman ruins in *The Ruin*, are evidence for their powers of original observation.

(d) Turns of phrase in the *Aeneid* and *Beowulf* are similar, e.g. *swîgedon ealle* (B. 1699) and *conticuere omnes* (A. 2.1); *wordhord onīēac* (B. 259) and *effundit pectore uoces* (A. 5. 482). (T. B. Haber, op. cit. in note *b*, 31 f.) My knowledge of Anglo-Saxon does not permit me to offer a useful opinion on this point; but from translations, the parallels look like coincidences of fairly obvious imagery (e.g. 'tossed on the waves of care') and the like, rather than imitations. And certainly the differences in language which can be observed are far more striking than the resemblances.

(e) Vergil's *Aeneid* was well known in northern Britain, and 'would surely have appealed to a poet versed in Germanic traditions' (Lawrence, *Beowulf and Epic Tradition*, 284–5). This argument is usually pushed much too far, and should be balanced by the following qualifications:

Footnote 11, continued:
(1) Priestly scholars knew Vergil during the Dark Ages in Britain, but they did not write long secular heroic poems in the vernacular. Aldhelm is reported to have sung vernacular songs to attract people to hear the gospel, but he was only making a one-way bridge over a gulf he would not cross. The greatest of these scholars, Alcuin, wrote a letter to a British bishop expressly decrying the taste for poems of heroic legend (Chadwick, *The Heroic Age,* 41 f.) and calling a hero like Beowulf a damned pagan.

(2) We do not hear, and it is difficult to imagine, that professional bards, like the maker of *Beowulf,* already steeped in their native tradition of heroic poetry, were enabled to learn enough Latin to study the *Aeneid.* In the Dark Ages, and for centuries afterwards, the way to learn Latin was to start with the Latin Bible. But the knowledge of the Bible shown in *Beowulf* is so extremely thin and vague that the poet can hardly have been able to read the Vulgate directly. Bede himself knew the Bible and the church fathers far better than Vergil, and Vergil was the only classical author he knew first-hand (M. L. W. Laistner, 'Bede as a Classical and a Patristic Scholar', *Transactions of the Royal Historical Society,* series 4, vol. 16, 73 f.). How then could a bard who barely knew the opening chapters of Genesis be so familiar with the difficult *Aeneid* as to imitate it in detail and in general plan? There is a parallel to this in the first appearance of the Trojan story in French medieval literature. Benoit de Sainte-Maure, who put the legends into French poetry, took them not from the *Aeneid* or the Latin *Iliad* but from a short romance in prose which was far easier to read; and even then he did not follow it carefully.

(3) When at last the two traditions, of Latin and of Anglo-Saxon poetry, blended, the results were grand. The blending begins with Cædmon, and goes on through the later poems attributed to him, through Cynewulf, to *The Dream of the Rood* and *Phoenix.* But all such poetry, although it uses the Anglo-Saxon poetic conventions, is religious in content as well as purpose. Anyone who at that time learnt enough Latin to understand the *Aeneid* would be dedicated to the service of God, and would not write a poem on monsters overcome in bloody battles, not by the power of the spirit but by strength of arm and magical weapons.

(4) In general, the sort of imaginative stimulus experienced by sensitive modern writers after reading a moving book is not likely to occur in primitive poets. As we see from *Phoenix,* when they copy a book, they copy it carefully and obviously. But they do not write poetry of their own containing 'reminiscences' of classical poetry. That road leads not to Grendel's cave, but to Xanadu.

---

from that of Greco-Roman civilization. Attempts have been made to prove that *Beowulf* imitates the *Aeneid,* but they consist mainly in showing that both poems describe distantly similar heroic incidents in heroic language; and on these lines we could prove that the Indian epic poets copied Homer. The differences in language, structure, and technique are so striking as to make any material resemblance merely coincidental, even if it were probable that a poet working in one difficult tradition at such a period would borrow from another even more difficult. When early craftsmen like the creator of *Beowulf* know any classical literature, they are forced by its superior power and elaboration to adapt it very carefully and obviously.

There is, however, a certain amount of Christian influence—although it is evidently peripheral, and later than the main conception of the poem. *Beowulf*, like the world in which it grew, shows Christian ideals superimposed upon a barbarous pagan substructure, and just beginning to transform it. We see the same thing in some of the Icelandic sagas and in the Gaelic legends. Lady Gregory tells how Oisin argued with St. Patrick from the old heroic standpoint, and said to him:

'Many a battle and many a victory was gained by the Fianna of Ireland; I never heard any great deed was done by the King of Saints (i.e. Jesus), or that he ever reddened his hand.'[12]

So *Beowulf* both begins and ends with a thoroughly pagan funeral. It is significant also that, when Heorot the haunted palace was first opened, a minstrel sang a song about the first five days of Creation (evidently based on Genesis, like Caedmon's hymn); but later, when the ogre began to attack the palace, the chiefs who debated about preventive measures vowed sacrifices to 'the slayer of souls' (= the devil = a pagan divinity). Such inconsistency can be a sign either of interpolation or of the confusion of cultures. What Christian influence does appear is strictly Old Testament tradition. The audience of *Beowulf*, the 'half-barbarous folk' to whom Aldhelm sang vernacular songs, was scarcely at an intellectual and spiritual level which would permit it to appreciate the gospels and the Pauline epistles. God is simply a monotheistic king, ruler, and judge, venerable because of his power. There is no mention of Jesus Christ, of the cross, of the church, of saints, or of angels.[13] One or two early Old Testament stories appear, as it were grafted upon paganism: the giant Grendel, together with 'ogres and elves and sea-monsters', is said to come of the race of the fratricide Cain; and there is a mention of the Flood.[14] But all this, although it comes through the Latin Bible, is classical influence at its very thinnest. Greece and Rome had no immediate influence on *Beowulf* and its kindred poems, any more than on the Welsh *Mabinogion*, the stories of Fingal and his warriors, the great legends of Arthur, and other heroic tales which grew up along the frontiers of the dissolving civilization of Rome. Classical influence, if it reached them and their makers at all, reached them through the church. After the Greek world had been cut off and the Roman world barbarized, the church civilized the barbarians. *Beowulf* allows us to see

[12] Lady Gregory, *Gods and Fighting Men* (London, 1910), 2. 11. 4.

[13] See H. M. Chadwick, *The Heroic Age* (Cambridge, 1912), 47–8. F. A. Blackburn, 'The Christian Coloring in the *Beowulf*' (*PMLA*, 12, n.s. 5 (1897), 205–25), analyses the passages which show acquaintance with certain elementary Christian doctrines, and shows that they could (and probably must) have been For instance, the numerous mentions of God could be replaced by *Wyrd*, 'fate', without in the slightest altering the meaning; and sometimes *Wyrd* has been allowed to remain in such passages.

[14] *Beowulf*, 107 f., 1261 f. (Cain and Abel): *orcnêas* in 112 is variously translated 'sea-monsters', and 'hellish things', from the Latin root of *Orcus*. The Flood appears in 1688–93.

how it began: gradually and wisely, by converting them. After many dark centuries, Europe regained civilization, urged forward largely by feeling, once again, the stimulus of the spirit of Greece and Rome; but it was the church which, by transmitting a higher vision through that influence, began the reconquest of the victorious barbarians upon the ruins of the defeated empire.

In *A Study of History* Mr. A. J. Toynbee discusses the very odd fact that none of the northern epics describes the greatest war-like achievement of their peoples, the overthrow of the Roman empire.[15] His explanation is that the barbarians found the Romans too complex to write about, and the chiefs who conquered them (such as Clovis and Theodoric) too dull. This answer is incomplete. Not all the victors were dull. Many were memorable figures like Attila (= Etzel and Atli in epic and saga). But the Roman empire was indeed too vast and complicated. Its conquest therefore took too long for the tribesmen and tribal poets to see it as one heroic effort. The *Iliad* is not about the siege of Troy— although, because of Homer's genius, it implies the ten years' fighting and the final capture: still less is it about the whole invasion of the Mediterranean area by the men from the north. For primitive man the stimulus to action and to poetry is single: an insult, a woman, a monster, or a treasure. Further, although they looted cities in the Roman empire, although they displaced officials and occupied territories, many of the barbarians did not think they were subjugating an alien enemy so much as taking over their due share in privileges from which they had been kept. They did not abolish the empire. They moved in and took it over. To adapt a phrase of Mommsen's, the conquest meant the romanization of the barbarians even more than the barbarization of the Romans.[16] And lastly (as Mr. Toynbee hints) the very process of conquering the empire tended to abolish their urge towards epic literature, for it was a successful operation, and a success that made them richer and more staid. Heroic poetry seldom describes successes, unless against fearful odds. It prefers to tell of the defeat which makes the brave man even braver and rounds off his life.[17] Not through conquering Rome would

[15] A. J. Toynbee, *A Study of History* (Oxford, 1939), 5. 610. f.

[16] This is the point of view expounded by J. B. Bury in *The Invasion of Europe by the Barbarians* (London, 1928): see also p. 478 of this book on Fustel de Coulanges.

[17] There is a fine example of this, reported by a Roman historian, from an earlier but similar era. After Hannibal had crossed the Alps, he determined to give his exhausted troops new courage for their first battle with the Romans in Italy. So, as a living example of the gallantry that despises death, he brought out some of the wild Alpine tribesmen (evidently Celts) whom he had captured en route. He offered them the chance of winning their liberty by fighting duels, the victor to be set free. They accepted gladly, seizing the weapons and dancing a highland fling, *cum sui moris tripudiis*. And then, during the fighting, the spectators expressed just as much admiration for the loser, if he died well, as for the winner: 'ut non uincentium magis quam bene morientium fortuna laudaretur' (Livy, 21. 42).

the barbarians' will become harder and their hearts keener.[18] But centuries later they re-created the heroic style. When they themselves, led by a new Caesar (a Christian of barbarian descent), were threatened by new pagans no less formidable, then, over high mountain and dark valley, rang out the dying trumpet of Roland.

[18] Hige sceal be heardra, heorte be cenre,
mod sceal be mare, be ure maegen lytlad   (*Maldon*, 312–13).

DANTE

E. M. W. Tillyard*

I must explain why I have so little to say about Dante when I said so much about Homer. Both poets are the head of different kinds of epic and as such would call for equal treatment. But whereas Homer led on to Virgil and Virgil to a great European form of poetry, Dante created no school. The epic attempts of Petrarch and Boccaccio were not after his fashion. The English medieval poet who owed most to him, Chaucer, was not an epic writer and valued him more as a learned man and the master of much substance than as a poet. The English medieval poet who most resembles him in substance and method, Langland, may have heard of him but shows no signs of having read him. If Dante and Langland both faced the problem of the righteous heathen and their fate, they derived their knowledge of the problem independently. Nor did Dante affect the course of the later English epic. From the Renaissance on he could not, as a model, compete with the classical epic writers. Milton read and admired him, but *Paradise Lost* would have been much the same if he had never done so. It was not till after the time-period covered by this book that the poets began to draw direct inspiration from the *Divine Comedy*. Shelley's *Triumph of Life* and Keats's revised *Hyperion* do indeed show a fundamental debt to it, but they are fragments and they come after the great tradition of English verse epic had expired. Dante scarcely counts as an influence on the English epic.

There are other reasons why I should say little about Dante. There is more agreement about his quality than about Homer's and Virgil's. Many people continue the belief that the Homeric poems are composite; and many continue the nineteenth-century habit of degrading Virgil from the highest rank. No one seeks to find more than one author for the *Divine Comedy* or thinks it inferior poetry. Where there is no controversy, there is less reason to intervene. In the reaction against the long dominance of the Greek and Latin Classics the modern reader has tended to cloak them with the dust of a now hated scholarship and to

* E. M. W. Tillyard, *The English Epic and Its Background* (London: Chatto and Windus; New York: Oxford University Press, 1954). Reprinted by permission.

think of them as more jejune and less human than the classics of other times and races. It is therefore wholesome to try to speak of them as literature like other literature. Dante has not suffered in the same way, and there is no reason to persuade the modern reader to put aside prejudice and to give him the chance to which all literature is entitled.

But though I should be wrong to write of Dante at length, it is fitting at this point to repeat the commonplace that Dante was the great poet of the Middle Ages and to say that this greatness was of the epic kind, in the way I use the word. Dante's span in the *Divine Comedy* equals that of any other poet. He ranged from the homely human passions to the highest religious emotion. He included theology and the whole medieval world picture. He sustained his will-power with a completeness surpassed by none. And though his structure resembles that of a great picture of Fra Angelico and not that of one by Titian, it is complete in every way. Probably no poem of comparable length is so elaborately interlocked. The *Divine Comedy* has never been questioned as the voice of its age and of Italy. Its subject is the great contemporary one; the pilgrimage of the human soul: not indeed through a realistically conceived journey but from a mental Hell through a mental Purgatory to a mental Paradise.[1] But this unquestioned choric character must not blind us to the high originality of the poem. Dante took much from the age's great poetic master, Virgil; and yet, except for the formal epic simile, he refrained from imitating him. He nourished himself on Virgil's spirit while transmuting it and making it his own. He broke with tradition by using his own language and not Latin for a very serious poem; and yet the seriousness he commanded was largely that of his age. Dante possessed every attribute of the epic poet in the fullest measure that appears humanly possible.

Samuel Taylor Coleridge*

In studying Dante, therefore, we must consider carefully the differences produced, first, by allegory being substituted for polytheism; and secondly and mainly, by the opposition of Christianity to the spirit of pagan Greece, which receiving the very names of its gods from Egypt, soon deprived them of all that was universal. The Greeks changed the ideas into finites, and these finites into *anthropomorphi*, or forms of men. Hence their religion, their poetry, nay, their very

---

[1] See H. O. Taylor, *The Medieval Mind* (4th ed. London 1925) ii. 579: 'The *Commedia* is the pilgrimage of the soul after all wisdom.'
* Samuel Taylor Coleridge, *A Course of Lectures* (1818).

pictures, became statuesque. With them the form was the end. The reverse of this was the natural effect of Christianity; in which finites, even the human form, must, in order to satisfy the mind, be brought into connexion with, and be in fact symbolical of, the infinite; and must be considered in some enduring, however shadowy and indistinct, point of view, as the vehicle or representative of moral truth.

Hence resulted two great effects; a combination of poetry with doctrine, and, by turning the mind inward on its own essence instead of letting it act only on its outward circumstances and communities, a combination of poetry with sentiment. And it is this inwardness or subjectivity which principally and most fundamentally distinguishes all the classic from all the modern poetry. Compare the passage in the Iliad (Z. vi. 119–236) in which Diomed and Glaucus change arms,—

They took each other by the hand, and pledged friendship—with the scene in Ariosto (Orlando Furioso, c. I. st. 20–22), where Rinaldo and Ferrauto fight and afterwards make it up:—

> Al Pagan la proposta non dispiacque:
> Così fu differita la tenzone;
> E tal tregua tra lor subito nacque
> Sì l'odio e l'ira va in oblivione,
> Che 'l Pagano al partir dalle fresche acque
> Non lasciò a piede il buon figliuol d'Amone:
> Con preghi invita, e al fin lo toglie in groppa,
> E per l'orme d'Angelica galoppa.

Here Homer would have left it. But the Christian poet has his own feelings to express, and goes on:—

> Oh gran bontà de' cavalieri antiqui!
> Eran rivali, eran di fè diversi,
> E si sentían degli aspri colpi iniqui
> Per tutta la persona anco dolersi;
> E pur per selve oscure e calli obbliqui
> Insieme van senza sospetto aversi!

And here you will observe, that the reaction of Ariosto's own feelings on the image or act is more fore-grounded (to use a painter's phrase) than the image or act itself.

THE ROMANCE EPIC*

Graham Hough

The romantic epic of Italy has its distant ancestry in the *chansons de geste* of France, but in form and spirit it belongs to such a different world that it could fairly be described as a complete perversion of these austere originals. There are several cycles of these old French epics all having for their theme or for the background of their adventures the struggle between Christendom and the Saracens. The Italian poems are derived from the central Carolingian cycle which has as its main characters Charlemagne and his peers. Happily this takes us back for purposes of illustration and contrast not to the subsidiary *chansons* such as *Le Charroi de Nimes* or *Le Couronnement de Louis*, but directly to the oldest, the grandest and the most famous of the French epics, the *Chanson de Roland* itself.

Le Chanson de Roland is different in almost all points, material, structure, style and temper, from the Italian poems that are derived from it or from its fellows (for the decent is doubtless not direct); and *a fortiori* different from Spenser. But to say something about it at the beginning is not altogether pointless. Spenser's romance-world is an ancient and well-cultivated soil, with the débris of many civilizations beneath its surface—more even than Spenser knew himself. There is interest and value in looking briefly at the remote origin of the literature that Spenser drew on. And the Carolingian cycle has I believe left one legacy of fundamental importance to all its successors.

The *Song of Roland* purports to have been composed by one Turoldus. It probably dates from the early years of the twelfth century. It is, as everybody knows, a tale of tragic heroism, told with bare passionate simplicity. There are no digressions from the tragic outline: and as for style there is but one simile, which takes two lines. The characters are warriors and heroes, royal and venerable, like Charlemagne, wise and temperate, like Oliver, or passionate and brave to the point of recklessness, like Roland; loyal, like Archbishop Turpin, or treacherous, like Ganelon. But none of them engages in irrelevant adventures, or falls in

* Reprinted from *A Preface to The Faerie Queene* by Graham Hough by permission of W. W. Norton & Company, Inc. and Gerald Duckworth & Co., Ltd. Copyright © 1962 by Graham Hough. First American Edition 1963, W. W. Norton & Company, Inc.

love, or is distracted in any way from his heroic and tragic destiny. The plot is essentially the ample treatment of a simple idea. Charlemagne and his host are returning from Spain after a successful campaign against the Saracens. In crossing the Pyrenees Roland is given the rear-guard. He refuses the offer of half the army and will take only twenty thousand men. But he has been betrayed by Ganelon who hates him; and arrived at Roncesvalles he finds himself ambushed by a huge Saracen army. Against the advice of his comrade Oliver he refuses to blow his horn to summon help from Charlemagne, and stands to fight it out. They make a heroic defence but it is hopeless. At last Roland does blow his horn; the sound carries thirty miles; Charlemagne hears it and turns back; but it is too late. Oliver dies, Roland dies, and Charlemagne arrives only in time to take revenge for the slaughter of his peers.

What has this heroic legend, in its noble simplicity, to do with the fluid intricacies of Ariosto or Spenser? Only this—that the blast of Roland's horn in Roncesvalles echoes through all medieval Europe, and gave rise to a whole new literature. The *Chanson* dates, as we said, probably from the early twelfth century. The events it describes are perhaps partly historical, but largely legendary. Charlemagne advanced into Spain and had his rearguard cut off in the Pyrenees on the return, in 778. But other parts of the Carolingian cycle tell of his being besieged in Paris by the Saracens; and of this history knows nothing. What we have here, however, is a picture of Christendom militant against a surrounding pagan foe. That Charlemagne actually accepted and identified himself with this idea is indeed historical. But that it has entered so deeply into *The Song of Roland* has another cause. The end of the eleventh century is the time of the first Crusade, when the idea of a holy war against the infidel again filled the mind of France. When Roland, after having struck the first blow in the first battle, cries out

Nos avons dreit mais cist gloton ont tort

it is doubtless the spirit of the first Crusade that speaks as much as that of his assumed historical period. And that crusading spirit, in which the mind of the eleventh century mingles with that of the eighth, is of great importance for later poetry: it means the beginning of the Christian epic.

"We are right and these miscreants are wrong." This is something new. The epic has always lived by conflict; but till now, simply by con-flict between two sides; both perhaps protected by gods; both probably noble; one destined to prevail—but only by superior prowess, or the accidental support of an immortal conceived in essentially human terms. Homer writes from a Greek point of view, but he does not suggest that the Greeks were right and the Trojans wrong; or the Trojans right and the Greeks wrong. Virgil has moved perceptibly nearer to the idea of a hero with a divine mission; but neither does he suggest when his Trojans arrive on the Lavinian shore that they have a sacred and pre-ordained superiority and that the Latins are perverse to oppose them. It is a consequence of polytheism (one of its great blessings, to my mind): when both sides are supported by equally reputable deities neither can claim supreme supernatural sanction for its position. It cannot be suggested that one side is of the family of the faith, while the other is in outer darkness, representing only evil or perversity or blindness. There is a difference, then, between two kinds of conflict—conflict between two sides which merely happen to be humanly and historically opposed; and conflict between two sides one of which is eternally and supernaturally right and the other eternally and supernaturally wrong.

The second notion, that of conflict with a supernatural sanction, is original with the Christian epic, and in various forms and with varying degrees of intensity runs all through it. It is not quite absent even in the more frivolous Italian epics, and it returns with all its weight in the operations of Spenser's Red Cross Knight and Sir Artegall. It is of central importance in *The Song of Roland*, first by reason of the subject of the poem, and then by reason of the crusading age in which it was written. When the Carolingian cycle was diversified and romanticized in Italy it might seem that this august theme would altogether disappear; but this is never entirely so. The characteristic of the Italian versions is that they are filled out with extravagant adventures in the East in which one of the paladins, usually Rinaldo, is entangled with a Paynim princess. But however many fantastic episodes and irrelevant characters may surround them, Charlemagne retains his character as the Christian king, and Roland as the Christian champion. Roland is even turned into a Roman that he may more appropriately function as a defender of the Catholic world. And the tale keeps returning to Charles beleaguered in Paris by the Saracen hordes, Christendom surrounded by the forces of outer darkness. To readers of Ariosto who are struck only by the fantasy and irony it may seem an absurdity to make anything of this aspect of the *Orlando Furioso*. But there is a case to be made for it all the same. And with Tasso the case needs no arguing. Writing in the full tide of the Counter-Reformation and completely expressing its spirit, he takes the holy war as his inspiration and his theme. The first Crusade which contributed its spirit and its feeling to the *Song of Roland* is the actual historical subject of *Jerusalem Delivered*. We might add that neither in Ariosto nor in Tasso do the exigencies of the faith exclude chivalry and courtesy to those outside its bounds.

French literature, including the Carolingian cycle, spread to North Italy about the end of the twelfth century,[1] and for the best part of a

---

[1] On the migration of Arthurian and Carolingian material into Italy, see J. A. Symonds, *Renaissance in Italy*, vol. 4, chaps. 1, 4, 7; Pio Rajna, *Le Fonti dell' Orlando Furioso*, Florence, 1876; E. G. Gardner, *Arthurian Legend in Italian Literature*, 1930; A. Viscardi, "Arthurian Influence on Italian Literature", in *Arthurian Literature in the Middle Ages*, ed. A. Loomis, 1959.

hundred years the north was a cultural province of France. But the influence was not confined to the courtly and the cultivated. The Carolingian tales were above all popular in their diffusion. The story of Roland and its various offshoots, notably that of Rinaldo, were sung in the market-places in a mixed dialect of Franco-Italian. They continued, proliferated and were elaborated throughout the thirteenth and fourteenth centuries; and finally, about the beginning of the fifteenth century, were combined into a huge prose compilation called the *Reali di Francia*, which performed much the same service for the Charlemagne legend in Italy as Malory did for the Arthurian legend in England.

However, at the very time the Carolingian cycle was gaining a new lease of life among the populace in Italy it was losing favour in courtly circles. It is of course pre-chivalric, and represents the manners of an earlier feudal age. The far more refined and sophisticated kind of courtly society that was growing up in the twelfth century had found its sustenance not in the rude and stern *chansons de geste* but in the mazy enchantments of the Arthurian romancers, of whom the type is Chrétien de Troyes. Love, hunting, tournaments, knight-errantry—the sentiments, pageantry and pastimes of courtly life replace the monotonous warfare of the earlier epics. And while the old Carolingian tales satisfied the people, it was this new matter, with its elaborate courtesy and refined sentiment, that was seized on by the courtly circles of northern Italy.

Arthurian literature is so vast and many-sided that it is important to realize just what it contributed to the Italian romance-epic. Like Charlemagne, Arthur was a Christian prince fighting against pagan enemies; but that aspect of his legend is of no interest for the tradition we are following. Already in Chrétien de Troyes the figure of Arthur has sunk into the background, and it is the exploits of the individual knights of the Round Table that provide the themes. And with the disappearance of the great theme of national and Christian war against a pagan foe these exploits are in the strictest sense individual—deeds of personal prowess, undertaken for love or personal renown. True, the knights of the Round Table sometimes fight against pagan or Saracen knights; but these are in no other way distinguished from the Christians; they are equally likely to be noble and brave; the code of chivalry embraces pagan and Christian alike. And failing a supply of suitable paynims the Christians are more likely to fight each other than to let their arms rust unused. There is no particular *point de repère* for the various adventures and this makes a further difference from the *chansons de geste,* where the siege of Paris or some other aspect of the continuing struggle against the infidel is constantly pulling us back towards an overriding central theme. And the disappearance of the holy war affects the supernatural no less than the natural events. They are no longer parts of a providential scheme, they are individual enchantments, infinitely various, and mysterious in means and motive, a parallel on the magical plane to the confused play of individual wills in the natural world. Ontological confusion no less: in the older layers of the Carolingian cycle the world is on two planes only—the will of God and the actions of men: but in the Arthurian world who would care to define the metaphysical status of Merlin or Morgan le Fay?

Above all it was the love theme that distinguished the Arthurian romances from the older epic. In the *chansons de geste* there are either no heroines or their role is restricted within the narrowest compass. Even if these tireless warriors could have found time for love the sternly limited emotional scope of the *Chanson de Roland* could hardly have admitted it. The style is perfectly adapted to stories of battle, heroism, treason and death: it could have done nothing with the elaboration of personal sentiments. In Italy it was above all the love stories, the stories of Lancelot and Guinevere, Tristan and Iseult, that represent the Arthurian cycle. It is curious to see the familiar northern tales in their Italian guise. *Qui conta della reina Isotta e di M. Tristano di Leonis; Qui conta come la damigella di Scalot morì per amore di Lancialotto del Lac*—these are two of the rubrics from the *Cento Novelle Antiche*. And the Paolo and Francesca episode in Inferno V—

> leggemmo insieme un giorno per diletto
> di Lancilotto e come amor lo strinse—

bears incidental but compelling witness to the way Arthurian romance could naturally be invoked as the predestined betrayer of gentle hearts. So a new motive enters Italian romance literature—love and the fatal power of the heroine. We are already within sight of Angelica and Bradamante. It is this grafting of the new Arthurian romance on to the old Carolingian stock that brings the romantic epic into being. It also accounts for the pervasive atmosphere of Arthurian romance in Spenser, with the absence of specific Arthurian tales or specific debts to Malory. We are right in feeling that the Arthurian element is there, but it has been filtered and transmuted through Spenser's Italian sources. And when a different and distinctly British Arthurian element enters into *The Faerie Queene* the ordinary reader probably fails to notice it.

The comparison of the old romance literature and the new was made by Boiardo,[2] Ariosto's predecessor, the first great poet of the revived romantic epic:

> Fo gloriosa Bertagna la grande
> Una stagion per l'arme e per l'amore,
> Onde ancora il nome suo si spande,
> Si che al re Artuse fa portare onore ...

[2] The best short account of Boiardo in English is in Symonds op. cit., vol. 4 chap. 7. See also C. S. Lewis, *The Allegory of Love, 1936;* and E. M. W. Tillyard, *The English Epic and its Background,* 1954.

> Re Carlo in Franza poi tenne gran corte,
> Ma a quella prima non fo sembiante . . .
> Perchè tiene ad Amor chiose le porte
> E sol se dette alle battaglie sante,
> Non fo di quel valore e quella estima
> Qual fo quell'altro che io contava in prima,
> Però che Amore è quel che da la gloria
> E che fa l'omo degno et onorato,
> Amore è quel che dona li vittoria,
> E dona ardire al cavalliero armato.

Britain the great was once glorious for arms and for love, whence its name is still spread abroad, and brings great honour to King Arthur. . . . Charlemagne then held a great court in France, but it was not like that former one. . . . Because it shut the door against Love and gave itself only to the holy war it was not of the same worth and reputation as that other one of which I spoke first. For it is Love that brings glory, and makes a man worthy and honoured; it is Love that brings victory and gives courage to the knight at arms.

(O.I., II. xviii. 1–3)

Matteo Boiardo, Count of Scandiano, wrote for the courtly society of Ferrara, a world already penetrated with the charms of Arthurian romance. We find members of the ducal house of Este bearing Arthurian names, Isotta and Ginevra; and the duke himself writes in 1470 to borrow as many French books as he can, especially those of the Round Table. Boiardo's poem *Orlando Innamorato* was roughly contemporary with Malory's *Morte d'Arthur*—begun about 1475 and first published in 1484. It inaugurates a new *genre,* and the principle of the new *genre* is a simple one—it is the fusion of the matter of Britain with the matter of France. Some contamination of the Carolingian stories with Arthurian material had already occurred sporadically in the popular tradition; but it was left for Boiardo systematically to infuse the spirit of chivalry and romantic love drawn from the courtly Arthurian romancers into the older cycle of legend. The very title of his poem indicates what he was doing. Who could think of Roland in love, as long as he remained in the sphere of the *chanson de geste*? Boiardo sets out to accept this challenge and to place Roland in another light.

> Non vi par già, Signor, meraviglioso
> Odir cantar de Orlando inamorato,
> Che qualunque nel mondo è piu orgoglioso,
> E da Amor vinto, al tutto subiugato;
> Nè forte braccio, nè ardire animoso,
> Nè scudo o maglia, nè brando affilato,
> Nè altra possanza può mai far diffesa,
> Che al fin non sia da Amor battuta e presa.

Do not let it seem surprising to you, Sir, to hear about Roland in love, for the proudest man in the world is conquered and totally subjugated by Love. Neither strong arm, nor fiery courage, nor shield nor mail nor sharp sword, nor any other power can serve as defence against it; in the end they are overcome and captured by Love.

(I. i. 2)

His method is to take the characters, Roland, Charlemagne, and the rest, and the general basis of the Carolingian tales, and then to diversify them by love, magic and chivalric adventure. The Arthurian tales are not used as such; their material and spirit are taken, rearranged and placed in another setting. The opening scene affords a good example. Charlemagne is in his great hall holding the feast of Pentecost, to be followed by a tournament. He is sitting at the *tavola ritonda* surrounded by his peers; and into the hall comes a beautiful maiden, attended by a single knight and guarded by four giants. She is Angelica. Orlando and a number of the other knights incontinently fall in love with her; and she brings a challenge which sets the whole story in motion. But what is Charlemagne doing sitting at a round table? And have we not met this scene before, or others remarkably like it? Of course it is like the beginning of *Sir Gawayne,* or any one of half-a-dozen other Arthurian stories —the great feast at Camelot, the appearance of a stranger, and the beginning of a quest or a series of quests. The *Faerie Queene* was to begin in the same way, though Spenser, affected by later notions of epic correctness, plunged *in medias res,* left what was chronologically the beginning to the end, and so never got to it at all. The two fountains of Cupid and Merlin, the one inspiring love and the other hate, which play a large part in the story, are similarly removed from the Carolingian and akin to the Arthurian spirit. Above all there is the central importance of the heroine, the delectable Angelica, whose caprices and enchantments control the whole intricate web.

Boiardo is the creator of this new romance world, where the peoples of the earth are in motion, the hordes of the pagan East gathered together for the assault on Christendom, and Charles calls all the nations of the Christian world to combat; where the action centres in France and Spain, but ranges over Tartary, Cathay and Africa; and where the great historical movements are crossed, tangled and ultimately controlled by the caprice of individual romantic love. He is of course building on a large body of popular and bourgeois *rifacimenti* of the Carolingian tales already in existence. They had already complicated the old outlines with fantastic adventures, the entanglement of the Paladins with Oriental princesses, and so forth. They had already handled the heroic material in a spirit of adventurous levity. But the colouring of the whole with the spirit of chivalry, the idea of love and arms as the two poles on which the romantic epic should turn, is Boiardo's own.

His style is straightforward, easy and a little rustic. He tells his tale with a rather grand carelessness and an undertone of irony that is nearer to simple humour than to the finesse of Ariosto. And his admiration for the virtues of chivalry is whole-hearted and perfectly genuine. Spenser read him—there are enough parallels to prove this, though they are not very significant[3]—and a certain old-fashioned simplicity of mind

[3] See H. H. Blanchard, "Spenser and Boiardo", PMLA, XL, 1925.

brings him in some ways near to Spenser. But more important is the fact that he created Ariosto's world, and therefore, at one remove, Spenser's world. He lays down the lines both of its adventures and its characters. All the principal characters in Ariosto are taken over from Boiardo. (There are slight changes in the forms of the names, and I will use the Ariostan ones to avoid confusion.) The principal heroes, Orlando, Rinaldo, Astolfo, Ferrau, all subject to the whims of Angelica; the faithful lovers Ruggiero and Bradamante, Brandimarte and Fiordiligi; the magician Atlante; the enchantresses Morgana, Alcina and Origille, with their beguiling gardens; the magic lance, the shield, the lions, the dragons, the hermits, the salvage men; all these that make up Boiardo's world are taken over bodily by Ariosto. And without them we should not have Arthur, Guyon, Calidore, Artegall and Britomart, Scudamour and Amoret, Archimage, Duessa and Acrasia. Intricate adventures proliferating into many episodes, feats of arms inspired by love, and a background, however treated, of religious conflict—these are the materials that Spenser was to inherit. It is even possible to find, besides one or two explicitly allegorical episodes, a general allegorical undertone to Boiardo's romance; and it is more than likely that Spenser read him in this way.

RENAISSANCE IDEAS*

Joel E. Spingarn

Epic poetry was held in the highest esteem during the Renaissance and indeed throughout the period of classicism. It was regarded by Vida as the highest form of poetry,[1] and a century later, despite the success of tragedy in France, Rapin still held the same opinion.[2] The reverence for the epic throughout the Renaissance may be ascribed in part to the mediaeval veneration of Virgil as a poet, and his popular apotheosis as prophet and magician, and also in part to the decay into which dramatic literature had fallen during the Middle Ages in the hands of the wandering players, the *histriones* and the *vagantes*. Aristotle[3] indeed had regarded tragedy as the highest form of poetry; and as a result, the traditional reverence for Virgil and Homer, and the Renaissance subservience to Aristotle, were distinctly at variance. Trissino (1561) paraphrases Aristotle's argument in favor of tragedy, but points out, notwithstanding this, that the whole world is unanimous in considering Virgil and Homer greater than any tragic poet before or after them.[4] Placed in this quandary, he concludes by leaving the reader to judge for himself whether epic or tragedy be the nobler form.

THE THEORY OF THE EPIC POEM

Vida's *Ars Poetica*, written before 1520, although no edition prior to that of 1527 is extant, is the earliest example in modern times of that class of critical poems to which belong Horace's *Ars Poetica*, Bolieau's *Art Poétique*, and Pope's *Essay on Criticism*. Vida's poem is entirely based on that of Horace; but he substitutes epic for Horace's dramatic

*Joel E. Spingarn, *A History of Literary Criticism in the Renaissance*, 2nd ed. (New York: Columbia University Press, 1908). Originally published in 1899. Reprinted by permission.

[1] Pope, i. 133.
[2] Rapin, 1674, ii. 2.
[3] *Poet.* xxvi.
[4] Trissino, ii. 118 sq.

studies, and employs the *Aeneid* as the model of an epic poem. The incompleteness of the treatment accorded to epic poetry in Aristotle's *Poetics* led the Renaissance to deduce the laws of heroic poetry and of poetic artifice in general from the practice of Virgil; and it is to this point of view that the critical works on the *Aeneid* by Regolo (1563), Maranta (1564), and Toscanella (1566) owe their origin. The obvious and even accidental qualities of Virgil's poem are enunciated by Vida as fundamental laws of epic poetry. The precepts thus given are purely rhetorical and pedagogic in character, and deal almost exclusively with questions of poetic invention, disposition, polish, and style. Beyond this Vida does not attempt to go. There is in his poem no definition of the epic, no theory of its function, no analysis of the essentials of narrative structure. In fact, no theory of poetry in any real sense is to be found in Vida's treatise.

Daniello (1536) deals only very cursorily with epic poetry, but his definition of it strikes the keynote of the Renaissance conception. Heroic poetry is for him an imitation of the illustrious deeds of emperors and other men magnanimous and valorous in arms,[5]—a conception that goes back to Horace's

Res gestae regumque ducumque et tristia bella.[6]

Trissino (1563) first introduced the Aristotelian theory of the epic into modern literary criticism; and the sixth section of his *Poetica* is given up almost exclusively to the treatment of heroic poetry. The epic agrees with tragedy in dealing with illustrious men and illustrious actions. Like tragedy it must have a single action, but it differs from tragedy in not having the time of the action limited or determined. While unity of action is essential to the epic, and is indeed what distinguishes it from narrative poems that are not really epics, the Renaissance conceived of vastness of design and largeness of detail as necessary to the grandiose character of the epic poem.[7] Thus Muzio says:—

Il poema sovrano è una pittura
De l' universo, e però in sè comprende
Ogni stilo, ogni forma, ogni ritratto.

Trissino regards *versi sciolti* as the proper metre for an heroic poem, since the stanzaic form impedes the continuity of the narrative. In this point he finds fault with Boccaccio, Boiardo, and Ariosto, whose romantic poems, moreover, he does not regard as epics, because they do not obey Aristotle's inviolable law of the single action. He also finds fault with the romantic poets for describing the improbable, since Aristotle

[5] Daniello, p. 34.
[6] *Ars Poet.* 73.
[7] Trissino, ii. 112 *sq.*

expressly prefers an impossible probability to an improbable possibility.

Minturno's definition of epic poetry is merely a modification or paraphrase of Aristotle's definition of tragedy. Epic poetry is an imitation of a grave and noble deed, perfect, complete, and of proper magnitude, with embellished language, but without music or dancing; at times simply narrating and at other times introducing persons in words and actions; in order that, through pity and fear of the things imitated, such passions may be purged from the mind with both pleasure and profit.[8] Here Minturno, like Giraldi Cintio, ascribes to epic poetry the same purgation of pity and fear effected by tragedy. Epic poetry he rates above tragedy, since the epic poet, more than any other, arouses that admiration of great heroes which it is the peculiar function of the poet to excite, and therefore attains the end of poetry more completely than any other poet. This, however, is true only in the highest form of narrative poetry; for Minturno distinguishes three classes of narrative poets, the lowest, or *bucolici*, the mediocre, or *epici*, who have nothing beyond verse, and the highest, or *heroici*, who imitate the life of a single hero in noble verse.[9] Minturno insists fundamentally on the unity of the epic action; and directly against Aristotle's statement, as we have seen, he restricts the duration of the action to one year. The license and prolixity of the *romanzi* led the defenders of the classical epic to this extreme of rigid circumspection. According to Scaliger, the epic, which is the norm by which all other poems may be judged and the chief of all poems, describes *heroum genus, vita, gesta*.[10] This is the Horatian conception of the epic, and there is in Scaliger little or no trace of the Aristotelian doctrine. He also follows Horace closely in forbidding the narrative poet to begin his poem from the very beginning of his story (*ab ovo*), and in various other details.

Castelvetro (1570) differs from Aristotle in regard to the unity of the epic fable, on the ground that poetry is merely imaginative history, and can therefore do anything that history can do. Poetry follows the footsteps of history, differing merely in that history narrates what has happened, while poetry narrates what has never happened but yet may possibly happen; and therefore, since history recounts the whole life of a single hero, without regard to its unity, there is no reason why poetry should not do likewise. The epic may in fact deal with many actions of one person, one action of a whole race, or many actions of many people; it need not necessarily deal with one action of one person, as Aristotle enjoins, but if it does so it is simply to show the ingenuity and excellence of the poet.[11]

[8] *Arte Poetica,* p. 9.
[9] *De Poeta,* pp. 105, 106.
[10] *Poet.* iii. 95.
[11] Castelvetro, *Poetica,* p. 178 *sq.*

EPIC AND ROMANCE

This discussion of epic unity leads to one of the most important critical questions of the sixteenth century,—the question of the unity of romance. Ariosto's *Orlando Furioso* and Boiardo's *Orlando Innamorato* were written before the Aristotelian canons had become a part of the critical literature of Italy. When it became clear that these poems diverged from the fundamental requirements of the epic as expounded in the *Poetics*, Trissino set out to compose an heroic poem which would be in perfect accord with the precepts of Aristotle. His *Italia Liberata*, which was completed by 1548, was the result of twenty years of study, and it is the first modern epic in the strict Aristotelian sense. With Aristotle as his guide, and Homer as his model, he had studiously and mechanically constructed an epic of a single action; and in the dedication of his poem to the Emperor Charles V. he charges all poems which violate this primary law of the single action with being merely bastard forms. The *romanzi*, and among them the *Orlando Furioso*, in seemingly disregarding this fundamental requirement, came under Trissino's censure; and this started a controversy which was not to end until the commencement of the next century, and in a certain sense may be said to remain undecided even to this day.

The first to take up the cudgels in defence of the writers of the *romanzi* was Giraldi Cintio, who in his youth had known Ariosto personally, and who wrote his *Discorso intorno al comporre dei Romanzi*, in April, 1549. The grounds of his defence are twofold. In the first place, Giraldi maintains that the romance is a poetic form of which Aristotle did not know, and to which his rules therefore do not apply; and in the second place, Tuscan literature, differing as it does from the literature of Greece in language, in spirit, and in religious feeling, need not and indeed ought not to follow the rules of Greek literature, but rather the laws of its own development and its own traditions. With Ariosto and Boiardo as models, Giraldi sets out to formulate the laws of the *romanzi*. The *romanzi* aim at imitating illustrious actions in verse, with the purpose of teaching good morals and honest living, since this ought to be the aim of every poet, as Giraldi conceives Aristotle himself to have said.[12] All heroic poetry is an imitation of illustrious actions, but Giraldi, like Castelvetro twenty years later, recognizes several distinct forms of heroic poetry, according as to whether it imitates one action of one man, many actions of many men, or many actions of one man. The first of these is the epic poem, the rules of which are give in Aristotle's *Poetics*. The second is the romantic poem, after the manner of Boiardo and Ariosto. The third is the biographical poem, after the manner of the *Theseid* and similar works dealing with the whole life of a single hero.

[12] Giraldi Cintio, i. 11, 64.

These forms are therefore to be regarded as three distinct and legitimate species of heroic poetry, the first of them being an epic poem in the strict Aristotelian sense, and the two others coming under the general head of *romanzi*. Of the two forms of *romanzi*, the biographical deals preferably with an historical subject, whereas the noblest writers of the more purely romantic form, dealing with many actions of many men, have invented their subject-matter. Horace says that an heroic poem should not commence at the very beginning of the hero's life; but it is difficult to understand, says Giraldi, why the whole life of a distinguished man, which gives us so great and refined a pleasure in the works of Plutarch and other biographers, should not please us all the more when described in beautiful verse by a good poet.[13] Accordingly, the poet who is composing an epic in the strict sense should, in handling the events of his narrative, plunge immediately *in medias res*. The poet dealing with many actions of many men should begin with the most important event, and the one upon which all the others may be said to hinge; whereas the poet describing the life of a single hero should begin at the very beginning, if the hero spent a really heroic youth, as Hercules for example did. The poem dealing with the life of a hero is thus a separate *genre*, and one for which Aristotle does not attempt to lay down any laws. Giraldi even goes so far as to say that Aristotle[14] censured those who write the life of Theseus or Hercules in a single poem, not because they dealt with many actions of one man, but because they treated such a poem in exactly the same manner as those who dealt with a single action of a single hero,—an assertion which is of course utterly absurd. Giraldi then proceeds to deal in detail with the disposition and composition of the *romanzi*, which he rates above the classical epics in the efficacy of ethical teaching. It is the office of the poet to praise virtuous actions and to condemn vicious actions; and in this the writers of the *romanzi* are far superior to the writers of the ancient heroic poems.[15]

Giraldi's discourse on the *romanzi* gave rise to a curious dispute with his own pupil, Giambattista Pigna, who published a similar work, entitled *I Romanzi*, in the same year (1554). Pigna asserted that he had suggested to Giraldi the main argument of the discourse, and that Giraldi had adopted it as his own. Without entering into the details of this controversy, it would seem that the priority of Giraldi cannot fairly be contested.[16] At all events, there is a very great resemblance between the works of Giraldi and Pigna. Pigna's treatise, however, is more detailed

[13] *Ibid.* i. 24.
[14] *Poet.* viii. 2.
[15] Giraldi, i. 66 *sq.*
[16] *Cf.* Tiraboschi, vii. 947 *sq.*, and Giraldi, ii. 153 *sq.* Pigna's own words are cited in Giraldi, i. p. xxiii.

than Giraldi's. In the first book, Pigna deals with the general subject of the *romanzi;* in the second he gives a life of Ariosto, and discusses the *Furioso,* point by point; in the third he demonstrates the good taste and critical acumen of Ariosto by comparing the first version of the *Furioso* with the completed and perfected copy.[17] Both Pigna and Giraldi consider the *romanzi* to constitute a new genre unknown to the ancients, and therefore not subject to Aristotle's rules. Giraldi's sympathies were in favor of the biographical form of the *romanzi,* and his poem, the *Ercole* (1557), recounts the whole life of a single hero. Pigna, who keeps closer to the tradition of Ariosto, regards the biographical form as not proper to poetry, because too much like history.

These arguments, presented by Giraldi and Pigna, were answered by Speroni, Minturno, and others. Speroni pointed out that while it is not necessary for the romantic poets to follow the rules prescribed by the ancients, they cannot disobey the fundamental laws of poetry. "The *romanzi,*" says Speroni, "are epics, which are poems, or they are histories in verse, and not poems." [18] That is, how does a poem differ from a well-written historical narrative, if the former be without organic unity?[19] As to the whole discussion, it may be said here, without attempting to pass judgment on Ariosto, or any other writer of *romanzi,* that unity of some sort every true poem must necessarily have; and, flawless as the *Orlando Furioso* is in its details, the unity of the poem certainly has not the obviousness of perfect, and especially classical, art. A work of art without organic unity may be compared with an unsymmetrical circle; and, while the *Furioso* is not to be judged by any arbitrary or mechanical rules of unity, yet if it has not that internal unity which transcends all mere external form, it may be considered, as a work of art, hardly less than a failure; and the farther it is removed from perfect unity, the more imperfect is the art. "Poetry adapts itself to its times, but cannot depart from its own fundamental laws."[20]

Minturno's answer to the defenders of the *romanzi* is more detailed and explicit than Speroni's, and it is of considerable importance because of its influence on Torquato Tasso's conception of epic poetry. Minturno does not deny—and in this his point of view is identical with Tasso's—that it is possible to employ the matter of the *romanzi* in the composition of a perfect poem. The actions they describe are great and illustrious, their knights and ladies are noble and illustrious, too, and they contain in a most excellent manner that element of the marvellous which is so important an element in the epic action. It is the struc-

[17] Canello, p. 306 *sq.*

[18] Speroni, v. 521.

[19] *Cf.* Minturno, *De Poeta,* p. 151.

[20] Minturno, *Arte Poetica,* p. 31. For various opinions on the unity of the *Orlando Furioso,* cf. Canello, p. 106, and Foffano, p. 59 *sq.*

ture of the *romanzi* with which Minturno finds fault. They lack the first essential of every form of poetry,—unity. In fact, they are little more than versified history or legend; and, while expressing admiration for the genius of Ariosto, Minturno cannot but regret that he so far yielded to the popular taste of his time as to employ the method of the *romanzi*. He approves of the suggestion of Bembo, who had tried to persuade Ariosto to write an epic instead of a romantic poem,[21] just as later, and for similar reasons, Gabriel Harvey attempted to dissuade Spenser from continuing the *Faerie Queene*. Minturno denies that the Tuscan tongue is not well adapted to the composition of heroic poetry; on the contrary, there is no form of poetry to which it is not admirably fitted. He denies that the romantic poem can be distinguished from the epic on the ground that the actions of knights-errant require a different and broader form of narrative than do those of the classical heroes. The celestial and infernal gods and demi-gods of the ancients correspond with the angels, saints, anchorites, and the one God of Christianity; the ancient sibyls, oracles, enchantresses, and divine messengers correspond with the modern necromancers, fates, magicians, and celestial angels. To the claim of the romantic poets that their poems approximate closer to that magnitude which Aristotle enjoins as necessary for all poetry, Minturno answers that magnitude is of no avail without proportion; there is no beauty in the giant whose limbs and frame are distorted. Finally, the *romanzi* are said to be a new form of poetry unknown to Aristotle and Horace, and hence not amenable to their laws. But time, says Minturno, cannot change the truth; in every age a poem must have unity, proportion, magnitude. Everything in nature is governed by some specific law which directs its operation; and as it is in nature so it is in art, for art tries to imitate nature, and the nearer it approaches nature in her essential laws, the better it does its work. In other words, as has already been pointed out, poetry adapts itself to its times, but cannot depart from its own laws.

Bernardo Tasso, the father Torquato, had originally been one of the defenders of the classical epic; but he seems to have been converted to the opposite view by Giraldi Cintio, and in his poem of the *Amadigi* he follows romantic models. His son Torquato, in his *Discorsi dell' Arte Poetica*, originally written one or two years after the appearance of Minturno's *Arte Poetica*, although not published until 1587, was the first to attempt a reconciliation of the epic and romantic forms; and he may be said to have effected a solution of the problem by the formulation of the theory of a narrative poem which would have the romantic subject-matter, with its delightful variety, and the epic form, with its essential unity. The question at issue, as we have seen, is that of unity; that is, does the heroic poem need unity? Tasso denies that there is any

[21] *Arte Poetica*, p. 31.

difference between the epic poem and the romantic poem as poems. The reason why the latter is more pleasing, is to be found in the fact of the greater delightfulness of the themes treated.[22] Variety in itself may be pleasing, for even a variety of disagreeable things may possibly please. But the perfect and at the same time most pleasing form of heroic poem would deal with the chivalrous themes of the romanzi, yet would possess that unity of structure which, according to the precepts of Aristotle and the practice of Homer and Virgil, is essential to every epic. There are two sorts of unity possible in art as in nature,—the simple unity of a chemical element, and the complex unity of an organism like an animal or plant,—and of these the latter is the sort of unity that the heroic poet should aim at.[23] Capriano (1555) had referred to this same distinction, when he pointed out that poetry ought not to be the imitation of a single act, such as a single act of weeping in the elegy, or a single act of pastoral life in the eclogue, for such a sporadic imitation is to be compared to a picture of a single hand without the rest of the body; on the contrary, poetry ought to be the representation of a number of attendant or dependent acts, leading from a given beginning to a suitable end.[24]

Having settled the general fact that the attractive themes of romanzi should be employed in a perfect heroic poem, we may inquire what particular themes are most fitted to the epic, and what must be the essential qualities of the epic material.[25] In the first place, the subject of the heroic poem must be historical, for it is not probable that illustrious actions such as are dealt with in the epic should be unknown to history. The authority of history gains for the poet that semblance of truth necessary to deceive the reader and make him believe that what the poet writes is true. Secondly, the heroic poem, according to Tasso, must deal with the history, not of a false religion, but of the true one, Christianity. The religion of the pagans is absolutely unfit for epic material; for if the pagan deities are not introduced, the poem will lack the element of the marvellous, and if they are introduced it will lack the element of probability. Both the marvellous and the verisimile must exist together in a perfect epic, and difficult as the task may seem, they must be reconciled. Another reason why paganism is unfit for the epic is to be found in the fact that the perfect knight must have piety as well as other virtues. In the third place, the poem must not deal with themes connected with the articles of Christian faith, for such themes would be unalterable, and would allow no scope to the free play of the poet's inventive fancy. Fourthly, the material must be neither too ancient nor too modern, for the latter is too well known to admit of fanciful changes

[22] T. Tasso, xii, 219 sq.
[23] T. Tasso, xii. 234.
[24] Della Vera Poetica, cap. iii.
[25] T. Tasso, xii. 199 sq.

with probability, and the former not only lacks interest but requires the introduction of strange and alien manners and customs. The times of Charlemagne and Arthur are accordingly best fitted for heroic treatment. Finally, the events themselves must possess nobility and grandeur. Hence an epic should be a story derived from some event in the history of Christian peoples, intrinsically noble and illustrious, but not of so sacred a character as to be fixed and immutable, and neither contemporary nor very remote. By the selection of such material the poem gains the authority of history, the truth of religion, the license of fiction, the proper atmosphere in point of time, and the grandeur of the events themselves.[26]

Aristotle says that both epic and tragedy deal with illustrious actions. Tasso points out that if the actions of tragedy and of epic poetry were both illustrious in the same way, they would both produce the same results; but tragic actions move horror and compassion, while epic actions as a rule do not and need not arouse these emotions. The tragic action consists in the unexpected change of fortune, and in the grandeur of the events carrying with them horror and pity; but the epic action is founded upon undertakings of lofty martial virtue, upon deeds of courtesy, piety, generosity, none of which is proper to tragedy. Hence the characters in epic poetry and in tragedy, though both of the same regal and supreme rank, differ in that the tragic hero is neither perfectly good nor entirely bad, as Aristotle says, while the epic hero must have the very height of virtue, such as Aeneas, the type of piety, Amadis, the type of loyalty, Achilles, of martial virtue, and Ulysses, of prudence.

Having formulated these theories of heroic poetry in his youth, Tasso set out to carry them into practice, and his famous *Gerusalemme Liberata* was the result. This poem, almost immediately after its publication, started a violent controversy, which raged for many years, and which may be regarded as the legitimate outcome of the earlier dispute in connection with the *romanzi*.[27] The *Gerusalemme* was in fact the centre of critical activity during the latter part of the century. Shortly after its publication, Camillo Pellegrino published a dialogue, entitled *Il Caraffa* (1583), in which the *Gerusalemme* is compared with the *Orlando Furioso*, much to the advantage of the former. Pellegrino finds fault with Ariosto on account of the lack of unity of his poem, the immoral manners imitated, and various imperfections of style and language; and in all of these things, unity, morality, and style, he finds Tasso's poem perfect. This was naturally the signal for a heated and long-continued controversy. The Accademia della Crusca had been

---

[26] T. Tasso, xii. 208.

[27] Accounts of this famous controversy will be found in Tiraboschi, Canello, Serassi, etc.; but the latest and most complete is that given in the twentieth chapter of Solerti's monumental *Vita di Torquato Tasso*, Torino, 1895.

founded at Florence, in 1582, and it seems that the members of the new society felt hurt at some sarcastic remarks regarding Florence in one of Tasso's dialogues. Accordingly, the head of the academy, Lionardo Salviati, in a dialogue entitled *L' Infarinato*, wrote an ardent defence of Ariosto; and an acrid and undignified dispute between Tasso and Salviati was begun.[28] Tasso answered the Accademia della Crusca in his *Apologia*; and at the beginning of the next century, Paolo Beni, the commentator on Aristotle's *Poetics*, published his *Comparazione di Omero, Virgilio, e Torquato*, in which Tasso is rated above Homer, Virgil, and Ariosto, not only in dignity, in beauty of style, and in unity of fable, but in every other quality that may be said to constitute perfection in poetry. Before dismissing this whole matter, it should be pointed out that the defenders of Ariosto had absolutely abandoned the position of Giraldi and Pigna, that the *romanzi* constitute a *genre* by themselves, and are therefore not subject to Aristotle's law of unity. The question as Giraldi had stated it was this: Does every poem need to have unity? The question as discussed in the Tasso controversy had changed to this form: What is unity? It was taken for granted by both sides in the controversy that every poem must have organic unity; and the authority of Aristotle, in epic as in dramatic poetry, was henceforth supreme. It was to the authority of Aristotle that Tasso's opponents appealed; and Salviati, merely for the purpose of undermining Tasso's pretensions, wrote an extended commentary on the *Poetics*, which still lies in Ms. at Florence, and which has been made use of in the present essay.[29]

EPIC POETRY

The Elizabethan theory of heroic poetry may be dismissed briefly. Webbe refers to the epic as "that princely part of poetry, wherein are displayed the noble acts and valiant exploits of puissant captains, expert soldiers, wise men, with the famous reports of ancient times";[30] and Puttenham defines heroic poems as "long histories of the noble gests of kings and great princes, intermeddling the dealings of gods, demigods, and heroes, and weighty consequences of peace and war."[31] The

[28] Nearly all the important documents of the Tasso controversy are reprinted in Rosini's edition of Tasso, *Opere*, vols. xviii.-xxiii.

[29] The question of unity was also raised in another controversy of the second half of the sixteenth century. A passage in Varchi's *Ercolano* (1570), rating Dante above Homer, started a controversy on the *Divine Comedy*. The most important outcome of this dispute was Mazzoni's *Difesa di Dante* (1573), in which a more or less novel theory of poetry is expounded in order to defend the great Tuscan poet.

[30] Haslewood, ii. 45.

[31] Puttenham, p. 40.

importance of this form of poetry, according to Puttenham, is largely historical, in that it sets forth an example of the valor and virtue of our forefathers.[32] Sidney is scarcely more explicit.[33] He asserts that heroic poetry is the best and noblest of all forms; he shows that such characters as Achilles, Aeneas, and Rinaldo are shining examples for all men's imitation; but of the nature or structure of the epic he says nothing.

The second part of Harington's *Apologie of Poetrie* is given up to a defence of the *Orlando Furioso*, and here the Aristotelian theory of the epic appears for the first time in English criticism. Harington, taking the *Aeneid* as the approved model of all heroic poetry, first shows that Ariosto has followed closely in Virgil's footsteps, but is to be preferred even to Virgil in that the latter pays reverence to false deities, while Ariosto has the advantage of the Christian spirit. But since some critics, "reducing all heroical poems unto the method of Homer and certain precepts of Aristotle," insist that Ariosto is wanting in art, Harington sets out to prove that the *Orlando Furioso* may not only be defended by the example of Homer, but that it has even followed very strictly the rules and precepts of Aristotle.[34] In the first place, Aristotle says that the epic should be based on some historical action, only a short part of which, in point of time, should be treated by the poet; so Ariosto takes the story of Charlemagne, and does not exceed a year or so in the compass of the argument.[35] Secondly, Aristotle holds that nothing that is utterly incredible should be invented by the poet; and nothing in the *Orlando* exceeds the possibility of belief. Thirdly, epics, as well as tragedies, should be full of περιπέτεια, which Harington interprets to mean "an agnition of some unlooked for fortune either good or bad, and a sudden change thereof"; and of this, as well as of apt similitudes and passions well expressed, the *Orlando* is really full.

In conclusion, it may be observed that epic poetry did not receive adequate critical treatment in England until after the introduction of the French influence. The rules and theories of the Italian Renaissance, restated in the writings of Le Bossu, Mambrun, Rapin, and Vossius, were thus brought into English criticism, and found perhaps their best expression in Addison's essays on *Paradise Lost*. Such epics as Davenant's *Gondibert*, Chamberlayne's *Pharonnida*, Dryden's *Annus Mirabilis*, and Blackmore's *Prince Arthur*, like the French epics of the same period, doubtless owed their inspiration to the desire to put into practice the classical rules of heroic poetry.[36]

[32] *Ibid.* p. 54.
[33] *Defence*, p. 30.
[34] Haslewood, ii. 140 sq.
[35] Cf. Minturno, *Arte Poetica*, p. 71; and Ronsard, (Œuvres, iii. 19.
[36] Cf. Dryden, *Discourse on Satire, in Works*, xiii. 37.

MILTON*

Arnold Stein

I shall begin with some of the immediate problems that Milton must have had to solve in order to solve his larger problem of building styles into style, variety into unity. It is toward the larger problem that I hope to work.

First there is the question of the dramatic in a poem which presents a large action and many smaller actions, which presents characters in a drama whose scope extends from the domestic to the cosmic. It is plain that the immediate, the local, and the individual cannot be allowed to dominate this epic situation. The stage is too vast—the panorama of hell, heaven, and earth, and their constant relationship. The events are too remote—the climax is on the threshold of time, and only at the end of the poem does the action move in a direct line into our time. (And these considerations must dominate, though there is a vision of history, and there are the frequent intrusive pressures of time, the echoes of the future that reverberate significantly on their source.)

The terms of the drama require that even Satan must realize himself as a public personality; it is not as a person but as a state of mind (however complex and far-reaching in significance) that he must express himself, less in speech than in speeches, and these never delivered without the audible overtones on God's providence. (The diminished Satan of *Paradise Regained* is more nearly individual.) Yet Satan is always interesting as a character; his public personality and his speeches have a liveliness of surface and a richness of depth; he has a history which is always bringing pressure upon the moment, and though the full dramatic illusion would violate the governing principles of this epic, at least there is an immediacy in the *impact* he makes. But if Satan must be presented under these controlling limitations, what of the human pair who are at the center of the drama? Intimations of personality there must be, but shadowed and requiring translation, for only as Adam and

* From: *Answerable Style: Essays on Paradise Lost* by Arnold Stein. The University of Minnesota Press, Minneapolis. Copyright 1953 by the University of Minnesota. Passages from *Milton's Complete Poems*, edited by Frank A. Patterson (New York: Appleton-Century-Crofts, 1947), reprinted by permission.

Eve approach the Fall can they begin to assume full human personality.

It may seem perverse to apply the term "dramatic" to a situation thus described—especially since visual imagery, colloquial language, and immediacy have usually been regarded by modern critics as indispensable to the "dramatic"; and hostile criticism of Milton has tended to emphasize his lack of these indispensables. Yet Milton plainly conceived of his epic as a great drama; and not merely because he first planned the material as a play; but because as an artist, and indeed as a man, he saw the most significant human experience and human destiny itself as a kind of drama. What the critic must do is obvious—accept Milton's terms and not insist on his own, at least if he wishes to see what Milton has done. And in Milton's kind of dramatic, which would ruin many other fine poems as their kind of dramatic would ruin his, the natural, the familiar, the sharply focused, the completely individual, and all aspects of the immediate must be subordinated to the larger considerations of context, perspective, and to the great order of dynamic interplay which is the total structure.

For instance, in *Paradise Lost* there is a constant and cumulative pressure of local context and its relationship to larger contexts, of local perspective and its relationship to the unfolding perspective which tests, purges, and unites parts into whole. In Milton's art the immediate, however striking it may be, is as likely to contradict as confirm. If it is Satan speaking, for example, there will be the immediate projection of his will, the rhetoric of his present intention; but there will also be a rich interplay of conflicting tensions which connect the most local context (which may be within Satan's own self-contradicting consciousness) with the chain of contexts leading ultimately to God's will. In such an art the elevation of perspective does not inhibit but rather creates variety and interior movement and counter-movement, which in turn test and prove the rightness of the perspective.

Most of these generalizations I have been making are based upon analyses of passages in *Paradise Lost* which I have previously used as arguments for interpretation. I assume that a kind of case for Milton's dramatic style has already been presented; but the issue is important enough to justify some fresh examples directly to the point, in order to illustrate more specifically the way this dramatic style works.

I take Satan's opening speech to Beelzebub, which is introduced by the specific reference to Satan's torment and to the bold words that break the horrid silence—bold in themselves, presumably, and bold because they express a will that can rise above the real terror of the numbing silence. The speech is followed by the choral commentary, "Vaunting aloud, but rackt with deep despare." Introduction and conclusion frame the speech and impose a formal perspective. This may seem to be a blemish and evidence of artistic inadequacy to the critic who regards commentary as the artist's personal intrusion on material that ideally should be able to speak for itself. But such a critical attitude, whatever its merits in other literary situations, can only be misleading here. For one thing, the formal perspective does not force itself upon Satan's speech, does not label and editorialize the impressive willfulness out of existence; but rather sets up a dramatic conflict between the local context of the immediate utterance and the larger context of which the formal perspective is expression. This conflict marks, with a literal accuracy and precision that are dazzling, the tormented relationship between the external boast and the internal despair. (Before he is through with the poem, Milton will have wrung all the rich possibilities for action out of his concept of despair.)

Dramatically, the immediate impact of Satan's great willfulness is more striking than the formal perspective, and this is as it should be; for then if there are small revelations that the external perspective is also expressed *within* the speech, that the despair does betray the boast, we shall have a tension within the speech as well, and the small quiet effects will clash advantageously with the large and loud effects. That is what does happen, and it is no mean dramatic accomplishment. The famous brassy effects come toward the middle of the speech, after Satan has pulled himself together. The opening lines keep trying for Satan's characteristic orchestration and assertiveness of rhythm, but lose their way and falter in a dazed and confused syntax. Mention of the good old cause almost regains him his voice, but memory of past and present interferes too violently and shakes loose the stunned surprise that must have been the shaping force of his first articulation, now finally stumbling its way into form:

> If thou beest he; But O how fall'n! how chang'd
> From him, who in the happy Realms of Light
> Cloth'd with transcendent brightnes didst outshine
> Myriads though bright: If he whom mutual league,
> United thoughts and counsels, equal hope,
> And hazard in the Glorious Enterprize,
> Joynd with me once, now misery hath joynd
> In equal ruin: into what Pit thou seest
> From what highth fal'n, so much the stronger provd
> He with his Thunder: and till then who knew
> The force of thos dire Arms?   (I, 84ff)

In the lines that follow Satan assumes his characteristic style, which weaves a fine tissue of ironies between Satan's perspective and God's providence. The boast of "that fixt mind" and "the unconquerable Will" glitter most and reflect most, but only the full evolving of the drama under the process of time will reveal all the particular meanings of the bright refractions. As he concludes his speech, though, the formal perspective which has been looking over his shoulder, as it were, becomes part of his own expressed perspective. The movement is subtle, like the skillful merging of two themes in music; one of them dominating the other, whether tenderly or gently or patronizingly or harshly, but with a fine sureness of its own identity. Only here the shaping skill which is the management of the inner logic of form is not in Satan's control; he and his consciousness, whatever it may divine of what is happening, act out the drama of the immediate context without knowing the full relationship of immediate perspective to the whole dramatic plan. Nor do we as readers, but we see enough to realize that it is drama.

The last two lines of the speech defiantly but ignorantly transfer Satan's own defeated hopes to his description of God, now triumphantly holding the "Tyranny of Heav'n" alone, and "in th' excess of joy." The approach to that ending is less defiant, a somewhat sobered letdown after the earlier largeness of statement. It is presented in the form of causal reasoning, a kind of scrambled syllogism. Since—"by Fate," the metaphysical source which Satan nominates and to which he nominates himself as casual prophet—the "strength" and the "substance" of gods cannot fail; and since, "through experience of this great event," we have lost nothing in arms and have gained in "foresight":

> We may with more successful hope resolve
> To wage by force or guile eternal Warr
> Irreconcileable, to our grand Foe. (I, 120ff)

It even has a nice internal cross-bolstering: the strength, arms, force lining up to demonstrate the series of unfailing continuance—the argument from soul or will, one might say; and then the more elevated and positive metaphysical argument, presumably from intelligence, the chain of substance, foresight, and guile. This latter series is itself a delicious metaphysical joke, one that comments with independent mischief on the argument, as substance humbly accepts the being of foresight and guile.

There is a rhetorical mischief too, in the disparity between the immediate thundering emphasis of the *eternal* and the *irreconcilable*, and the remarkably shy string of hesitant advances toward the positive committal, which even then still remains governed by the carefully laid down *may*: We may . . . with more . . . successful . . . hope . . . resolve. The formal perspective of despair has permeated the formal logic of the syllogism and acted out the drama of resolved hopelessness founding its hope on the irreconcilable maintenance of that state. The grand defiance of eternal war has quietly excluded the question of possible victory and Satan has embraced despair as if he were no unwilling victim but an eager lover seeking to prove himself and to learn the nature of the beloved.

This example, though it is especially useful in demonstrating that familiar canons of the dramatic cannot arbitrarily be applied to Milton's style, is by no means unusual. The same basic control of materials, however varied, occurs time and again. Satan, of course, by nature of his role provides Milton with the best opportunities; the unfallen and still untainted creatures are too nearly in harmony with the great perspective to admit much conflict. Adam's first speech (Book IV), for instance, is dignified and simple, securely removed from the individual and the immediate. It is pure of internal conflict and yet does not lack external conflict; for it expresses the simplicity of unfallen nature in the great conflict that is shaping, and it follows immediately after Satan's fertile demonstration of internal conflict in the "melting" soliloquy that "wonders" at Paradise and man, and dances love and pity and duty into hatred and self-pity and evasive compulsion.

But Adam's speeches do not remain so simple, nor do Eve's, and the style—the voice—of each is successfully differentiated from the other. That is one kind of variety Milton skillfully maintains within his elevation. The most virtuoso display is, I suppose, that by the speakers in the Parliament of Hell. There we find stylistic characterization with broad and heavy strokes—the energetic stolidity of the die-hard general, the flat language and rhythms of the business executive. But there are subtly drawn differences too—as between the rhythms and sensuousness of Satan's first public speech and those of Belial's oration. Satan puts the pressure of his personality and feeling and will on every word and rhythm; Belial starts, at least, by creating the illusion of cool distance, by the curve of his rhythms, by the graceful syntax of apparently objective contemplation, though he ends in a sensuousness of attitude and direction that has no object for contemplation but the deliciousness of self.

God's speeches have hardly aroused critical enthusiasm, though Milton's skill in providing and adapting biblical phrases has been admired. Perhaps it is no answer to say that Milton's God is not presented as a dramatic character. Metaphysically He would seem to be properly outside the universe of action, though He is also the biblical God revealing Himself in His chosen terms, however symbolically, to angelic and human understanding. Milton certainly did not expect his fit audience to read literally, and with no consciousness of the literary problem of presenting God's words. (Language and cadence are as unsensuous as if Milton were writing a model for the Royal Society and attempting to speak purely to the understanding.) There at the fountain of light, where there can be no shadow and no reflection, the words themselves can have no overtones or echoes; though after they have been heard and interpreted one may become aware of reflections, less to eye or ear than to understanding, reflections that are the images of the words. The grand style would be presumptuous, and what Milton aims at is a particular kind of bare language that will rise above the familiar associations of such bareness with austerity and harshness. Much, not all, of God's speech is delivered in rhythms that are markedly shorter than usual with Milton, and yet successfully avoid the effects of brokenness or crabbedness. They are no mean achievement of Milton's ear, which has too often received credit for near-perfection at the expense of recognizing the range of its imaginative accomplishments.

Poetry is human and metaphorical, and the Father's speeches are intended to express divine Justice as if directly: to seem without seeming: to create the illusion of no illusion. I pass the problem of trying to judge them—and say only that in Milton's plan it is necessary that God be present and speak; that Justice reveal, however imperfectly in human words, its Idea; which then can be translated perfectly, in the universe where poetry is valid, by the words and actions of God's creatures. The Son is the authorized Word and has the greatest range of speech: He is the Logos creating, the interpreter and declared will of God, He uses "I" gently to Adam and Eve as creator, sternly as judge. He expresses the fullness of divine love, God's "dearest mediation" between eternity and time, immortality and mortality, justice and love.

The scene where He chooses sacrifice in order to fulfill justice is one of Milton's great triumphs of style. Again, all the conflict is external, in what this untroubled simplicity of utterance represents in the whole drama—in the way it will echo when Satan, also "freely," volunteers as individual sacrifice; when Eve chooses the ambitious death of putting off human "to put on Gods" and resolves to share with Adam "all deaths" or "equal Joy, as equal Love"; when Adam chooses death with Eve, for "Death is to mee as Life"; and when Eve, as the drama moves into the myth of redemption, prays that all the sentence fall on her; and Adam, in the forgiveness of renewed love and the acceptance of justice, gently says that if prayers could alter high decrees he would, first and more loudly, pray "That on my head all might be visited." The Son's speech has no internal conflict, for it is above human drama. But it expresses the divine order against which conflict is free to try itself— the expression of justice in terms of the immortal love for the mortal. It speaks with grace and beauty and purity to human senses, as the sanctioned mediation between the human metaphor of poetry and reality:

> Father, thy word is past, man shall find grace;
> And shall grace not find means, that finds her way,
> The speediest of thy winged messengers,
> To visit all thy creatures, and to all
> Comes unprevented, unimplor'd, unsought,
> Happie for man, so coming; he her aide
> Can never seek, once dead in sins and lost;
> Attonement for himself or offering meet,
> Indebted and undon, hath none to bring:
> Behold mee then, mee for him, life for life
> I offer, on mee let thine anger fall;
> Account mee man; I for his sake will leave
> Thy bosom, and this glorie next to thee
> Freely put off, and for him lastly die
> Well pleas'd, on me let Death wreck all his rage . . .
>   (III, 227ff)

In *Paradise Lost* there are many detachable moments that are projected with striking beauty. Time seems to stop, and the illusion grants the enclosed moment a great intensity, which is always modified significantly as the moment re-enters the continuum of time. An obvious example is the sudden illusion of magnification in Satan's encounters with Death and with Gabriel. Some more important examples, which occur most liberally in hell, are the beautiful military review of the fallen angels marching forward in the momentary unification of music and discipline, with the illusion of past and present and future boldly but despairingly fused into one; or the whole building of Pandemonium, and the sub-moment of Mulciber's fall; or the whole experience of Paradise as a beautiful but impossible moment in time, with sub-moments complete in their purity, and others, like Eve's dream or Adam's praise to Raphael of Eve's apparent absoluteness; or the creation by Sin and Death of the causeway between hell and earth; or the sustained moments of many of the epic similes which rise out of the narrative to furnish great adventures in perspective. All of these, and countless more, gain enormous intensity from being seen both as they immediately are and as they are in the unfolding perspectives which lead finally to God's Idea of time, which includes as a smaller circle man's creation, fall, and redemption. The great circle, which begins with the creation of the angels, and proceeds from God to God, is described as finally ending thus with the last judgment:

> Hell, her numbers full,
> Thenceforth shall be for ever shut. Mean while
> The World shall burn, and from her ashes spring
> New Heav'n and Earth, wherein the just shall dwell
> And after all thir tribulations long
> See golden days, fruitful of golden deeds,
> With Joy and Love triumphing, and fair Truth.
> Then thou thy regal Scepter shalt lay by,
> For regal Scepter then no more shall need,
> God shall be All in All. (III, 332ff)

Under this positive vision of the whole, the powerful play of Satan's immediacy is contained while given the full expression that dramatically demonstrates its opportunism, its essentially negative evil. He has no real place to go, as his syllogism of despair argues; he vacillates between an impossible stasis and a real retreat. The great assertions of individual will which, with their counterplay of conscious and unconscious inner conflict, endow him with the illusion of dramatic being, drive him inevitably to allegorical being. He is drawn gradually into the mechanical existence of his unwilled creations, Sin and Death. It is part of their structural role to show this, for their allegorical being constitutes a kind of stable measure; but their author changes, to become more like his images. When they first meet at the gate of hell Satan ungallantly de-

clares that he has never seen "Sight more detestable then him and thee."
But when he returns to find his success anticipated by their "connatural"
sympathy, he expresses unreserved admiration for their work, for their
very selves, and for their relationship to him:

> Fair Daughter, and thou Son and Grandchild both,
> High proof ye now have giv'n to be the Race
> of *Satan*.   (X, 384ff)

He has been demonstrating the logic of sin, the thraldom of self,
the progressive deaths of spirit and will; now he passes on to the final
mechanistic demonstration, his role in the mass metamorphosis. At this
point he equals the abstract grotesqueness of Sin and Death, and he is
himself a monster illustrating an allegory. The infernal trinity do more
than parody the supernal trinity and true creation (though I agree with
Mr. Tillyard's recent observation that they do this); they demonstrate
another order of being, the crude mechanistic existence of allegorical
being. Their career constitutes a negative proof that also has some
bearing on Milton's attitude toward the imagination; for they oppose,
in a mechanical metaphor cut off from true reality, the whole imaginative vision of true creation and the true poem, with its degrees of
metaphor leading up to the great source which allows imaginative freedom, under love and order, to the human and natural.

The moments not detachable from time are less gorgeous and exciting, freed from the dramatic burden of intensity. I think of the Son's
volunteering for sacrifice, of the contrasting forward march to music
by the loyal angels in heaven, of the reconciliation between Adam and
Eve, of Adam's final recital of his lesson:

> with good
> Still overcoming evil, and by small
> Accomplishing great things, by things deemd weak
> Subverting worldly strong, and worldly wise
> By simply meek; that suffering for Truths sake
> Is fortitude to highest victorie,
> And to the faithful Death the Gate of Life.   (XII, 565ff)

The whole of Book VII is the great example. The Creation occurs as an
authentic miracle which can take itself for granted. Everything is easy
and natural and right. All the creatures do the typical things, which are
interesting for themselves, but are loved because they express the order
and harmony of the created world. There is no extravagance of image
or diction or rhythm. By contrast the building of Pandemonium is a
dazzling piece of self-conscious conjuring.

But there are two other moments that are perhaps more significant
in their contrast. First, the intoxicated extravagance of image and diction
that celebrates the infernal creation by Sin and Death; especially this:

> The aggregated Soyle
> Death with his Mace petrific, cold and dry,
> As with a Trident smote, and fix't as firm
> As *Delos* floating once; the rest his look
> Bound with *Gorgonian* rigor not to move,
> And with *Asphaltic* slime.   (X, 293ff)

And then, the beautiful and quiet moment of natural description presented by the simile which concludes the consultation in Pandemonium:

> Thus they thir doubtful consultations dark
> Ended rejoycing in thir matchless Chief:
> As when from mountain tops the dusky clouds
> Ascending, while the North wind sleeps, o'respread
> Heav'ns chearful face, the lowring Element
> Scowls ore the dark'nd lantskip Snow, or showre;
> If chance the radiant Sun with farewell sweet
> Extend his ev'ning beam, the fields revive,
> The birds thir notes renew, and bleating herds
> Attest thir joy, that hill and valley rings.   (II, 486ff)

The natural beauty is as innocent here as in Book VII, but packed down into this moment is the human consciousness of change, of the certainty of uncertainty. The intense moment that prolongs day is made intense by the knowledge that it is a moment; man responds joyously as a part of nature because he is in the moment, but it is a mixed joy because he knows about time. And so the reader shares fallen feelings with these angels; he participates in the experience, which is his experience too, but he is also outside it by virtue of the controlled perspective and its comment on this illusion. He will marvel at Milton's imaginative sympathy, but he will remember other moments: and he may remember particularly the delayed morning of the night-foundered skiff, the long summer's day, which ends, of Mulciber's fall; and the image that concludes Mammon's speech, the true and false illusion of the echoes in the craggy bay after the tempest; and he may be reminded later by the images of false light; and by Satan's sea finding a shore in the dubious light on the border of chaos, and by evening and morning in Paradise; and by the unknown beauty of the fruit of Paradise described in an image drawn from the known beauty on the edge of the border of change:

> On which the Sun more glad impress'd his beams
> Then in fair Evening Cloud, or humid Bow,
> When God hath showred the earth.   (IV, 150ff)

And by the final sunset image that formally begins human time and the long day's dying.

The wealth and variety of the answerable style is a vision of the whole, a vision that can accommodate natural beauty, and the necessary discipline in heaven and on earth, and the extravagant hope for man (who is made *to delight*, "and delight to Reason joyn'd")—it is an affirmation of hope in God's love for creation, and a sober realization of the now under the great promise of Time. The *poetic* authority for the great vision of time is also poetic authority for the answerable style. This may be seen in its most direct expression in the passage that follows the Son's free offer to die for man:

> His words here ended, but his meek aspect
> Silent yet spake, and breath'd immortal love
> To mortal men, above which only shon
> Filial obedience.   (III, 266ff)

The variety is unity through the sanction of the immortal love for the mortal under obedience: with the stage, the focus of the feelings, successfully human, allowing the full play of human interest in the drama of freedom, fall, and redemption under the sanctioned perspective of love fulfilling justice. It is a vision that demands love from the style, under an Idea that authorizes and encourages love for created things, and does not require love for the Idea to dry up all other love. It holds to a Platonic insistence on the responsibility of reason, but with no drawing back from the natural and material; man knows God because God has given man the true means, which have dignity.

In his style Milton can trust the springs of the natural, because the "simple" end loves the sensuous and passionate means to it, and does not withdraw its love completely from the means that tend away. Beauty is not blotted out of evil: the fallen angels lie like autumnal leaves "that strow the Brooks/In *Vallombrosa*"; and Mulciber's fall is neither an "unconscious" beauty nor merely (as I have thought) a deliberate irony—there is a place for that beauty finally. Love is the solution of the insoluble. The vision that can contain the necessity and beauty of Eve, the certain but not necessary fall, through misdirected love, and the certain but not necessary redemption in love, can contain in true perspective the individual beauty of each created part in the harmony of the whole creation. Song and dance in heaven express the same harmonious relationship between part and whole:

> No voice exempt, no voice but well could joine
> Melodious part, such concord is in Heav'n.   (III, 370f)

>   mazes intricate,
> Eccentric, intervolv'd, yet regular
> Then most, when most irregular they seem.   (V, 622ff)

When Adam becomes conscious that he has been created, he feels with a knowledge as spontaneous as love that he is happier than he knows. The last two books are not to be explained away historically, as the esthetic result of the seventeenth century's being more interested in biblical history than is the twentieth century. These books fulfill the rhythm of the poem, and they satisfy two kinds of time; they allow Adam a necessary interval to convalesce as man and hero under the aspects of human history and eternity. During this time he becomes a conscious tragic hero (both actor and spectator) accepting, with all passion spent, fully man's condition, and he himself now a fully experienced man; and becomes a mythic hero reborn; and finally becomes man, with all his history behind and before him.

The complex is the dramatic, the dust and heat of the world trying truth in no simple contest. But the clarity shines through the complexity. The style returns through full complexity to a source beyond innocence, without losing any of the wisdom of the whole experience—or the knowledge that it must be lived through again and again.

DRYDEN*

William K. Wimsatt, Jr. and Cleanth Brooks

At about the same time as he was writing his *Essay of Dramatic Poesy* Dryden signed a contract with the King's Theater to write three plays a year. Shortly afterwards he became Poet Laureate and Historiographer Royal and entered upon the palmiest phase of his career. In a critical sense this phase had two main features: it was heroic and it was courtly, and in neither of these ways was it modest.

Both the theory and to some extent the practice of heroic poetry were the outcome of a theory of ideal literary genre which had waxed in the later 16th century.[1] Thus Sir Philip Sidney:

> There rests the heroical, whose very name, I think, should daunt all backbiters. For by what conceit can a tongue be directed to speak evil of that which draweth with it no less champions than Achilles, Cyrus, Aeneas, Turnus, Tydeus, Rinaldo? who doth not only reach and move to truth, but teacheth and moveth to the most high and excellent truth; . . . But if anything be already said in the defense of sweet poetry, all concurreth to the maintaining the heroical, which is not only a kind, but the best and most accomplished kind of poetry. For, as the image of each action stirreth and instructeth the mind, so the lofty image of such worthies most inflameth the mind with desire to be worthy, and informs with counsel how to be worthy.[2]

The term "poem" (which since the time of Wordsworth and Keats has meant for us a short piece of verse, characteristically, let us say, an ode or sonnet) meant in Dryden's time par excellence a long story in verse (an epic or heroic poem) or a drama like an epic. (D'Avenant argued

---

[1] The theory begins at least as early as Vida's *De Arte Poetica*. See B. J. Pendlebury, *Dryden's Heroic Plays* (London, 1913), pp. 9 ff; C. V. Deane, *Dramatic Theory and the Heroic Play* (London, 1930).

[2] *A Defense of Poesy*, ed. A. S. Cook (Boston, 1890), p. 30. Cf. Scaliger, *Poetics* III, 96: "In epic poetry, which describes the descent, life, and deeds of heroes, all other kinds of poetry have . . . a norm, so that to it they turn for their regulative principles."

that the epic should be fashioned after the drama in five main parts;[3] Dryden argued that the narrative epic was the correct model for the mighty drama.) A shorter poem was likely to be dubbed a "paper of verses."[4] Nobody in Dryden's day would have understood (or at least nobody would have admitted understanding) Edgar Allan Poe's typically romantic thesis that a long poem is a contradiction in terms and that such an apparently successful long poem as Milton's *Paradise Lost* is really a collection of short poems, intense moments, held together by prose.[5] As tragedy was the norm of Aristotle's theory, and epistolary satire implicitly that of Horace's best insights, so the heroic epic was the more or less explicit norm of poetry in the latter part of the 17th century (and was a rather unhappily dilated focus for critical theory). Witness not only the numerous original epic attempts and the epic translations of the century but the epic straining of even such a topical poem as Dryden's *Annus Mirabilis* and the dreams of strong poets like Dryden and Pope about writing a British epic. Heroic poets, says the Earl of Mulgrave in his *Essay upon Poetry,* 1682, are "gigantic souls;" the heroic poem is the "chief effort of human sense." And Dryden was sure that the heroic poem not only always had been but always would be "estemed . . . the greatest work of human nature."[6] As late in his career as 1697 (long after the passion for heroic drama had cooled) he opened the Dedication of his translated *Aeneis* with the sentence: "A HEROIC POEM, truly such, is undoubtedly the greatest work which the soul of man is capable to perform."

Partly as a result of such ideas, partly as a result of grandiose political trends (which doubtless underlay the literary doctrine), and in some small part through the Puritan interdict of the stage which drove the poet Davenant in 1656 to adopt in lieu of a real play the expedient of a musical and recitative spectacle (*The Siege of Rhodes*), the English heroical play was born. At its most glorious the heroical play was an amalgam of Marlovian and Cornelian passion drama, of Fletcherian romantic melodrama, of French nine-volume pastoral romance, of

[3] Letter to Hobbes prefixed to *Gondibert,* 1651. D'Avenant's letter and Hobbes's answer, the earliest full-bloom pronouncements in English of heroic theory, first appeared, together, at Paris in 1650.

[4] See Howard, Preface to *Four Plays* (D. D. Arundell, *Dryden and Howard,* Cambridge, 1929, p. 8) and Dryden, *Essay of Dramatic Poesy:* "Blank verse is acknowledged to be too low for a poem, nay more, for a paper of verses; but if too low for an ordinary sonnet, how much more for Tragedy, which is by Aristotle, in the dispute betwixt the epic poesy and the dramatic, for many reasons he there alleges, ranked above it?" (Ker I, 101).

[5] But cf. Dryden's opinion: Milton "runs into a flat of thought, sometimes for a hundred lines together . . ." (*Original and Progress of Satire,* Ker II, 29); and cf. *post* Chapter 20.

[6] *Apology for Heroic Poetry and Poetic Licence,* Ker I, 181.

masque and Italian opera. It was Homeric and Aristotelian in its aim at action, largeness, and elevation; it was Virgilian and Heliodoran[7] in its tender concern for the union of a pair of lovers and the founding of an illustrious house. It urged the themes of love, honor, and civic virtue, in high places, and with furious confusion and rivalry, before an exotic and pseudo-historical setting, to the continuous fanfare of trumpets and clash of arms on nearby plains.

The English heroic drama consisted most conspicuously of Dryden's five plays of this kind, from *The Indian Queen*, written in collaboration with Howard and produced in 1664, to *Aurengzebe*, produced in 1677. Heroic theory, Dryden's justification for the magnitude, the uproar, and the constant oratorical altitude at which he found himself moving, appears in his *Essay of Heroic Plays*, prefixed to his two-part heroic play *The Conquest of Granada*, 1672, and in his *Apology for Heroic Poetry and Poetic Licence* prefixed to his operatic rhymed rendition of Milton's *Paradise Lost*, *The State of Innocence and the Fall of Man*, a work printed in 1677, though never acted. Heroic theory was a coarse parody of Aristotelian epic theory: the Homeric hero inflated to a colossus and paragon of prowess, honor, and passion, the element of the wonderful (*to thaumaston*) magnified both in the direction of the amazing and in that of the admirable, and the element of fear, in the direction of terror. Withal a dash of Longinianism and Petronianism[8] was convenient to justify the liberal introduction of the supernatural (ghosts and heavenly signs) to the main end of hair-raising. Were it not for Dryden's unparalleled aplomb, which makes him at all times amusing, it might be a sorry shock to find his hand lent to this task.

> But I have already swept the stakes; and, with the common good fortune of prosperous gamesters, can be content to sit quietly; to hear my fortune cursed by some, and my faults arraigned by others, and to suffer both without reply.[9]

Critical resistance to heroic insensibility in England was furnished not so much by reasoned argument as by ruthless burlesque, the first effort being that of Buckingham and his friends in *The Rehearsal*, 1671, which hit Dryden himself and may in part have provoked his defences. Later, came the retrospective sortie of Fielding, *The Tragedy of Tragedies; or the Life and Death of Tom Thumb the Great*, 1731 which parodies every element of inflation in English drama from Shakespeare to Addison.

---

[7] See Sidney's and Scaliger's statements about the *Theagenes and Chariclea* of Heliodorus compared by Cornell M. Dowlin, "Sidney and Other Men's Thoughts," *RES*, XX (October, 1944), pp. 257-71.

[8] Petronius is quoted in *Of Heroic Plays* (Ker I, 152); Longinus is cited in the *Apology for Heroic Poetry and Poetic Licence* (Ker. I, 181).

[9] *Of Heroic Plays*, Ker I, 159.

EPIC, COMEDY, AND PROSE*

Henry Fielding

AUTHOR'S PREFACE

As it is possible the mere English reader may have a different idea of romance from the author of these little volumes, and may consequently expect a kind of entertainment not to be found, nor which was even intended, in the following pages, it may not be improper to premise a few words concerning this kind of writing, which I do not remember to have seen hitherto attempted in our language.

The Epic, as well as the Drama, is divided into tragedy and comedy. Homer, who was the father of this species of poetry, gave us a pattern of both these, though that of the latter kind is entirely lost; which Aristotle tells us, bore the same relation to comedy which his Iliad bears to tragedy. And perhaps, that we have no more instances of it among the writers of antiquity, is owing to the loss of this great pattern, which, had it survived, would have found its imitators equally with the other poems of this great original.

And farther, as this poetry may be tragic or comic, I will not scruple to say it may be likewise either in verse or prose: for though it wants one particular, which the critic enumerates in the constituent parts of an epic poem, namely metre; yet, when any kind of writing contains all its other parts, such as fable, action, characters, sentiments, and diction, and is deficient in metre only, it seems, I think, reasonable to refer it to the epic; at least, as no critic hath thought proper to range it under any other head, or to assign it a particular name to itself.

Thus the Telemachus of the archbishop of Cambray appears to me of the epic kind, as well as the Odyssey of Homer; indeed, it is much fairer and more reasonable to give it a name common with that species from which it differs only in a single instance, than to confound it with those which it resembles in no other. Such are those voluminous works, commonly called Romances, namely, Clelia, Cleopatra, Astraea, Cassandra, the Grand Cyrus, and innumerable others, which contain, as I apprehend, very little instruction or entertainment.

Now, a comic romance is a comic epic poem in prose; differing from comedy, as the serious epic from tragedy: its action being more

* Henry Fielding, *Joseph Andrews.*

extended and comprehensive; containing a much larger circle of incidents, and introducing a greater variety of characters. It differs from the serious romance in its fable and action, in this; that as in the one these are grave and solemn, so in the other they are light and ridiculous: it differs in its characters by introducing persons of inferior rank, and consequently, of inferior manners, whereas the grave romance sets the highest before us: lastly, in its sentiments and diction; by preserving the ludicrous instead of the sublime. In the diction, I think, burlesque itself may be sometimes admitted; of which many instances will occur in this work, as in the description of the battles, and some other places, not necessary to be pointed out to the classical reader, for whose entertainment those parodies or burlesque imitations are chiefly calculated.

But though we have sometimes admitted this in our diction, we have carefully excluded it from our sentiments and characters; for these it is never properly introduced, unless in writings of the burlesque kind, which this is not intended to be. Indeed, no two species of writing can differ more widely than the comic and the burlesque; for as the latter is ever the exhibition of what is monstrous and unnatural, and where our delight, if we examine it, arises from the surprising absurdity, as in appropriating the manners of the highest to the lowest, or è *converso;* so in the former we should ever confine ourselves strictly to nature, from the just imitation of which will flow all the pleasure we can this way convey to a sensible reader. And perhaps there is one reason why a comic writer should of all others be the least excused for deviating from nature, since it may not be always so easy for a serious poet to meet with the great and the admirable; but life everywhere furnishes an accurate observer with the ridiculous.

I have hinted this little concerning burlesque, because I have often heard that name given to performances which have been truly of the comic kind, from the author's having sometimes admitted it in his diction only; which, as it is the dress of poetry, doth, like the dress of men, establish characters (the one of the whole poem, and the other of the whole man), in vulgar opinion, beyond any of their greater excellences: but surely, a certain drollery in stile, where characters and sentiments are perfectly natural, no more constitutes the burlesque, than an empty pomp and dignity of words, where everything else is mean and low, can entitle any performance to the appellation of the true sublime.

And I apprehend my Lord Shaftesbury's opinion of mere burlesque agrees with mine, when he asserts, There is no such thing to be found in the writings of the ancients. But perhaps I have less abhorrence than he professes for it; and that, not because I have had some little success on the stage this way, but rather as it contributes more to exquisite mirth and laughter than any other; and these are probably more wholesome physic for the mind, and conduce better to purge away spleen, melancholy, and ill affections, than is generally imagined. Nay, I will appeal to common observation, whether the same companies are not found more full of good-humour and benevolence, after they have been sweetened for two or three hours with entertainments of this kind, than when soured by a tragedy or a grave lecture.

But to illustrate all this by another science, in which, perhaps, we shall see the distinction more clearly and plainly, let us examine the works of a comic history painter, with those performances which the Italians call Caricatura, where we shall find the true excellence of the former to consist in the exactest copying of nature; insomuch that a judicious eye instantly rejects anything *outré,* any liberty which the painter hath taken with the features of that *alma mater;* whereas in the Caricatura we allow all licence—its aim is to exhibit monsters, not men; and all distortions and exaggerations whatever are within its proper province.

Now, what Caricatura is in painting, Burlesque is in writing; and in the same manner the comic writer and painter correlate to each other. And here I shall observe, that, as in the former the painter seems to have the advantage; so it is in the latter infinitely on the side of the writer; for the Monstrous is much easier to paint than describe, and the Ridiculous to describe than paint.

And though perhaps this latter species doth not in either science so strongly affect and agitate the muscles as the other; yet it will be owned, I believe, that a more rational and useful pleasure arises to us from it. He who should call the ingenious Hogarth a burlesque painter, would, in my opinion, do him very little honour; for sure it is much easier, much less the subject of admiration, to paint a man with a nose, or any other feature, of a preposterous size, or to expose him in some absurd or monstrous attitude, than to express the affections of men on canvas. It hath been thought a vast commendation of a painter to say his figures seem to breathe; but surely it is a much greater and nobler applause, that they appear to think.

But to return. The Ridiculous only, as I have before said, falls within my province in the present work. Nor will some explanation of this word be thought impertinent by the reader, if he considers how wonderfully it hath been mistaken, even by writers who have professed it: for to what but such a mistake can we attribute the many attempts to ridicule the blackest villanies, and, what is yet worse, the most dreadful calamities? What could exceed the absurdity of an author, who should write the comedy of Nero, with the merry incident of ripping up his mother's belly? or what would give a greater shock to humanity than an attempt to expose the miseries of poverty and distress to ridicule? And yet the reader will not want much learning to suggest such instances to himself.

Besides, it may seem remarkable, that Aristotle, who is so fond and free of definitions, hath not thought proper to define the Ridiculous. Indeed, where he tells us it is proper to comedy, he hath remarked that villany is not its object: but he hath not, as I remember, positively asserted what is. Nor doth the Abbé Bellegarde, who hath written a treatise on this subject, though he shows us many species of it, once trace it to its fountain.

The only source of the true Ridiculous (as it appears to me) is affectation. But though it arises from one spring only, when we consider the infinite streams into which this one branches, we shall presently cease to admire at the copious field it affords to an observer. Now, affectation proceeds from one of these two causes, vanity or hypocrisy: for as vanity puts us on affecting false characters, in order to purchase applause; so hypocrisy sets us on an endeavour to avoid censure, by concealing our vices under an appearance of their opposite virtues. And though these two causes are often confounded (for there is some difficulty in distinguishing them), yet, as they proceed from very different motives, so they are as clearly distinct in their operations: for indeed, the affectation which arises from vanity is nearer to truth than the other, as it hath not that violent repugnancy of nature to struggle with, which that of the hypocrite hath. It may be likewise noted, that affectation doth not imply an absolute negation of those qualities which are affected; and, therefore, though, when it proceeds from hypocrisy, it be nearly allied to deceit; yet when it comes from vanity only, it partakes of the nature of ostentation: for instance, the affectation of liberality in a vain man differs visibly from the same affectation in the avaricious; for though the vain man is not what he would appear, or hath not the virtue he affects, to the degree he would be thought to have it; yet it sits less awkwardly on him than on the avaricious man, who is the very reverse of what he would seem to be.

From the discovery of this affectation arises the Ridiculous, which always strikes the reader with surprise and pleasure; and that in a higher and stronger degree when the affectation arises from hypocrisy, than when from vanity; for to discover any one to be the exact reverse of what he affects, is more surprising, and consequently more ridiculous, than to find him a little deficient in the quality he desires the reputation of. I might observe that our Ben Jonson, who of all men understood the Ridiculous the best, hath chiefly used the hypocritical affectation.

Now, from affectation only, the misfortunes and calamities of life, or the imperfections of nature, may become the objects of ridicule. Surely he hath a very ill-framed mind who can look on ugliness, infirmity, or poverty, as ridiculous in themselves: nor do I believe any man living, who meets a dirty fellow riding through the streets in a cart, is struck with an idea of the Ridiculous from it; but if he should see the same figure descend from his coach and six, or bolt from his chair with his hat under his arm, he would then begin to laugh, and with justice. In the same manner, were we to enter a poor house and behold a wretched family shivering with cold and languishing with hunger, it would not incline us to laughter (at least we must have very diabolical natures if it would); but should we discover there a grate, instead of coals, adorned with flowers, empty plate or china dishes on the sideboard, or any other affectation of riches and finery, either on their persons or in their furniture, we might then indeed be excused for ridiculing so fantastical an appearance. Much less are natural imperfections the object of derision; but when ugliness aims at the applause of beauty, or lameness endeavours to display agility, it is then that these unfortunate circumstances, which at first moved our compassion, tend only to raise our mirth.

The poet carries this very far:

> None are for being what they are in fault,
> But for not being what they would be thought.

Where if the metre would suffer the word Ridiculous to close the first line, the thought would be rather more proper. Great vices are the proper objects of our detestation, smaller faults, of our pity; but affectation appears to me the only true source of the Ridiculous.

But perhaps it may be objected to me, that I have against my own rules introduced vices, and of a very black kind, into this work. To which I shall answer: first, that it is very difficult to pursue a series of human actions, and keep clear from them. Secondly, that the vices to be found here are rather the accidental consequences of some human frailty or foible, than causes habitually existing in the mind. Thirdly, that they are never set forth as the objects of ridicule, but detestation. Fourthly, that they are never the principal figure at that time on the scene: and, lastly, they never produce the intended evil.

Having thus distinguished Joseph Andrews from the productions of romance writers on the one hand and burlesque writers on the other, and given some few very short hints (for I intended no more) of this species of writing, which I have affirmed to be hitherto unattempted in our language; I shall leave to my good-natured reader to apply my piece to my observations, and will detain him no longer than with a word concerning the characters in this work.

And here I solemnly protest I have no intention to vilify or asperse any one; for though everything is copied from the book of nature, and scarce a character or action produced which I have not taken from my own observations and experience; yet I have used the utmost care to obscure the persons by such different circumstances, degrees, and colours, that it will be impossible to guess at them with any degree of certainty; and if it ever happens otherwise, it is only where the failure characterised is so minute, that it is a foible only which the party himself may laugh at as well as any other.

As to the character of Adams, as it is the most glaring in the whole, so I conceive it is not to be found in any book now extant. It is designed a character of perfect simplicity; and as the goodness of his heart will recommend him to the good-natured, so I hope it will excuse me to the gentlemen of his cloth; for whom, while they are worthy of their sacred order, no man can possibly have a greater respect. They will therefore excuse me, notwithstanding the low adventures in which he is engaged, that I have made him a clergyman; since no other office could have given him so many opportunities of displaying his worthy inclinations.

WORDSWORTH: THE PERSONAL EPIC*

Karl Kroeber

The White Doe, in fact, not only belongs to a later phase in Wordsworth's career but stands on the threshold of a later phase of Romanticism in which the simple poetic tale ceased to exist.[1] We have noted that Wordsworth refused the opportunity to develop his story in the way in which Byron or Scott might have, and that deliberate refusal marks The White Doe as a significant dividing point in the history of Romantic narrative art. On one side, Byron and Scott, rejecting any pretense of epical significance and grandeur, developed what we shall call the adventurous narrative: a story poem concerned with physical action and adventure, usually based on historical fact, more or less realistic in manner, and most significant in its exploration of sociological reality—the relationship of the individual to the social group and the interaction of supra-individual forces. The adventurous narrative is most closely associated with (and contributed much to) the evolution of prose fiction during the early years of the nineteenth century. On the other side, the older Wordsworth, followed by Shelley and Keats, developed narrative poetically. Their stories became less and less like prose fiction and more and more the form or medium for the expression of personal, visionary experience. They became private myths. Whereas Byron's and Scott's language became progressively simpler and more colloquial as their subjects became more realistic, the language of Wordsworth, Shelley, and Keats became progressively richer and more literary as their subjects became less realistic. Byron and Scott moved in the direction of the novel.

* Reprinted with the permission of the copyright owners, the Regents of the University of Wisconsin, from Karl Kroeber, Romantic Narrative Art, 1960, the University of Wisconsin Press.

[1] Not literally true, of course. Keats's Isabella, for example, is a simple poetic tale. But both Keats and Shelley attempted visionary personal epics much earlier in their careers than had the first generation of Romantics. Endymion and Alastor, moreover, originate in a confidence in the validity of personal vision as truth and of private myth as an appropriate form for that truth, a confidence which Wordsworth attained only in The Excursion.

Wordsworth, Shelley, and Keats (who were, we may note, the Romantics most influenced by Milton) moved in the direction of the epic.

Romantic epics,[2] however, are not like the traditional epics of the Renaissance and antiquity. They express personal rather than social experience; their truth is not that of reason but of supra-rational vision; their manner is mythical and dynamic, not formal and conventional. No single form is more characteristic of Romantic poetry than these personal epics, but like all types of Romantic verse they originate in reactions against specific Neo-classic theories and in modifications of specific Neo-classic practices, and to understand them we must understand something of their literary antecedents.

Of all narrative forms genuine epic is the most impressive and enduring. That tenet of Renaissance genre theory was not profoundly challenged by either Neo-classic or Romantic poets,[3] who, nevertheless, if they were competent artists, almost ostentatiously eschewed the traditions of the form. A good writer knows his limitations as an inferior one may not. But we recognize in the history of eighteenth-century literature an increasing pressure upon poets to write epically. Partly the pressure was economic; Pope's *Iliad* was a money-making venture, and some atrocious original epics of the period sold reasonably well. Partly it was critical; one could scarcely accept the doctrine of epic supremacy and not urge practicing poets to prove their worth by attempting that "highest" genre. And partly it was philosophical; the growing appreciation of sublimity in art pointed toward epic grandeur. By the end of the eighteenth century these combined pressures could not be ignored, and Romantic poets had either consciously to deny any epic intention, as Scott and Byron did, or to try their hand at something like epic, as Wordsworth, Shelley, and Keats did.

[2] I am thinking specifically of Wordsworth's two longest poems, Shelley's *The Revolt of Islam*, and Keats's *Hyperion*, though several other Romantic narratives might be considered in this connection. Let me repeat, however, that to analyze adequately the verse narratives of Shelley and Keats alone would require another book. However like their immediate predecessors they may be, they worked changes in narrative practice that are important to the history of the Romantic style and perhaps even more important to the history of the influence of that style upon later nineteenth-century poets. To mention but one minor instance: Shelley and Keats were by no means averse, as the earlier Romantics had been, to using old stories and old mythologies as the basis of their "original" visions. (Wordsworth's *Laodamia*, written after *The Excursion*, provides an important exception which seems almost literally to prove this rule.) It is apparent that Tennyson, Browning, and Morris developed and enriched Shelley's and Keats's method rather than returning to the inventiveness of the earlier Romantics.

[3] But see Donald M. Foerster, "The Critical Attack upon the Epic in the English Romantic Movement," *Publications of the Modern Language Association,* LXIX (1954), 432–47.

If we are to discuss intelligently the fortunes of the epic during this period we must have some definite idea of what constitutes genuine epic. As touchstones of authentic epic we propose three characteristics.[4] First, an epic is a narrative poem. About this point all critics since Aristotle have agreed. Second, the story of an epic must be real, that is, in Professor Abercrombie's words, "must be founded deep in the general experience of men. . . . No [mere] fiction will ever have the air . . . not merely of representing, but of unmistakably *being*, human experience" (pp. 44–45). About this point there has been some critical quibbling, but most of it a matter of word-chopping. But our third touchstone, although probably acceptable to most modern students of epic literature, is one that many early critics might have had trouble understanding: The epic story must embody some profoundly significant idea. By "idea" we do not mean merely a rational abstraction, nor do we mean exactly what Milton, for instance, called his "argument." Rather we mean that sort of implicit lesson which Goethe said he learned from *The Iliad:* "From Homer I learn every day more clearly, that in our life here above ground we have, properly speaking, to enact Hell."

If we apply these touchstones to the epics or pseudo-epics of the eighteenth century we see why an age that talked so much about epics is so barren of genuine heroic poetry.[5] It has become a platitude to say that in the Augustan era poets and critics alike tended to distinguish between imaginative truth and rational truth, assigning reality to the sphere of the latter alone. Even if modern scholarship has exaggerated that tendency, its existence is indisputable and even in latent form is bound to be fatal to the creation of epic stories that are "real" in the sense of our definition. For related reasons the Augustans thought of the animating force of epic as its argument or fable rather than as its idea. Hence eighteenth-century criticism and practice seldom penetrated beyond the ornaments of epic—its obvious subjectmatter, its supernatural machinery, its special diction. The Augustan discussions of the rules and techniques of epic (largely derived from Le Bossu) make tedious reading today not because they are silly (they are not) but because they never come near the experience we feel when

[4] There are now many fine studies of the nature of epic, most notable perhaps among works in English those of Bowra, Chadwick, Lewis, Routh, and Tillyard. But in some ways even more valuable is Lascelles Abercrombie's brief essay *Epic* in *The Art and Craft Letters* Series. To this essay my discussion of epic problems is indebted. Professor Abercrombie, for example, renders suspect the hoary distinction between primary and secondary epic, upon which rests the major argument of even so recent a book as Professor C. S. Lewis' brilliant *Preface to Paradise Lost.*

[5] An exhaustive study of Augustan epic criticism is Hugh Thomas Swedenberg's *The Theory of Epic in England, 1650–1800* (Berkeley, 1944).

we read epic poetry.[6] One is struck, for instance, by the Augustan reluctance to condemn poetry which even superficially meets the formal requirements of its particular genre. The eighteenth-century epics of Blackmore, Glover, and Willkie are bad by any standards because they are destitute of genuine poetic feeling. But that charge, as Macneile Dixon pointed out long ago, was only seldom and feebly raised against them by eighteenth-century critics, who wasted most of their energies on discussions of the appropriateness of their "machinery." [7]

One may examine the problem from a different angle. In a very real sense the true epics of the late seventeenth and early eighteenth centuries are Dryden's translation of the *Aeneid* and Pope's translation of the *Iliad*. Douglas Knight has argued persuasively that to the degree that Pope's *Iliad* is not Homer it is a positive and original contribution to the European heroic tradition.[8] One can only agree with Dr. Knight, but one may feel, as he does not, that Pope's translation is too like its original to contribute much to the European tradition of heroic poetry. In what large sense, after all, is Pope's *Iliad* not like Homer's? Richard Bentley, the classical scholar, is reputed to have remarked, "A very pretty poem, Mr. Pope, but you musn't call it Homer." Seldom has pedantic hostility to poetry been better disguised in aphoristic grace. If the story, characters, and setting of Pope's *Iliad* are not Homer's, whose are they? If Bentley meant that Pope's diction differs from Homer's he could have saved breath by confining himself to the observation that Greek and English are different languages. If he meant that Pope's translation is animated by a different spirit from that which animates Homer's poem he is in one obvious way correct, in another way ambiguous, but mostly obtuse. To the degree that Pope's version is faithful it necessarily must be animated by the same spirit as Homer's original. But the fact that Pope translates means that nothing in his version can embody Homer's spirit, which does not exist separately from the Greek language which expresses it. Bentley's comment deserves belaboring because, if we are interested in poetry rather than in scholarship, we must recognize that the fault of Pope's *Iliad* is that it is too faithful to Homer. Pope was a poetic genius of the first order, yet his one contribution to the European heroic tradition is a careful translation, which is as much as to say no contribution. Had Pope treated Homer with the happy freedom that some

[6] This is, possibly, why Addison's *Spectator* papers on *Paradise Lost* are still interesting. Addison seems to have been deeply impressed by Milton's poem and his enthusiasm infects the rather mechanical form of his critique.

[7] W. Macneile Dixon, *English Epic and Heroic Poetry* (London, 1912), pp. 242–43.

[8] Douglas Knight, *Pope and the Heroic Tradition*, Yale Studies in English, Vol. 117 (New Haven, 1951), pp. 82–110.

medieval translators used toward their originals, his contribution to epic would surely have been more significant and viable. That he did not do so may be ascribed to his being infected by the same kind of anti-poetic pedantry which Bentley exhibits in his criticism. Insofar as he was a poet Pope wasted his talents trying to copy, literally copy, another man's verse. His *Iliad* is actually a manifestation of, rather than as Dr. Knight contends, a protest against, his age's "growing opposition [to] the idea that one can look to poetry for an expression of human significance and value." [9]

Faith in the power of poetry to express the profoundest kind of truth is the necessary condition of all Romantic attempts at epic. Something of the nature of that faith is suggested by the distinctively anti-historical character of the Romantic personal epic. From the time of Pope until the writing of *The Prelude*[10] all epic poetry was to some degree historical or pseudo-historical.[11] A growing historical consciousness, one of the most significant eighteenth-century developments, perhaps most climactically exemplified by Gibbon's monumental *Decline and Fall* (published between 1776 and 1788), worked against the creation of authentic epic. Not only is the idea of a rational history hostile to faith in poetic truth, but also the historical method is antagonistic to the epical method. The essence of the historical method is research, research to discover factual truth. The essence of the epical method lies in its imposition of an imaginative ideal upon the facts of history. Epic asserts or celebrates rather than discovering; it is anti-historical. It can work only with that kind of history which has been transformed by tradition or imaginative enthusiasm into legend.[12] The historian's "grand design" is always, in theory at least, a tentative one.[13] It is always subject to modification, however slight, through

[9] Knight, p. 107.

[10] And, later, since all of Southey's epics, for example, belong to the eighteenth-century tradition of historical narrative.

[11] Keith Stewart in his article "Ancient Poetry as History in the 18th Century" *Journal of the History of Ideas,* XIX (1958), 335–47, which discusses that "kind of poetry whose truth (in the sense of historical fact) was on numerous occasions taken to be of a significance at least equal to that attached to it conventionally as art" (p. 347). See also Lois Whitney, "English Primitivistic Theories of Epic Origins," *Modern Philology,* XXI (1924), 337–78. To my mind, however, all studies in this area must consider A. C. Bradley's "The Long Poem in the Age of Wordsworth," *Oxford Lectures on Poetry* (2nd ed.; London, 1923), which sensitively and perceptively investigates Matthew Arnold's assertion that the peculiar characteristics of early nineteenth-century long narratives are the result of their authors' lack of knowledge.

[12] Some of Milton's greatest difficulties arise in *Paradise Lost* at those places where his commitment to the biblical story as historically true cramps the imaginative freedom of his conception. Virgil's advantage in this respect lies precisely in the amorphousness of his legendary material.

[13] I oversimplify. History is an art, too.

the introduction of new evidence. The epic writer's grand design, being a function of his art, not an organization of external facts, cannot be dependent on extrinsic materials. Recent discoveries of Mycenean civilization do not affect the value of the *Iliad*. Or, to put the matter differently, the opinion of some modern historians that what Homer describes as the siege of Troy was in fact merely a freebooters' raid has no bearing on our opinion of Homer's poem but does affect our judgment of Thucydides' discussion of the Trojan War at the opening of his history. This is so well understood as to be scarcely worth repeating, except that the effort to treat history epically defines the basic fault in many eighteenth-century and early nineteenth-century long narrative poems, most of which are burdened by too great a respect for the grandeur of history. More important, the effort to escape the limiting conditions of history goes far to explain the form and the subject of Wordsworth's most ambitious poem, *The Prelude*, which attempts a new kind of epic system.

We are not the first by any means to call attention to the epic nature and structure of *The Prelude*,[14] although our definition of the poem as epic is perhaps derived from a more particularized consideration of its place amidst the many historical verse narratives of Wordsworth's era. *The Prelude* is, in part, a history of the French Revolution, but Wordsworth subordinates that history to his autobiography. The mighty events of contemporary history are presented only as they appear to, and exert influence upon, the life of a private individual. But without the French Revolution there would be no *Prelude*. *The Prelude* is not in any sense literal, consistent autobiography, as Wordsworth's later biographers have all had to emphasize. Wordsworth distorts his autobiography, in the first place, by suppressing certain important occurrences in his personal life. Many of his omissions, most strikingly, of course, that of his affair with Annette, reveal his determination not

---

[14] Among others see Ernest de Selincourt's introduction to *The Prelude or Growth of a Poet's Mind by William Wordsworth, Edited from the Manuscripts* (Oxford, 1926), esp. p. xxvii (from this edition are taken all subsequent quotations from the 1850 version of *The Prelude*), Sir Herbert Read, *Phases of English Poetry* (New York, 1929), and Abbie Findley Potts, *Wordsworth's Prelude* (Ithaca, 1953). Of special interest is R. A. Foakes's chapter "The Unfinished Journey" in *The Romantic Assertion* (New Haven, 1958). Mr. Foakes's treatment of *The Prelude* as an epic journey, his comparison of it to *The Ancient Mariner*, and his explication of several imagaic patterns, notably those of the journey, the sea, and the mountain, are substantially identical with my observations and conclusions in the original version of this chapter, which was written before Mr. Foakes's book appeared. Consequently I have eliminated, insofar as was possible, anything in my discussion that duplicates his lucid and reasonable exegesis, and I urge interested readers to consult his excellent chapter. My interpretation of Wordsworth's poem, however, is very different from Mr. Foakes's, though complementary, I hope, rather than antagonistic.

to treat of exclusively private matters. What critics of *The Prelude* have stressed insufficiently is that the organization of the poem is founded upon a continuous and systematic dialectic between public and private affairs, between social developments and personal growth, between the objective drama of political events and the subjective drama of psychological change. At no point is either term in the dialectic dismissed. The public and the private may interpenetrate or may stand in opposition, or may be more complexly related, but neither exists without reference to the other. Hence Wordsworth, besides suppressing some matters important to him personally, freely rearranges the actual chronology of his experience to make it accord with the social evolution he dramatizes. To take a famous example, the climactic vision from the top of Snowdon in Book XIV records an experience that in fact took place before—not after—the poet had undergone the psychic travail of abandoning his faith in revolutionary reform.[15] If in *The Prelude* public events are subordinated to the individual's vision of them, both public and private history are adjusted to the demands of Wordsworth's narrative embodiment of a profound and enduring conception of "the general experience of men."

The subject of *The Prelude* is power. Wordsworth is first of all interested in the power of the imagination, an individual power and one peculiarly the attribute of the poet. But in *The Prelude* the power of imagination is defined, dramatized, and evaluated according to its relationship to other kinds of power, most notably, on the one hand, the power of Nature, which is the "express resemblance" of the individual's imagination—

> The power, which all
> Acknowledge when thus moved, which Nature thus
> To bodily sense exhibits, is the express
> Resemblance of that glorious faculty
> That higher minds bear with them as their own. (XIV, 86–90)—

and, on the other hand, the contrasting power of social action, heroic service to one's fellow men, a power which Wordsworth tasted in the fervid days of revolutionary ardor:

> I began
> To meditate with ardour on the rule
> And management of nations; what it is
> And ought to be; and strove to learn how far
> Their power or weakness, wealth or poverty,
> Their happiness or misery, depends
> Upon their laws, and fashion of the State.
> .   .   .   .

[15] Following Havens and Foakes; see in the latter's book note 1 on page 67, an excellent summary of the evidence. But compare also de Selincourt, *Poetical Works*, I, 328, for a discussion of the relation of this image to its model in the 1793 version of *Descriptive Sketches*, ll. 492–511.

> Now was it that *both* found, the meek and lofty
> Did both find helpers to their hearts' desire,
> And stuff at hand, plastic as they could wish,—
> Were called upon to exercise their skill,
> Not in Utopia,—subterranean fields,—
> Or some secreted island, Heaven knows where!
> But in the very world, which is the world
> Of all of us,—the place where, in the end,
> We find our happiness, or not at all!   (XI, 98–104, 136–44)

Imagination, as Wordsworth conceives it, is not restricted to aesthetic matters. The poet, we must remember, is to Wordsworth's way of thinking the least specialized of human beings. He is simply "a man speaking to men." He addresses himself not to one particular faculty nor to a limited range of experience but to those capacities and experiences which are common to all human beings.

> The Poet writes under one restriction only, namely, the necessity of giving immediate pleasure to a human Being possessed of that information which may be expected from him, not as a lawyer, a physician, a mariner, an astronomer, or a natural philosopher, but as a Man. Except this one restriction, there is no object standing between the Poet and the image of things; between this, and the Biographer and Historian, there are a thousand.[16]

In choosing as his subject the power of imagination, Wordsworth was not, as it may at first appear, confining himself to the egotistical and aesthetic, but was, rather, selecting what seemed to him the best available means of conveying the whole truth about the place and function of the individual in both the macrocosm of Nature and the microcosm of his society.

The story *The Prelude* tells, then, is of the birth and early growth of the imaginative power (Books I–VI), its impairment (Books VII–XI), and its eventual restoration (Books XII–XIV). The "idea" which the story embodies is that modern civilization, the human creation which is meant to foster and to protect man's dignity as man, is itself the most dangerous enemy of those "civil" virtues which distinguish man from beast. Thus in *The Prelude* we find the first expression of the typically modern conviction that only by resisting his civilization can a man preserve his individuality and all the common decencies that appertain thereto. Wordsworth as he appears in *The Prelude* is the prototype of the contemporary hero: the man who fights against his culture.

Because we have become accustomed to identifying heroism with the capacity to resist, instead of to represent, the culture of which one

---

[16] "Preface," Cambridge Edition, p. 794.

is a part,[17] we underestimate the vigor of self-consciousness required by such heroism 150 years ago. It demands, above all, that we become conscious of our culture as a culture. What makes that difficult is that any culture is pervasive and all-encompassing. If a salmon were to become aware that it is swimming in water and then further that the river it swims up in order to spawn is fresh rather than salt water, its awareness, however impressive an achievement for a fish, would be less astonishing than a man's consciousness of the culture in which he operates. For human culture is not only an external environment, it is also a way of thinking and feeling, and it determines to a large extent what we perceive and how we respond to those perceptions. To become aware of one's culture and then to reject it, even partially, is, in consequence, an enormous experience and a shattering one.

The Prelude, then, is epic in its rejection of the traditional principles of epic narrative. Quietism is celebrated over heroic activity; imagination is rated above physical prowess; autobiography supersedes political history; individual adherence to basic, perhaps even primitive, loyalties is praised beyond individual sacrifice to social causes. Yet it is precisely these reversals of conventional epic standards, not Wordsworth's half-century of labor on his poem or references to and echoes of previous epic poems, that command for The Prelude the title of epic. The Aeneid is an authentic epic in part, perhaps largely, because it embodies a conception of virtue and an ideal of life unalterably hostile to the virtues and ideals of life embodied in previous epics, most notably the Iliad. And in Paradise Lost Milton rejects the Virgilian ideal. Genuine literary epic, that is, epic written by a poet conscious of earlier examples of the form, must be inspired by the pressing sense that the great literary monuments of the past convey only a partial, a limited, and hence a misleading consciousness of the human predicament. That sense pervades every line of Wordsworth's Prelude.

Even if one finds it difficult to accept The Prelude as part of the old European epic tradition, one must recognize that it has given its form to much of the heroic literature of revolution that has succeeded it. The Prelude, in fact, is one of the first representatives of a form created in the early years of the nineteenth century which, whether or not itself a kind of epic, has usurped the function of traditional epic. That form we may call the mythical journey. It is a form characterized by its tendency to find the profoundest order, significance, and satis-

---

[17] This is probably why we all secretly sympathize with Milton's Satan, although we all know better, and why we have difficulty in estimating the heroism of Aeneas at its proper worth. It is to me significant that it was not until the beginning of the nineteenth century that literary men began genuinely to prefer The Iliad to The Aeneid, though of course since the time of Petrarch Homer had been paid lip service.

faction in individual experience, in the fulfillments or defeats of the individual soul operating amidst the chaotic impersonalities of modern civilization. Its hero rejects, or is rejected by, his civilization; hence his journey is above all a spiritual journey through "The Heart of Darkness" to a personal salvation that may—but need not—be Christian salvation.

THE POSSIBILITY OF A LONG POEM*

Herbert Lindenberger

The fact that the Romantic age was so rich in ambitious fragments—Goethe's attempt at an *Achilleïs*, Keats's *Hyperion*, Wordsworth's *Recluse*, not to speak of poems of less lofty conception, such as Coleridge's *Christabel*—may well have something to do with the transitional nature of the age: a transition from a concept of poems as imitations of established structures to self-expressions of the individual poet, with the consequent narrowing down of the province of poetry from a wide variety of discursive forms to those few forms which could aspire to the condition either of the dreamlike or the impassioned lyric. When Keats, in answer to Leigh Hunt's question, "Why endeavor after a long Poem?" attempted to defend the form, he left both the older and the newer concept of poetic structure implicit in his reply: "Do not the Lovers of Poetry like to have a little Region to wander in where they may pick and choose, and in which the images are so numerous that many are forgotten and found new in a second Reading: which may be food for a Week's stroll in the Summer? Do not they like this better than what they can read through before Mrs. Williams comes down stairs? a Morning work at most. Besides a long Poem is a test of Invention which I take to be the Polar Star of Poetry, as Fancy is the Sails, and Imagination the Rudder."[1]

The very notion of a long poem as a collection of images among which the reader may "pick and choose" need be taken only one step further to arrive at the Symbolist idea that the long poem is but a series of individual lyrics, and hence does not exist at all. Perhaps Keats was aware of the latent paradox when, at the end of his defense, he assumed the neo-classic stance, which could take for granted the high and singular accomplishment of a man who could meet the "test of Invention" necessary to successful completion of a long poem. But the above statement was made during the composition of *Endymion;* it is significant that when he announced the final abandonment of

* Reprinted from *On Wordsworth's Prelude* by Herbert Lindenberger by permission of Princeton University Press. Copyright 1963.

[1] *Letters*, ed. H. E. Rollins (Cambridge, Mass., 1958), I, 170.

Hyperion, Keats stated his predicament as the inability to "make the division properly" between "the false beauty proceeding from art" and "the true voice of feeling":[2] the demands of imitation—in his case, the need to imitate Milton's language in order to sustain the style necessary for his epic structure—are rejected in favor of the demands of original expression, with the result that he is unable to complete his poem.

When A. C. Bradley surveyed "The Long Poem in the Age of Wordsworth" at the beginning of this century, he concluded that the relative failure of the larger Romantic structures was a consequence of the essentially lyrical impulse which characterized the age:

"It may be suggested . . . that the excellence of the lyrical poetry of Wordsworth's time, and the imperfection of the long narratives and dramas, may have a common origin. Just as it was most natural to Homer or to Shakespeare to express the imaginative substance of his mind in the 'objective' shape of a world of persons and actions ostensibly severed from his own thoughts and feelings, so, perhaps, for some reason or reasons, it was most natural to the best poets of this later time to express that substance in the shape of impassioned reflections, aspirations, prophecies, laments, outcries of joy, murmurings of peace. The matter of these might, in another sense of the word, be 'objective' enough, a matter of general human interest, not personal in any exclusive way; but it appeared in the form of the poet's thought and feeling. Just because he most easily expressed it thus, he succeeded less completely when he attempted the more objective form of utterance."[3]

Bradley's essay is remarkable, not only for the incisive way with which he accounted for the weakness of Romantic long poems, but also for the fact that he argued for the validity of the long poem at a time when the Symbolist aesthetic—which in certain of its manifestations stands behind his own best criticism—was at its height in England: "To speak as if a small poem could do all that a long one does, and do it much more completely, is to speak as though a hummingbird could have the same kind of beauty as an eagle, the rainbow in a fountain produce the same effect as the rainbow in the sky, or a moorland stream thunder like Niagara. . . . It would be easy to show that [a long poem] admits of strictly poetic effects of the highest value which the mere brevity of a short one excludes."[4]

Yet even if we grant the weakness of Romantic long poems and note the fragmentary nature of so many ambitious attempts, it is significant that the age was singularly productive in longer works, that, in fact, every major English poet from Blake through Browning—with the obvious exception of Coleridge—produced at least one, in some cases

[2] *Ibid.,* II, 167.

[3] *Oxford Lectures on Poetry* (London, 1909), pp. 184-185.

[4] *Ibid.,* p. 204.

several long poems. It is also significant that most of the Romantic long poems, whether or not they succeed in their total effect, are characterized by far greater unity of conception and structure than such eighteenth-century "composite" poems—to use Wordsworth's term—as *Nights Thoughts* and *The Task*. Even a brief glance at the major poems of Thomson, Young and Cowper—as well as that anomalous modern poem, Bridges' *Testament of Beauty*—reveals a loose, episodic mixture of objective description, didactic matter, and, except for Cowper, narrative interlude. (Dr. Johnson even complained of the "want of method" in *The Seasons*.) The form of these poems, of course, ultimately derives from the *Georgics* (or, rather, the eighteenth century's conception of the form of the *Georgics*), and as a result they share far less of the spirit of classical epic than does *The Prelude*, which, for all its georgic elements, seeks to emulate, if not exactly imitate, *Paradise Lost*.

If we can speak of both the eighteenth- and nineteenth-century longer poems as uneven, we should also distinguish the nature of their unevenness. The former are uneven by virtue of a discursiveness of tone that motivates them as a whole and which is inherent in the models they seek to imitate; the latter, through the sharply varying degrees of intensity that result from a lyrical impulse which they can only partially sustain. One could, in fact, describe the history of the long poem since the end of the eighteenth century as a search for a form that would adequately embody—to borrow Bradley's words— those "impassioned reflections, aspirations, prophecies, laments, outcries of joy, murmurings of peace" which could not be satisfied by the limited framework of lyric and ballad. Though Bradley is doubtless right in stressing the lyrical impulse as a prime characteristic of the age, we can also, with our larger historical perspective, discern still another prevailing tendency of the age—its attempts to propound and vividly present a new world-view. And the shorter forms, however much they sought to serve this purpose (many of Wordsworth's short lyrics, for instance, "To the Cuckoo," when seen in the context of his total work, attempt to express a transcendental view of things) clearly did not suffice.

It is not merely the fact that the Romantic writers were concerned with ideas—so, indeed, are all serious poets, including the Symbolists, in their own, very indirect way—but rather, each of the Romantics, whether or not he succeeded in finding an adequate form, was concerned with a whole body of related ideas and attitudes which in their totality add up to a larger, though not necessarily consistent or even original, view of reality. When we speak of the primacy of the lyrical impulse in Romanticism we refer to the peculiar way in which the Romantics perceived the world and also to the manner in which they sought to communicate their perceptions. Yet the lyrical impulse in each of the Romantics existed side by side, and often in conjunction with, a sense of epic grandeur, the feeling that Keats, for instance, was trying to define when he wrote, "I feel more and more every day, as my imagination strengthens, that I do not live in this world alone but in a thousand worlds—No sooner am I alone than shapes of epic greatness are stationed around me, and serve my Spirit the office (of) which is equivalent to a king's body guard." [5] Like all the Romantics at one time or another, Keats was describing a state of mind wholly within the area of sublimity, of *pathos* as opposed to *ethos*. If the lyrical and epic impulses were not always compatible in the creation of successful works of art, both nonetheless sought expression and helped determine the particular forms of the long poems of the age.

To return to the "objective" forms of the past was no solution, as Keats eventually learned while struggling with *Hyperion*. At first glance a poem like Landor's *Gebir* seems an anomaly in its age. In its dignity and control, its impeccably Miltonic diction, its occasional use of epic machinery—invocation, descent to the underworld—it would seem a serious attempt to revive not only the spirit but the letter of classical epic. Yet, despite its claim of ethical content and national, contemporary relevance—"[These] twenty verses . . . describe the equality which nature teaches, the absurdity of colonizing a country which is peopled, and the superior advantage of cultivating those which remain unoccupied" [6]—*Gebir* remains at bottom an exotic Oriental tale, a romance rather than an epic, a Dido-and-Aeneas episode (in this case, one in which the hero, rather than abandoning the heroine, is murdered by her servant) lifted from a still unwritten larger epic. Indeed, in the lines preceding his hero's descent into the underworld Landor poignantly expresses the plight of a poet who lives in an age too late to realize his highest ambitions:

> O for the spirit of that matchless man
> Whom Nature led throughout her whole domain,
> While he, embodied, breath'd etherial air!
> Though panting in the play-hour of my youth,
> I drank of Avon, too, a dang'rous draught,
> That rous'd within the fev'rish thirst of song—
> Yet, never may I trespass o'er the stream
> Of jealous Acheron, nor alive descend
> The silent and unsearchable abodes
> Of Erebus and Night, nor unchastized
> Lead up long absent heroes into day.
> When on the pausing theatre of earth
> Eve's shadowy curtain falls, can any man
> Bring back the far-off intercepted hills,
> Grasp the round rock-built turret, or arrest
> The glittering spires that pierce the brow of Heav'n?
> Rather, can any, with outstripping voice,
> The parting Sun's gigantic strides recall? [7]

[5] *Letters*, I, 403.
[6] *Works*, ed. Stephen Wheeler, XIII, 48.
[7] *Ibid.*, p. 16.

Landor's yearning for a vanished age of poetry—though in one sense a traditional assertion of the poet's modesty—all too easily recalls the plight depicted by Wordsworth in that introductory passage to *The Prelude* which describes his troubles coming to terms with his proposed epic themes. In both, written, as they were, within a year or two of one another, we hear a farewell to the possibility of traditional epic.

If the epic strain could no longer be sustained in poetry, the less lofty demands of romance could at least provide a form for the long poem. In romance the very need of getting one's story told made possible a structure more cohesive than that of the discursive eighteenth-century poems. And by setting his romance in a distant time or place the poet could lay the groundwork for those lyrical effects of atmosphere which he was so bent on capturing. In romance, moreover, he could call upon a style less demanding than the sublime and, above all, one less dependent upon Milton, whose examples had determined, for better or worse, the nature of the sublime in English. Thus, when Scott defended the method he employed in *The Lay of the Last Minstrel,* he made clear that his genre was one essentially different from epic or georgic: "As the description of scenery and manners was more the object of the author than a combined and regular narrative, the plan of the Ancient Metrical Romance was adopted, which allows greater latitude in this respect than would be consistent with the dignity of a regular Poem." [8] It is significant that Scott came closest to the spirit and content of epic—though not by its neo-classic definition—when he turned away from the long poem to the novel. The so-called epics of Southey, though endowed with a certain atmosphere of loftiness through those violent aspects of nature which the author was wont to to evoke, are distinctly within the realm of exotic romance, as are the less pretentious Oriental tales of his enemy Byron; indeed, the very idea of a new epic issued regularly at four and five year intervals—*Joan of Arc* in 1796, *Thalaba* in 1801, *Madoc* in 1805, *The Curse of Kehama* in 1810, *Roderick* in 1814—is antithetical to that conception of an epic as the single goal toward which a poet directs his life-work. If Wordsworth sometimes approaches the forms of romance—in *The White Doe of Rylstone,* for instance, or, on a more modest scale, in the short narratives of *Lyrical Ballads*—one must note the sharp distinction in language and meter between these attempts and the ambitious, uncompleted poem of which *The Prelude* is a part. It is also worth noting how rigorously he excluded the trappings of romance from his great poem, except for the compliments he pays to older romances in Book v of *The Prelude* for the role they play in a child's educational process.

Wordsworth dispensed not only with exotic content to fashion

[8] Oxford Standard Authors edition, p. 1.

his long poem, but also with myth, which made possible such long poems as Blake's prophetic books and Shelley's *Revolt of Islam*. The invention of a private myth, built out of a self-enclosed world of traditional Neoplatonic symbols, gave Blake and Shelley the opportunity to voice their moral concerns—concerns as weighty as those of any epic poet of the past—with a tone of prophetic urgency, though at the obvious cost of that clarity which not only makes a long poem readable, but which can make its prophecy meaningful within the public as well as the private realm. When Wordsworth assumes the prophetic tone in *The Prelude*, he does so by means other than myth or allegory, that is, through formal rhetoric and, most conspicuously and successfully, in those culminating passages within the spots of time in which his explorations of his personal past lead naturally, and by a process of gradual intensification, into generalizations of public significance.

If there is any single longer form which is distinctly a product of the age and which could provide the cosmic scope which was once a property of epic, it is the dramatic poem—not, certainly, the dreary pseudo-Shakespearean closet drama that can be found among the works of virtually every nineteenth-century English poet, including Wordsworth, but rather the type of poem exemplified at its best in Goethe's *Faust* and Shelley's *Prometheus Unbound* and which produced a distinguished late example in Hardy's *Dynasts*. While obviously sacrificing that semblance of unity and self-containment which results from regularity of meter, the dramatic form provides a more compelling vehicle for the presentation of ideas than the more frank and open didacticism traditional to the long poem. One need only compare *Queen Mab*, which has only the rudiments of dialogue, with *Prometheus Unbound*, whose dramatic form allowed full play to Shelley's didactic and lyric, though also quite undramatic, talents. Indeed, the dramatic convention often provided an ideal outlet for an essentially lyric impulse which, not resting satisfied with the modest framework of the short poem, demanded a more comprehensive structure to express a larger vision.

In comparison with works such as *Faust* and *Prometheus*, *The Prelude* seems a peculiarly bare and restrained performance, one governed by a classical rigor which Shelley never knew and which Goethe, with his fine sense of decorum, relegated to other, less ambitious works. *The Prelude's* bareness and restraint are even more conspicuous when we set it next to a poem to which it has more obvious affinities, Byron's *Childe Harold*, which, like *The Prelude*, could be viewed generically as an eighteenth-century loco-descriptive poem inflated by romantic introspection. But Byron's most successful approach to the longer form came neither in *Childe Harold* nor in the Oriental tales, but in *Don Juan*, which manages to entertain us throughout by that illusion of improvisation by which, to use the words of Northrop Frye, "we simultaneously read the poem and watch the poet at work writing it." [9]

In his long poem, *Luise,* a work much admired by Wordsworth, the distinguished German translator of Homer, Johann Heinrich Voss, attempted to give new life to the epic by using the German hexameter line, which his readers could naturally associate with the world of epic, to focus upon the everyday details of middle-class life. The resulting form, known in Germany as the "domestic idyll," is the sort of narrative that might be created by lifting the pastoral similes out of the *Iliad* and ignoring matters of more heroic import. The greatest examples of the genre, Goethe's *Hermann und Dorothea* (which Wordsworth, because of his deep prejudice against Goethe, was unable to appreciate) is in fact set during the French Revolution, whose rumbles are heard only distantly while the poet concentrates on the more stable realities of ordinary life. The genre is essentially a kind of pastoral, though, in the hands of the Germans, a pastoral not of shepherds but of small-town burghers. Its affinities are not with Virgilian epic, but with Homer, whom it tries to emulate in directness of perception and in evenness, though not loftiness, of tone. In its celebration of the ordinary rather than the extraordinary details of life it represents a full withdrawal from the world of *pathos* and a correspondingly total immersion in the world of *ethos.* Wordsworth approaches this genre at occasional moments in *The Prelude,* as in the description of the card games and other "home amusements" in Book I, and at far greater length in *The Excursion,* especially in those tedious descriptions of local families in the two books entitled "The Churchyard among the Mountains." Yet he could never successfully have sustained a longer work in the form, for the characters and incidents which most excited his imagination, though pastoral in setting, tend toward the extraordinary rather than the ordinary, toward a somber rather than a serene world. The very fact that he concentrated on solitaries, and many of the most eccentric kind, testifies to the distance he maintained from the realities of daily life.

Yet the example of domestic idyll directly inspired one of the most successful epic efforts—if one can judge by translations and the testimony of others—of the nineteenth century, the Polish national epic *Pan Tadeucz* by Adam Mickiewicz, who started out with the modest intention of imitating *Hermann und Dorothea* and gradually found himself creating a heroic poem. Mickiewicz, unlike his contemporaries in the more firmly established literary traditions, had the double fortune of a language in whose loftier reaches there were still new claims to be staked out and, second, of a burning national theme, that of

[9] *Anatomy of Criticism* (Princeton, 1957), p. 234.

liberation from Russia, for which he found fictional embodiment in a heroic interlude from the Napoleonic wars. What ultimately gives his poem universal significance is his success in setting his heroic action against a fully realized background of everyday life: what Voss and Goethe had, so to speak, removed from Homer was now restored to the larger epic structure.

Had Coleridge had his way, still another work in German, the extended "prose poem" *The Death of Abel* by the Swiss writer Salomon Gessner, would have served Wordsworth as a model for a longer work. In 1798 the two poets, at Coleridge's instigation, set out to write a sequel to Gessner's work, calling it *The Wanderings of Cain*.

"My partner," Coleridge tells us, "undertook the first canto: I the second: and which ever had *done first,* was to set about the third. Almost thirty years have passed by; yet at this moment I cannot without something more than a smile moot the question which of the two things was the more impracticable, for a mind [Wordsworth's] so eminently original to compose another man's thoughts and fancies, or for a taste so austerely pure and simple to imitate the Death of Abel? Methinks I see his grand and noble countenance as at the moment when having despatched my own portion of the task at full finger-speed, I hastened to him with my manuscript—that look of humourous despondency fixed on his almost blank sheet of paper, and then its silent mock-piteous admission of failure struggling with the sense of the exceeding ridiculousness of the whole scheme—which broke up in a laugh; and the Ancient Mariner was written instead." [10]

Whether or not Wordsworth was capable of "imitation" or whether his taste was too "austerely pure and simple" to rework materials as sentimental as Gessner's, it is evident that *The Death of Abel,* with its far-off Biblical setting, would have provided Wordsworth with an even less suitable model for his talents than *Luise.* Above all, both Gessner and Voss had nothing to offer Wordsworth's heroic impulse, which, side by side with his attraction to pastoral, was to demand expression in his longer work.

The history of the long poem in England and France in the later nineteenth century is a history, if not exactly of the death of the form, at least of its gradual fragmentation. Lamartine's remarks on *Jocelyn,* which he published in 1836 as one unit in a series of never-completed long poems which were to constitute a national epic, are an attempt to redefine epic: "I looked for an epic subject suitable to our epoch," he tells us in his introduction, and what he found was an "intimate epic," the story of a Protestant pastor (as, indeed, the hero of Voss' *Luise* had been, not to speak of *The Excursion*). But *Jocelyn* is less a story than a series of lyrical meditations tied loosely together; and its sub-

---

[10] *Complete Poetical Works,* ed. E. H. Coleridge (Oxford, 1912), I, 286–287.

title, "Journal trouvé chez un curé de campagne," reveals its essentially introspective nature.

If *Jocelyn* approached the private realm, it was still possible for poets to maintain at least the semblance of a public voice by retelling traditional tales, as Tennyson's *Idylls of the King*, Morris' *Earthly Paradise*, and Hugo's *Légende des Siècles*. Of these the last-named is most self-consciously epic in intent. Drawing its tales from a large range of epochs and traditions, it is created on the assumption that a collection of small epics will somehow add up to a larger one; yet for all its pretensions it is less informed by a truly unifying idea than two other collections of poems that appeared only a few years before—*Leaves of Grass* and *Les Fleurs du Mal*.

Although Baudelaire's collection belongs primarily to the history of lyric poetry, Whitman's is characterized by a distinctly epic impulse. Its longest poem, *Song of Myself*, through its attempt to mediate between the public and private realm, its prophetic strivings, its cultivation of the egotistical sublime, and even its organization into spots of time, has perhaps more affinities with *The Prelude* (which Whitman gives no evidence of having read) than any other poem of the century. Like *The Prelude* it portrays the poet as hero and advertises its essentially heroic argument through its ceremonious, though also quite un-Miltonic, language. Yet to the extent that it lacks any overt formal structure analogous even to the chronological development within *The Prelude*—it is less the growth than the lyrical outpourings of the poet's mind—*Song of Myself* is yet another example of the fragmentation process that has characterized the long poem since Wordsworth's time.

Browning came to terms with the problem of form by making his most amibitious poem, *The Ring and the Book*, a series of thematically connected dramatic monologues. As a result he could dispense with rhetorical connectives as well as the embellishments of language which were traditionally the right of the poet when he spoke in his own voice. Its affinities are less with any other long poem, past or present, than with the modern experimental novel, as Henry James was perhaps the first to point out.[11] If *The Ring and the Book* failed to serve as a model for later long poems, Tennyson's *Princess*, which includes short poems of the highest lyric intensity interspersed within a fairly flat narrative which is essentially a novel in meter, suggests a method which, in one way or another, has made possible certain long poems of our own day. The method might be described as the alternation of various levels of intensity.

T. S. Eliot, who employs the method in *Four Quartets*, has described it thus: "In a long poem some parts may be deliberately planned to be less 'poetic' than others: these passages may show no lustre when

[11] *Notes on Novelists* (New York, 1914), pp. 385–411.

extracted, but may be intended to elicit, by contrast, the significance of other parts, and to unite them into a whole more significant than any of the parts. A long poem may gain by the widest possible variations of intensity." [12] *Four Quartets,* of course, is a meditative poem and makes no such epic pretensions as does that other long poem of our day, William Carlos Williams' *Paterson,* which utilizes the principle of alternating intensities to the degree that its "flatter" passages often take the form of prose, and, in fact, the prose of newspaper clippings and lists of statistics.

The very notion of different levels of intensity is, of course, a consequence of the gradual narrowing down, during the nineteenth century, of what could appropriately be called "poetic." As soon as rhetoric was no longer considered poetic, it could only find its way back into poetry if the poet was willing to include the lower levels of intensity. Since the stricter adherents of Poe's theory could hardly justify their inclusion, we cannot properly speak of a Symbolist epic, as we can of a Renaissance or even Romantic epic. Yet the concept of what is poetic has radically changed during the half-century since the Symbolist aesthetic has become influential in the English-speaking countries, and since the revolution effected by Eliot and Pound our notion of what makes for high intensity has shifted from the ecstatic lyric flight which Poe called for in his essay to the tightly controlled, indeed, often somewhat "prosaic" concrete image. It is symptomatic of the modern tendency to fragmentize poetic structures that we speak of the individual image—the ideogram of Pound, or the epiphany of Joyce— as the central unit of meaning instead of the larger structure of which it is a part; indeed, Wordworth's idea of the "spot of time," though he did not allow it to replace or distort his conception of a total poem, can be viewed as one step on the way to the autonomous image which has been the goal of the Symbolist poet.

Despite the obstacles which Symbolist conceptions of poetic structure have set in the way of the creation of long poems, the major contemporary poets have been only slightly less deterred in their ambitions to create longer works than were their nineteenth-century predecessors. Certainly nearly all have tried their hand at a long poem, although they have often sought rather the semblance of length than actual length. *The Waste Land,* whose obscurity was early defended on grounds that Eliot had left out the rhetorical connectives which would formerly have clarified, as well as relaxed the intensity of a long poem, is perhaps the model epic within the Symbolist tradition, for within the space of 400 lines (only two or three times the length of most Wordsworthian spots of time) it presents a series of highly charged images and undeveloped dramatic situations that create the illusion of a larger

[12] "From Poe to Valéry," p. 334.

vision of history. A similar illusion of amplitude was achieved by Hart Crane in *The Bridge*, which, hardly less concise but considerably more heroic in its intentions than *The Waste Land*, succeeds in uniting the introspective concerns characteristic of the modern lyric with the ceremoniousness traditional to epic. Wallace Stevens' *Notes Toward a Supreme Fiction*, though more modest in its range of interests than *The Waste Land* or *The Bridge*, also strives toward an illusion of length. It bears close affinities to *The Prelude* than perhaps any other modern long poem, not only in its verse form and overtly didactic intent, but in its very argument for the primacy of the poetic imagination. Yet through its relatively small scope it succeeds in fusing its diverse components—fragments of memory, parables, and large blocks of discursive argument—into a far more tightly integrated whole than the much more sprawling *Prelude*, many of whose individual books are longer than Stevens' whole poem; Stevens' achievement, one might say, was to order the more loosely organized materials of most older meditative poems into a single, sustained spot of time.

If Eliot, Crane, and Stevens could create at least the semblance of a long poem by Symbolist method, Ezra Pound and St. John Perse have employed the method to create genuinely long poems. Pound, in fact, has undertaken the most ambitious epic effort of our time and, true to his Symbolist principles, has presented his view of history, both public and personal, by concentrating on certain pregnant moments which follow one another without transition, commentary, or even, for that matter, chronology. By a strange irony the boredom and relaxation of intensity which Poe and his followers deplored in the rhetoric of long poems is also inherent in the ideogrammic method of the *Cantos;* it is as though the very existence of length relaxes tension, however highly charged the components of the structure may be. But Symbolist method, like that of the dramatic poem, makes possible a vividness of presentation rarely attainable in the traditional type of long poem and thus has provided an opportunity for the return of heroic action to the long poem: such works as the *Anabasis* of Perse and the *Conquistador* of MacLeish succeed as evocation, though emphatically not as re-enactment, of action.

At the present time, when we have come to recognize the limitations of the Symbolist aesthetic and, indeed, to long for a return to rhetoric and public statement, *The Prelude* can perhaps serve us as an example. Through its introspectiveness it speaks to us as a record of the modern sensibility as no earlier long poem can do; yet it is also rooted in an older rhetorical system which, however foreign to us its premises may be, may teach us how to reconcile the public and private world within a larger poetic structure and, above all, to recapture for poetry that fullness of development and presentation which, as poetic structures became more and more fragmented, passed inevitably into the domain of the novel.

THEORY OF GENRES*

Northrop Frye

In the high mimetic we reach the structure that we think of as typically epic, the form represented by Homer, Virgil, and Milton. The epic differs from the narrative in the encyclopaedic range of its theme, from heaven to the underworld, and over an enormous mass of traditional knowledge. A narrative poet, a Southey or a Lydgate, may write any number of narratives, but an epic poet normally completes only one epic structure, the moment when he decides on his theme being the crisis of his life.

The cyclical form of the Classical epic is based on the natural cycle, a mediterranean known world in the middle of a boundlessness (apeiron) and between the upper and the lower gods. The cycle has two main rhythms: the life and death of the individual, and the slower social rhythm which, in the course of years (periplomenon eniauton in Homer, volvibus or labentibus annis in Virgil), brings cities and empires to their rise and fall. The steady vision of the latter movement is possible only to gods. The convention of beginning the action in medias res ties a knot in time, so to speak. The total action in the background of the Iliad moves from the cities of Greece through the ten-year siege of Troy back to Greece again; the total action of the Odyssey is a specialized example of the same thing, moving from Ithaca back to Ithaca. The Aeneid moves with the household gods of Priam, from Troy to New Troy.

The foreground action begins at a point described in the Odyssey as hamothen, "somewhere": actually, it is far more carefully chosen. All three epics begin at a kind of nadir of the total cyclical action: the Iliad, at a moment of despair in the Greek camp; the Odyssey, with Odysseus and Penelope furthest from one another, both wooed by importunate suitors; the Aeneid, with its hero shipwrecked on the shores of Carthage, citadel of Juno and enemy of Rome. From there, the action moves both backward and forward far enough to indicate the general shape of the historical cycle. The discovery of the epic action is the sense of the end of the total action as like the beginning, and hence of a consistent order and balance running through the whole. This consis-

* Reprinted from *Anatomy of Criticism: Four Essays* by Northrop Frye by permission of Princeton University Press. Copyright 1957.

tent order is not a divine fiat or fatalistic causation, but a stability in nature controlled by the gods, and extended to human beings if they accept it. The sense of this stability is not necessarily tragic, but it is the kind of sense that makes tragedy possible.

It does so in the *Iliad*, for example. The number of valid reasons for praising the *Iliad* would fill a bigger book than this, but the relevant reason for us here is the fact that its theme is *menis*, a song of wrath. It is hardly possible to overestimate the importance for Western literature of the *Iliad's* demonstration that the fall of an enemy, no less than of a friend or leader, is tragic and not comic. With the *Iliad*, once for all, an objective and disinterested element enters into the poet's vision of human life. Without this element, poetry is merely instrumental to various social aims, to propaganda, to amusement, to devotion, to instruction: with it, it acquires the authority that since the *Iliad* it has never lost, an authority based, like the authority of science, on the vision of nature as an impersonal order.

The *Odyssey* begins the other tradition of the epic of return. The story is a romance of a hero escaping safely from incredible perils and arriving in the nick of time to claim his bride and baffle the villains, but our central feeling about it is a much more prudent sense, rooted in all our acceptance of nature, society, and law, of the proper master of the house coming to reclaim his own. The *Aeneid* develops the theme of return into one of rebirth, the end in New Troy being the starting-point renewed and transformed by the hero's quest. The Christian epic carries the same themes into a wide archetypal context. The action of the Bible, from the poetic point of view, includes the themes of the three great epics: the theme of the destruction and captivity of the city in the *Iliad*, the theme of the *nostos* or return home in the *Odyssey*, and the theme of the building of the new city in the *Aeneid*. Adam is, like Odysseus, a man of wrath, exiled from home because he angered God by going *hyper moron*, beyond his limit as a man. In both stories the provoking act is symbolized by the eating of food reserved for deity. As with Odysseus, Adam's return home is contingent on the appeasing of divine wrath by divine wisdom (Poseidon and Athene reconciled by the will of Zeus in Homer; the Father reconciled with man in the Christian atonement). Israel carries its ark from Egypt to the Promised Land just as Aeneas carries his household goods from the fallen Troy to the eternally established one.

Hence there is, as we go from the Classical to the Christian epic, a progress in completeness of theme (not in any kind of value), as Milton indicates in such phrases as "Beyond the Aonian mount." In Milton the foreground action of the epic is again the nadir of the total cyclical action, the fall of Satan and Adam. From there the action works backward through the speech of Raphael, and forward through the speech of Michael, to the beginning and end of the total action. The beginning is God's presence among the angels before the Son is manifested to them; the end comes after the apocalypse when God again is "all in all," but the beginning and end are the same point, the presence of God, renewed and transformed by the heroic quest of Christ. As a Christian, Milton has to reconsider the epic theme of heroic action, to decide what in Christian terms a hero is and what an act is. Heroism for him consists in obedience, fidelity and perseverance through ridicule or persecution, and is exemplified by Abdiel, the faithful angel. Action for him means positive or creative act, exemplified by Christ in the creation of the world and the recreation of man. Satan thus takes over the traditional qualities of martial heroism: he is the wrathful Achilles, the cunning Ulysses, the knight-errant who achieves the perilous quest of chaos; but he is from God's point of view a mock-hero, what man in his fallen state naturally turns to with admiration as the idolatrous form of the kingdom, the power, and the glory.

In the low mimetic period the encyclopaedic structure tends to become either subjective and mythological, or objective and historical. The former is usually expressed in epos and the latter in prose fiction. The main attempts to combine the two were made, somewhat unexpectedly, in France, and extend from the fragments left by Chenier to Victor Hugo's Legéndes des Siècles. Here the theme of heroic action is transferred, consistently with low mimetic conventions, from the leader to humanity as a whole. Hence the fulfilment of the action is conceived mainly as social improvement in the future.

In the traditional epic the gods affect the action from a continuous present: Athene and Venus appear epiphanically, on definite occasions, to illuminate or cheer the hero at that moment. To gain information about the future, or what is "ahead" in terms of the lower cycle of life, it is normally necessary to descend to a lower world of the dead, as is done in the nekyia, or katabasis, in the eleventh book of the Odyssey and the sixth of the Aeneid. Similarly in Dante the damned know the future but not the present, and in Milton the forbidden knowledge which "brought death into the world" is actualized in the form of Michael's prophecy of the future. We are thus not surprised to find a great increase, in the low mimetic period of future hopes, of a sense of Messianic powers as coming from "underneath" or through esoteric and hermetic traditions. Prometheus Unbound is the most familiar English example: the attempt to insert a katabasis into the second part of Faust, first as the descent to the "mothers" and then as the Classical Walpurgis Night, was evidently one of the most baffling structural problems in that work. Sometimes, however, the katabasis is combined with and complemented by the more traditional point of epiphany. Keats's Endymion goes "down" in search of truth and "up" in search of beauty, discovering, not surprisingly for Keats,

that truth and beauty are the same. In *Hyperion* some alignment between a Dionysian "below" and an Apollonian "above" was clearly
on the agenda. Eliot's *Burnt Norton* is founded on the principle that
"the way up and the way down are the same," which resolves this
dichotomy in Christian terms. Time in this world is a horizontal line,
and God's timeless presence is a vertical one crossing it at right
angles, the crossing point being the Incarnation. The rose garden and
subway episodes outline the two semi-circles of the cycle of nature, the
upper one the romantic mythopoeic fantasy world of innocence and the
lower the world of experience. But if we go further up than the rose
garden and further down than the subway we reach the same point.

Comedy and irony supply us with parody-symbolism, of which
the relation of the bound Gulliver in Lilliput to Prometheus, of the
staggering hod-carrier in *Finnegans Wake* to Adam, of the madeleine
cake in Proust to the Eucharist, are examples on varying levels of
seriousness. Here too belongs the kind of use of archetypal structure
made in *Absalom and Achitophel,* where the resemblance between the
story and its Old Testament model is treated as a series of witty
coincidences. The theme of encyclopaedic parody is endemic in satire,
and in prose fiction is chiefly to be found in the anatomy, the tradition
of Apuleius and Rabelais and Swift. Satires and novels show a relation
corresponding to that of epics and narratives; the more novels a novelist
writes the more successful he is, but Rabelais, Burton, and Sterne build
their creative lives around one supreme effort. Hence it is in satire and
irony that we should look for the continuing encyclopaedic tradition,
and we should expect that the containing form of the ironic or satiric
epic would be the pure cycle, in which every quest, however successful or heroic, has sooner or later to be made over again.

In Blake's poem *The Mental Traveller* we have a vision of the
cycle of human life, from birth to death to rebirth. The two characters
of the poem are a male and a female figure, moving in opposite directions, one growing old as the other grows young, and vice versa. The
cyclical relation between them runs through four cardinal points: a
son-mother phase, a husband-wife phase, a father-daughter phase, and
a fourth phase of what Blake calls spectre and emanation, terms corresponding roughly to Shelley's alastor and epipsyche. None of these
phases is quite true: the mother is only a nurse, the wife merely "bound
down" for the male's delight, the daughter a changeling, and the
emanation does not "emanate," but remains elusive. The male figure
represents humanity, and therefore includes women—the "female will"
in Blake becomes associated with women only when women dramatize
or mimic the above relation in human life, as they do in the Courtly
Love convention. The female figure represents the natural environment which man partially but never wholly subdues. The controlling
symbolism of the poem, as the four phases suggest, is lunar.

To the extent that the encyclopaedic form concerns itself with the cycle of human life, an ambivalent female archetype appears in it, sometimes benevolent, sometimes sinister, but usually presiding over and confirming the cyclical movement. One pole of her is represented by an Isis figure, a Penelope or Solveig who is the fixed point on which the action ends. The goddess who frequently begins and ends the cyclical action is closely related. This figure is Athene in the *Odyssey* and Venus in the *Aeneid;* in Elizabethan literature, for political reasons, usually some variant of Diana, like the Faerie Queen in Spenser. The *alma Venus* who suffuses Lucretius' great vision of life balanced in the order of nature is another version. Beatrice in Dante presides over not a cycle but a sacramental spiral leading up to deity, as does, in a far less concrete way, the *Ewig-Weibliche* of *Faust.* At the opposite pole is a figure—Calypso or Circe in Homer, Dido in Virgil, Cleopatra in Shakespeare, Duessa in Spenser, sometimes a "terrible mother" but often sympathetically treated—who represents the opposite direction from the heroic quest. Eve in Milton, who spirals man downward into the Fall, is the contrasting figure to Beatrice.

In the ironic age there are naturally a good many visions of a cycle of experience, often presided over by a female figure with lunar and femme fatale affiliations. Yeats's *Vision,* which Yeats was quite right in associating with *The Mental Traveller,* is based on this symbolism, and more recently Mr. Robert Graves' *The White Goddess* has expounded it with even greater learning and ingenuity. In Eliot's *Waste Land* the figure in the background is less "the lady of situations" than the androgynous Teiresias, and although there is a fire sermon and a thunder sermon, both with apocalyptic overtones, the natural cycle of water, the Thames flowing into the sea and returning through death by water in the spring rains, is the containing form of the poem. In Joyce's *Ulysses* a female figure at once maternal, marital, and meretricious, a Penelope who embraces all her suitors, merges in her sleep with the drowsy spinning earth, constantly affirming but never forming, and taking the whole book with her.

But it is *Finnegans Wake* which is the chief ironic epic of our time. Here again the containing structure is cyclical, as the end of the book swings us around to the beginning again. Finnegan never really wakes up, because HCE fails to establish any continuity between his dreaming and waking worlds. The central figure is ALP, but we notice that ALP, although she has very little of the Beatrice or Virgin Mary about her, has even less of the femme fatale. She is a harried but endlessly patient and solicitous wife and mother: she runs through her natural cycle and achieves no quest herself, but she is clearly the kind of being who makes a quest possible. Who then is the hero who achieves the permanent quest in *Finnegans Wake?* No character in the book itself seems a likely candidate; yet one feels that this book gives us something more than the merely irresponsible irony of a turning cycle. Eventually it dawns on us that it is the reader who achieves the quest, the reader who, to the extent that he masters the book of Doublends Jined, is able to look down on its rotation, and see its form as something more than rotation.

In encyclopaedic forms, such as the epic and its congeners, we see how the conventional themes, around which lyrics cluster, reappear as *episodes* of a longer story. Thus the panegyric reappears in the *klea andron* or heroic contests, the poem of community action in the convention of the games, the elegy in heroic death, and so on. The reverse development occurs when a lyric on a conventional theme achieves a concentration that expands it into a miniature epic: if not the historical "little epic" or epyllion, something very like it generically. Thus *Lycidas* is a miniature scriptural epic extending over the whole range covered by *Paradise Lost,* the death of man and his redemption by Christ. Spenser's *Epithalamion* also probably contains in miniature as much symbolic range as the unwritten conclusion to his epic would have had. In modern times the miniature epic becomes a very common form: the later poems of Eliot, of Edith Sitwell, and many cantos of Pound belong to it.

Often too, in illustration of our general principle, a miniature epic actually forms part of a bigger one. The prophecy of Michael in *Paradise Lost* presents the whole Bible as a miniature contrast-epic, with one pole at the apocalypse and the other at the flood. The Bible itself contains the Book of Job, which is a kind of microcosm of its total theme, and is cited by Milton as the model for the "brief" epic.

Similarly, oratorical prose develops into the more continuous forms of prose fiction, and similarly too the growing points of prose, so to speak, which we called the commandment, parable, aphorism, and oracle, reappear as the kernels of scriptural forms. In many types of prose romance verse or characteristics of verse are prominent: the old Irish epics, euphuism in Elizabethan romance, the rhyming prose of the Arabian Nights, the use of poems for cultivated dialogue in the Japanese *Tale of Genji,* are random examples showing how universal the tendency is. But as *epos* grows into epic, it conventionalizes and unifies its metre, while prose goes its own way in separate forms. In the low mimetic period the gap between the subjective mythological epic and the objective historical one is increased by the fact that the former seems to belong by its decorum to verse and the latter to prose. In prose satire, however, we notice a strong tendency on the part of prose to reabsorb verse. We have mentioned the frequency of the verse interlude in the anatomy tradition, and in the *melos* of Rabelais, Sterne and Joyce the tendency is carried much farther. In scriptural forms, we have seen, the gap between prose and verse is very narrow, and sometimes hardly exists at all.

We come back to where we started this section, then, to the Bible, the only form which unites the architectonics of Dante with the disintegration of Rabelais. From one point of view, the Bible presents an epic structure of unsurpassed range, consistency and completeness; from another, it presents a seamy side of bits and pieces which makes the *Tale of a Tub, Tristram Shandy,* and *Sartor Resartus* look as homogeneous as a cloudless sky. Some mystery is here which literary criticism might find it instructive to look into.

When we do look into it, we find that the sense of unified continuity is what the Bible has as a work of fiction, as a definitive myth extending over time and space, over invisible and visible orders of reality, and with a parabolic dramatic structure of which the five acts are creation, fall, exile, redemption, and restoration. The more we study this myth, the more its descriptive or sigmatic aspect seems to fall into the background. For most readers, myth, legend, historical reminiscence, and actual history are inseparable in the Bible; and even what is historical fact is not there because it is "true" but because it is mythically significant. The begats in Chronicles may be authentic history; the Book of Job is clearly an imaginative drama, but the Book of Job is more important, and closer to Christ's practice of revelation through parable. The priority of myth to fact is religious as well as literary; in both contexts the significance of the flood story is in its imaginative status as an archetype, a status which no layer of mud on top of Sumeria will ever account for. When we apply this principle to the gospels, with all the variations in their narratives, the descriptive aspect of them too dissolves. The basis of their form is something other than biography, just as the basis of the Exodus story is something other than history.

At this point the analytic view of the Bible begins to come into focus as the thematic aspect of it. In proportion as the continuous fictional myth begins to look illusory, as the text breaks down into smaller and smaller fragments, it takes on the appearance of a sequence of epiphanies, a discontinuous but rightly ordered series of significant moments of apprehension or vision. The Bible may thus be examined from an aesthetic or Aristotelian point of view as a single form, as a story in which pity and terror, which in this context are the knowledge of good and evil, are raised and cast out. Or it may be examined from a Longinian point of view as a series of ecstatic moments or points of expanding apprehension—this approach is in fact the assumption on which every selection of a text for a sermon is based. Here we have a critical principle which we can take back to literature and apply to anything we like, a principle in which the "holism," as it has been called, of Coleridge and the discontinuous theories of Poe, Hulme, and Pound are reconciled. Yet the Bible is "more" than a work of literature, so perhaps the principle has a wider range of extension even than literature.

EPICAL ACTIONS*

Paul Goodman

EPICS AND EPICAL ACTIONS

The remarks on epic poetry in the *Poetics* are quite unsatisfactory. They are made by analogy with complex tragedy and from a surprisingly poor induction from the *Iliad* and *Odyssey*. In the peculiar contest between Epic and Tragedy (xxvi), tragedy, and especially *Oedipus*, wins the palm because it can attain the "end" (namely, the end of plays like *Oedipus*) with less space and time and fewer words, and it has a tighter unity. The analysis of the epic poems themselves seeks to show the tragic unity of the action and then explains the remainder of the poems as "episodes . . . to relieve the uniformity of the narrative" (xviii. 1459ª30); the action of the *Odyssey* is essentially the slaying of the suitors; the rest is episode (xvii. 1455ᵇ16 ff.). This is not a profitable approach.

Here let us start afresh with a little collection of epical actions, find what they have in common, and draw a kind of generalized scheme of the epic plot. This will be merely a discussion of genre and not the structure of any actual experience.

Consider a few poems that are called "epics" or actions that are called "epical." The deeds of purgative heroes, like Beowulf or Hercules, are epic; and also donative heroes, like Prometheus; battles against odds, like *Roland* or *Malden;* wars with individual heroes, like the *Iliad*. Real voyages are epical, like the *Odyssey* or the *Lusiad*. Also allegorical voyages through difficult terrain, like the *Commedia*. Also the initiation of great enterprises, as the *Aeneid* is a voyage with difficulties and temptations, and a war, to found a city. The laying of the Atlantic cable, the winning of the West, Sherman's march to the sea, would all be called "epical"; and, in general, many battles and triumphs over nature.

* Reprinted from *The Structure of Literature* by Paul Goodman by permission of The University of Chicago Press. Copyright 1954.

PERFORMING EXPLOITS

DISTINCTION FROM TRAGEDY

These are all heroes or heroic groups performing exploits, great, important, and admirable actions accompanied by difficulty and danger. Poems with such actions must be called "serious."

But first let us distinguish between the seriousness of an epic exploit and of a tragic action. The tragic action is serious because it is essential to the integration or breakdown of the character—we noted the breakdown in *Oedipus*, the integration in *Philoctetes*. If the action turns out well, he becomes himself or finds his identity; if it turns out badly, he changes. In this sense the episode of Dido in the *Aeneid* is tragic for Dido and Aeneas; and the action of Achilles is tragic throughout the *Iliad*, except precisely when he is fighting.

It is not this relation that makes an epic exploit serious and essential, but because it is something important and necessary, that must be done, in itself. What concerns many people is important; what has lasting and useful consequences; what is divinely ordained; etc. It is true that (a) the hero must perform the exploit and that (b) he is threatened with destruction in performing it; but it is just these two that in the epic exploit are not the same, whereas in the tragedy what the hero must do is to be threatened with destruction.

a) The exploit and the character are externally, though essentially, related. The exploit must be done because it is necessary. The hero must perform it because he can, he has the requisite virtue; and it is his task, otherwise he is not acting out his habit.

b) The difficulty and danger of the exploit are, of course, vital threats to the hero, as Aeneas may be sunk in Aeolus' waves or be lost in Hell. But it is not these risks that are his concern; they are merely incidental to the founding of Rome. Or Roland takes the risk, faces the danger, as his task; but his exploit is not in what he is threatened with but in what he does, saving the army.

The distinction may be put formally as follows: Tragic action and passion involve character change; the epic exploit follows from the character as fixed: some habitual virtue. Thus the actions in epic are more external to the character and may win more interest in themselves, just as the hero may have a tragic or romantic plot that is not directly essential to his exploit. In the *Iliad* strong bonds of probability connect Achilles' tragic plot and his exploit, but both are allowed independent development. The same is true in the *Aeneid* of Aeneas' relations to Dido and to Anchises, which are tragically essential, yet are importantly connected with his exploit.

DISTINCTION FROM "EPIC NOVELS"

Further, the epic hero *performs* the exploits. They belong to his nature to do, and he does them. In this the *Aeneid* differs from an "epic novel" like *War and Peace,* where there are battles and other epic incidents, but such major characters as Prince André respond sentimentally to them rather than perform them. It is not in the Prince's nature, as such, to be in these incidents.

To be sure, Aeneas himself is not a very active hero; his exploits are often fatalities that he bears with a pious fortitude, his chief virtue. And a very large part of the beauty of the *Aeneid* is its sentimentality, the Virgilian reflectiveness and melancholy.

MEANING OF EPIC SERIOUSNESS

Since the exploits follow from an habitual virtue, the same hero can perform more than one exploit (which would be impossible of a tragic action); and he can even, because the plot is narrated rather than presented, be engaged in more than one at the same time, as Aeneas, seeking his *antiqua mater* Italy, pauses to conduct the funeral games for Anchises. (Of course he must pay this honor before he goes to mother-Italy, just as he must descend to propitiate the *inferos* when he first lands. His ritual is not very different from that in the Creed.)

Seriousness means some or all of the following relations: each of the exploits flows from the essential virtue of the hero, as from the piety of Aeneas; thus he cannot omit the performance and may be involved in danger. He is threatened with the destruction of his life and purpose if he is not successful in the exploit. But further—and this is a capital point for epic poetry and explains much about the plotting—the exploit is vicariously essential to him as a member of a group, the group, namely, to whom the exploit is objectively important. By "vicariously essential" I mean the essential relation not of a man and his antagonist but of a representative and the group he represents. Thus Oedipus is a representative hero in unriddling the Sphinx, for the solution of the riddle is vital to the Thebans; but he is a tragic hero when the oracle turns against himself.

THE EPIC HERO

The epic hero is thus always a double role: the person (with his virtue) and the representative of the group to whom the exploit is important. In either of these roles there may be a frailty laying him open to dangers and reversals; Aeneas the Trojan is frail, the object of Juno's wrath, but the pious Aeneas is not. (This is what makes him a savior hero rather than a tragic epic hero like Achilles, who is frail in both roles.) Again, there may be an important plot between the two roles, as where Achilles sits in his tent and the Greek ships are burned, or, contrariwise, where the sailors of Columbus want to turn back, but Columbus drives them to their own glory.

In general, since the performance of the exploit is important because of the group rather than the person, the man may be destroyed by his frailty, like Roland, and yet the group be saved by the virtue of its representative.

Again, because of the essential relevance of the group, episodes may occur in which the hero himself does not appear at all, as Lausus and Mezentius, part of the war. (This episode is also a character foil to Aeneas and Pallas.)

It might be useful, in considering the double role of the epic hero, to refer back to what was said above about the hero of tragic history, who is both a tragic character and a figure of history.

THE EPIC PLOT IS EPISODIC

The action must of course have a beginning, middle, and ending, otherwise it would not be one poem. Yet, from what has just been said, the hero can finish an exploit and his habitual virtue survive for another, and within limits the other characters may perform independent exploits, for the group may have other representatives. All these considerations point to the following type of plot: an episodic plot in which the episodes are partial actions of the one action.

The over-all action of the existing poems lend themselves to this arrangement. A voyage home may include many adventures, a siege many battles, and founding a city the overcoming of many difficulties. In the handling, two contrary problems arise. On the one hand, the unity of the over-all action must not be lost. In some stories (e.g., a voyage) there is an obvious progression, but in others the order must be made clear, as why to descend to the underworld upon landing in Italy. On the other hand, the greatness of the individual exploits must not be lost; they must not be underwritten to hasten to the end, or they will not be epic. The whole must not fall apart into an "episodic plot"; yet each episode must not be pusillanimous.

A fine arrangement is for the episodes to lead up to a tragic episode, as in Roland, the Odyssey, Götterdämmerung, for at the same time this achieves the goal and destroys or completes the hero. (Or, likewise a miraculous episode, a wedding, or any other finale.)

In the Iliad the tragic conflict, moved by Achilles' wrath, persists through most of the poem; yet meantime the epic exploits are performed by other representatives until the death of Patroclus brings back the virtuous Achilles—yet with a cognate frailty, for he exchanges wrath for ruthlessness. This general pattern of a personal story against a background of epic incident is even usual in the historical novels, from *War and Peace* to *Ben Hur*; but in such cases, as we have said, the personal actors do not perform the epic incidents, or at least not as champions.

Again, where in an epic novel the responses of Prince André to the great events may be very numerous, in the epic poem it is the events themselves that are greatly presented; and, if these are great, they cannot be infinite. So formally: The epic plot contains not one or very many but a few great incidents.

THE EPIC EPISODE

An epic episode differs from a tragic episode (what we call an act of the play) in being relatively self-contained, so that even a new hero may be introduced for the exploit, as Lausus or Glaucon, if he is a representative champion. "Relatively self-contained" would have to be analyzed for each case in the whole of the particular poem. Frequently it means that the beginning of the episode grows out of the main action, as the meeting of Glaucon and Diomed flows from the battle yet is the beginning of their conversation; and the same with the ending, as they return to the battle (which they have made so pathetic).

Most of the episodes are active exploits; but some may be great descriptions, etc., as the Building of Carthage or the Storm, or the Catalogue of the Ships.

THE HERO OF THE EPISODIC PLOT

We have mentioned the hero's habitual virtue and his being representative of a group, and these motivate an episodic epic plot, for he may perform several exploits, and the group may have other champions. Let us go a little further into this.

The hero's virtue is specific to the kind of exploit, as Aeneas is pious to transfer the Penates. Now the "goodness" of a tragic hero is not specific; it means simply that he is serious and will cope with the problem. But of course it is, in a special sense, his *own* problem; the tragic character is responsible for his plight. But the epic hero need not be responsible for the existence of his task but only for its performance; he overcomes difficulties either imposed from outside altogether or brought on by the guilt of his group; and he may receive outside aid, usually from a god (though not in the respect in which he is virtuous— the fatal bird in Aeneas' flight with Turnus is not too impressive). These things give occasions to introduce historical causes and divine destiny from the beginning.

Since he must persist in crises from outside, the hero cannot be passionate; his passion is weaker than his habit (except in the tragic episode). Obviously it is impossible to construct a passionate episodic plot with unity, since the character is changed and the passion is purged once and for all. But this restriction does not apply to sentiment, which, like the sadness of the *Iliad* or the melancholy of the *Aeneid*, may pervade the whole; and it is really the expression of the Narrator.

The hero may be a single man, like Aeneas, or, as in the *Iliad*, rival groups: the Greeks and the Trojans. In the latter case, the group itself has a character; in the *Iliad* it is wonderfully drawn, the adventuring soldiers quarreling over their booty, against the people of the city, including wives and children.

To sum up with an example: Roughly the plot of the *Aeneid* is that Juno retards the founding of Rome with difficulties which are met by the heroic virtues of Aeneas—patience for the retarding, courage for the difficulties, and piety for the main action. As a man, the hero is virtuous; as a Trojan, he is frail, but he makes up for their frailty by his virtues, until Juno relents. (In the *Iliad* it is the other way, for the Greeks suffer by their leaders.)

EPIC EMOTIONS: THE NARRATOR

What are the emotions of an epic plot as an experience? The destructive and tragic episodes are fearful, pitiful, and resolving, not too unlike the tragic plots we have been discussing.

But with regard to the exploits, the epic part, it seems to me that again we must take into account the doubleness that comes from the more external relation between the hero and the action.

1. The feeling of performing an exploit is pride, as if to say, "One of us is doing this." Unlike the tragic feelings, pride can be cumulative from episode to episode. It is even likely that it is best felt when there are several episodes, for then it is securely grounded in an habitual expectation, as a father says of his son, or a son says of his father, "See! I told you so; that's how he always does. Look at *him!*" Also, this is not the kind of feeling that requires discharge or catharsis; we may carry it away with us.

(Psychologically, the feeling of epic pride seems to be precisely the means of expansively showing off by belonging to the pride group; for this avoids, on the one hand, the feeling of envy of the exploit of the "other" and, on the other hand, the fear of castration in showing off one's self in a possibly hostile company. In epic pride it is *we* who display our prowess.)

2. The feeling of the exploit performed is importance, as if to say,

"This is a necessary or great thing for us." An exploit is what is, so to speak, objectively important. By "objectively" I mean what belongs to our habitual physiological, civic, or religious needs rather than to our personal crisis. If there is not this underlying sense of importance, there cannot be the pride. We are proud of our friend who saves someone from drowning, because life-saving is important.

Of course the important and the proud-making are historically relative. To slay a dragon is important when there are dragons but romantic when there are none. Tragic themes are also historically relative, of course, as adultery was serious in England but comic in France; but somewhere in the psyche there are always the contrary evaluations, and the play can evoke one or the other. But with epic themes it is a question whether it is not indispensable for them to be grounded in "our" history or institutional mythology; for what is a great, extrinsic, merely fictional action? This raises the question of "suspension of disbelief"; and I think it is best handled by the following consideration.

3. These exploits are narrated. In the art experience in which the plot is the sequence of our foreground attention, the background is always the presence of the Narrator; we are listening to or reading the story. And it is the attitude, conviction, selection, and emphasis of the Narrator that implies the importance of the exploits. (Let us call this attitude, etc., of the Narrator simply the "narrator"; later, in the third analysis in chapter iii and throughout chapter iv, we shall explore the narrator part as a structural part of the plot.)

Aristotle praises Homer for speaking little in his own person but rather being always the imitator; "he brings in forthwith a man or woman or some other character, no one of them characterless" (xxiv. 1460ª5ff.). This is very sound in principle, when in fact the imitation is part of the important life-experience of the audience; that is, when the exploits are important exploits "for us." But with the lapse of history we find that the aesthetic experience has turned inside out: it is because of Homer, his style and attitude, that those exploits are still exploits; he proves their human worth. Even from antiquity this has been recognized; the difference between Achilles and other heroes of history is simply that "they have no Homer and are dead." And when we come to a modern "epic" writer like Milton, almost in his own time and certainly in ours it is that a Milton tells it that makes his myth important.

In brief, the question of credibility, to repeat this, depends not on our willingness to suspend disbelief but on the ongoing art experience itself: in narrative works it is the narrator who convinces, and in principle we ought to be able to demonstrate this in the details of the work. A talking horse does not make sense, but Homer makes sense of Achilles' talking horse, and "Homer" is a certain rhythm, diction, selection, and arrangement of episodes.

THE NARRATIVE MANNER AND THE EPISODIC PLOT

Speaking of the narrative manner, Aristotle says (xxiv. 1459^{b}24–25):

"In a play one cannot represent an action with a number of parts going on simultaneously . . . but in epic poetry the narrative manner makes it possible to describe a number of simultaneous incidents; and these, if germane to the subject, increase the body of the poem . . . there is room for episodes of diverse kinds."

Strictly speaking, what he says about plays is false. By crosscutting the scenes, as Shakespeare and most moderns do, the playwright can present simultaneous actions: we know simultaneously about Lady Macduff in her castle, Malcolm in England, and Macbeth in his castle. Yet, more deeply, every such interruption of the unity of place and time, whether by pulling the curtain or emptying the stage and rebeginning, strongly implies the author and takes us into the narrative manner. In our fourth chapter we shall try to define formally "dramatic manner" and "narrative manner" and shall explore the meaning of unity of time and place.

Obviously the narrative manner is capital in preserving the unity of the main action through the relatively independent episodes of the episodic plot. The narrator gives continuity, either explicitly by explanatory statements of the relation of the episodes (e.g., "Et iam finis erat, cum Iuppiter despiciens," etc.), or implicitly by his tone and attitude, rising and falling with the incidents but not to such extremes as the actors, so that the whole is kept in attention. In plays like *Oedipus* such a problem of continuity does not exist, for the action and time coincide (the action tragically speeded up), and the time coincides precisely with the actual flow of the speeches. The epic action is usually much longer than the time of narrating. Sometimes it has the same serial order as the flow of the words; at other times, as in the *Odyssey* or the *Aeneid*, there are incidents that flash back in time; and the narrator must make this clear.

THE EPIC DICTION OF THE NARRATOR

Speeches have the characteristic diction of the speakers in the situation. Here, too—as in not rising and falling to the same extremes in describing the action—a certain tone of the narrator makes all the speeches somewhat more alike than they would be in a tragic play. And even more so when the narrator is speaking in his own person. (*Except*, of course, when there is a special plot of the narrator that appears as he narrates the various incidents, like Milton's apostrophe to Light.)

To say what is important, overt, and an exploit, the epic style is in various modifications grand and earnest, vivid, reserved, realistic and objective. Thus, to use contrasts, ballad is simple, epic is grand; novel is sentimental, epic is objective; romance is fantastic, epic realistic; in drama the speech becomes the action, in epic something is reserved for the whole narrative. Homer is "rapid, simple, clear, and noble," says Matthew Arnold; Virgil is solemn, elegant, and pathetic; Dante is portentous and minute. Further, the meters in the existing poems are grand: they are hexameters, assonantal *laisses, terza rima*, the blank-verse paragraph. Dryden rather curiously notices this in his Preface to *Annus mirabilis* when he objects to couplets as too brief and chooses pentameter quatrains, as if four lines were twice as grand as two. (Yet his *Aeneis*, in couplets, is not meaner than Virgil but a little too salty and vigorous.) Again, epic poems find place for impressive enumerations like the Catalogue of the Ships or the list of Fallen Angels; for repeated lines and epithets; descriptions of ritual actions; formal similes; and formal proemiums and invocations. All these things belong to the narrator and imply the importance of the exploit.

ON TRANSLATING HOMER ONCE MORE*
Belief in Nobility in Our Time

> For Homer is not only rapid in movement, simple in
> style, plain in language, natural in thought; he is also,
> and above all, *noble*.[1]—Matthew Arnold, *On Translating
> Homer.*

[1] *Essays of Matthew Arnold* (London: Oxford University Press, 1925), p.
273. There were three lectures, given at Oxford in 1861 (pp. 243-312). In this
edition the three lectures are followed by Francis W. Newman's reply to
Arnold, "Homeric Translation in Theory and Practice" (pp. 313–376), and
Arnold's final lecture on the subject, "On Translating Homer: Last Words"
(pp. 377–424).

Kenneth G. Wilson

Homer is rapid, plain, direct, and noble, Matthew Arnold says. Arnold
makes clears the nature of rapidity, plainness, and directness in illustrating his points with what still remain the most accurate and useful descriptions of Homeric qualities. But what of nobility? To Arnold, nobility
was the ultimate, the most important quality of all. The translator might
imitate Homer perfectly in the first three qualities, but if his translation
lacked nobility, it could not succeed. Arnold's descriptions of nobility
are maddeningly vague, and his examples of it are often far from explicit.
Speaking of the translator's choice of diction, he remarks, "No doubt a
true poetic feeling is the Homeric translator's best guide in the use of
words . . ." Other means of attaining nobility appear to be equally a
matter of intuition or luck. If all goes well, nobility, according to
Arnold's description, will inhere in the translation which achieves the
other three qualities—the rapidity, the plainness, and the directness
which the translator *can* attempt consciously to achieve.

Among recent translators of Homer into English, Richmond Latti-

* Kenneth G. Wilson, "On Translating Homer Once More," *University of
Kansas City Review*, XXV (Spring and Summer, 1959), pp. 227–235. Reprinted
by permission of the author.

more[2] achieves nobility, while W. H. D. Rouse[3] assumes that nobility is no longer to be hoped for, and refuses even indirectly to seek it. Forgetting for the moment the distinctions between poetry and prose, let us consider this difference of assumption in order to discover how it happens that, although in rapidity and directness Rouse's *Iliad* has never been exceeded, and in plainness—the lack of ornament—it has good success, yet in nobility his translation is so completely lacking. Lattimore's translation, on the other hand, achieves rapidity, directness, and plainness—and nobility too. That is, although both translators strive for three of the qualities Arnold describes, one comes naturally to achieve the fourth, while the other omits it completely.

To be sure, neither translator attempts nobility. Richmond Lattimore only hopes for it. W. H. D. Rouse assumes instead that nobility does not concern the modern reader and offers him nothing which he can understand or will want to experience. Rouse believes, it seems to me, that nobility is a quality which the modern reader cannot grasp, and that even if he could grasp it, he would not admire it. Surely, if these assumptions are to be granted, Rouse's rapid, direct, modern prose translation deserves our praise (and it has received a good deal of it). The character of the translation is strikingly different from the tradition of Lang, Leaf, and Myers. Rouse stresses the comic, the farcical, the colloquial, the slangy. His gods speak a good deal of cheerful chatter. "What ho!" Hera says to Zeus, "You dreadful creature! What a thing to say!" They are rather like musical comedy deities. They converse in a half-whimsical style most of the time, so that Rouse's gods might well walk into a Shavian comedy without appearing out of place. They are fully aware of their own amusing behavior, sensitive to others' judgments of seriousness, anticipating and warding off any suggestion of their being "sincere." Above all they are gods who disarm our criticism of their actions by means of a full, modern self-consciousness which through its own sense of irony protects them from the irony of others. There is none of this in Lattimore's gods, and I conclude that by avoiding it he has caught the flavor of nobility. I believe also that in the translators' differences of opinion there are important implications for contemporary moral values.

First of all, however, let us consider the nature of nobility itself as it appears in heroic poetry. In *The Song of Roland* this quality is surprisingly simple to discover. It is often inexactly described as a childlike quality which makes the hero stand erect and deliver himself

[2] *The Iliad of Homer* (Chicago: University of Chicago Press, 1951). Lattimore translates the Greek into six-stressed unrimed English verse.

[3] Homer, *The Iliad: The Story of Achilles.* This English prose translation was first published in London by Thomas Nelson and Sons, in 1938. I have worked from the Mentor Book edition (New York: The New American Library of World Literature, 1950).

of long, proud speeches full of confidence in himself and his values, and
without a trace of doubt of the worth of his efforts. Roland announces
his virtues again and again, and he insists on his ability to perform. He
states directly his earnest desire to do well, nor does he ever doubt
that he will. As the late Erich Auerbach has pointed out, Roland's world
is without real problems.[4] Roland believes in his God and in the right
as he sees it, and he has no moments of doubt about possibly virtuous
pagans on the one hand or possibly fallible courage or ability in himself
on the other. Above all, he never asks whether he is fighting for the
right, or whether in his simple values there may be some flaw. In the
following, the battle at Roncevals is about to begin, and the pagans
approach with trumpets blaring.

> Then saith Oliver: "Sir comrade, methinks we shall have ado with the
> Saracens." "Now God grant it be as thou sayest," Roland answers him,
> "for to make stand here for our King is to do as good men ought to
> do. Verily for his liege a man well ought to suffer pain and woe, and
> endure both great heat and great cold, and should hold him ready to
> lose both hide and hair in his lord's service. Now let each have a care
> that he strikes good blows and great, that no man may mis-say us in
> his songs. These misbelieving men are in the wrong, and right with the
> Christians, and for my part I will give ye no ill example."[5]

Nowhere in the poem is there any change from the position stated
in this simple credo; none of these values ever comes under question.
Most contemporary heroes could not make such a speech, or, if one did,
either *his* sense of it or ours would be ironic. He might be a Felix Krull
or some other *picaro* whose view of such sentiments would be completely calculated, or else he would be filled with conflicting doubts,
either then or later. A modern hero—Raskolnikov or Julien Sorel, for
example—does not live in such a simple world. A modern heroic narrative (if we may ignore the implicit contradictions in the term *heroic*
used here) would almost inevitably concern itself with the examination
and the revaluation of the ideas so calmly accepted in *The Song of Roland*. Auerbach concludes his splendid essay on *The Song of Roland* by
remarking on the nature of the "elevated style" of the poem, and by
pointing out its grip on reality:

> Confronting the reality of life, this style is neither able nor willing to
> deal with its breadths or depths. It is limited in time, place, and social
> milieu. It simplifies the events of the past by stylizing and idealizing
> them. The feeling it seeks to arouse in its auditor is admiration and
> amazement for a distant world, whose instincts and ideals, though they
> certainly remain his own, yet evolve in such uncompromising purity

[4] *Mimesis—The Representation of Reality in Western Literature*, translated by Willard R. Trask (Princeton: Princeton University Press, 1953), p. 110.
[5] *The Song of Roland*, translated by Isabel Butler (Boston: Houghton
Mifflin Company, 1932), p. 36.

and freedom, in comparison with the friction and resistance of real life, as his practical existence could not possibly attain. Human movements and great, towering exemplary figures appear with striking effect; his own life is not there at all.[6]

The "uncompromising purity and freedom" of the world of the narrative make the difference. Within that frame, the narrator and his heroes may stand unafraid of laughter and judgment. They may be absolutely un-selfconscious.

It is this lack of self-consciousness (it may be childlike in some respects, but children fear laughter aimed at themselves; perhaps the best use of the word is in the distinction between *childlike* and *childish*) which makes poems like *The Song of Roland* seem almost to be parodies if they are read in the rigorously self-conscious frame of mind and protectively ironic tone of voice peculiar to the modern intellectual. One need argue only that Roland has mistaken his value or that the things in which he believes are foolish, and at once *The Song of Roland* becomes a parody. There is always only a narrow circle of protection for the man who takes himself seriously; we can accept him only by willingly suspending our disbelief in the "uncompromising purity and freedom" of his world. If we will not make that suspension, if we cannot accept a world without compromise—and Rouse cannot— then *The Song of Roland* certainly becomes a parody, and *The Iliad* may too.

The Iliad and *The Song of Roland* are of course very different in other important ways, but in this respect it seems to me that their difference is one of degree rather than of kind. I would argue that the quality of unselfconsciousness is, in fact, peculiar to all the great heroic narratives of Western literature, and that it is the major force in that quality in Homer which Arnold calls nobility. The heroic posture is that of a man standing erect, fearing no laughter, human or cosmic. The great heroic poems have the peculiar quality of making that posture appear glorious, never ludicrous.

The problem for the translator is therefore how to make acceptable to the reader the necessity for this world of no compromise, this world where the ironic sense of human futility and triviality is ultimately put away in favor of a glorious, reverent belief in human courage. The problems raised in translating such a poem can perhaps be illustrated simply enough if we describe *The Iliad* as a poem dealing with either "the wrath of Achilles" or "the squabble between Achilles and Agamemnon;" the choice of the latter phrasing implies the triviality, the fallibility of the motivations. The choice of "the wrath of Achilles," or Lattimore's "the anger of Peleus' son Achilleus and its devastation," simply ignores the possibility that anything might be questioned. Such

---

[6] *Mimesis*, pp. 120–121.

diction argues rather that this wrath and these actions are of the highest dignity and importance. That there could be any question never enters the narrator's mind.

Nobleness, the most important of Arnold's list of Homeric characteristics, can be illustrated in the heroes and their actions and in the style, the manner in which the poet tells their story. Arnold called it "the grand manner." A comparison of the translations by Lattimore and Rouse will illustrate the point. Consider first this simple little discussion of Euchenor, a very minor Achaian, as Lattimore translates it. Paris, seeking to avenge the death of a friend,

> let fly a bronze-shod arrow.
> There was a man, Euchenor, son of the seer Polyidos,
> a rich man and good, who lived in his house at Korinth,
> who knew well that it was his death when he went on shipboard,
> since many times the good old man Polyidos had told him
> that he must die in his own house of a painful sickness
> or go with the ships of the Achaians and be killed by the Trojans.
> He therefore chose to avoid the troublesome price the Achaians
> would ask, and the hateful sickness so his heart might not be afflicted.
> Paris struck him by jaw and ear, and at once the life spirit
> fled from his limbs, and the hateful darkness closed in about him.
> —Lattimore, p. 289

The statement of Euchenor's troubled choice is clear; there are two possibilities, with a minor economic advantage accompanying the choice of the heroic death. Irony is not stressed in the modern way; the man's choice is dignified and brave; he is noble. Rouse tells the story thus.

> [Paris] took a shot in revenge. There was a man there, the son of Polyidos the diviner, one Euchenor of Corinth, a man both wealthy and brave. He knew well what his fate would be before he embarked; for the good old man Polyidos had told him often enough, that he was either to die of a cruel disease in his own house, or to fall by a Trojan hand in the great war. *So he avoided two evils at the same time, the fatal disease and a heavy fine, and saved himself a great deal of discomfort.* Paris hit this man near the jawbone under the ear: a quick death for him when the darkness took him.
> —Rouse, p. 160, italics mine

The understatement of the italicized sentence avoids nobility and adds a touch of the modern's vaunted irony; it is almost flippant. What the sentence does is to make Euchenor's choice acceptable to a modern realist. In the brevity of the statement and the stress on the logic, any idealistic quality in Euchenor's character which might have been suggested in the Lattimore translation is removed. Euchenor here is a sensible, courageous businessman, not a hero exemplifying Arnold's nobleness. He may also be the butt of ironic laughter.

Diction and syntax both accomplish these different ends, but the whole distinction involves a grasp of what seems "properly explained and adequately motivated" for the modern reader. Rouse's assumption is that no one now can accept men who act with the naïveté of Boy Scouts or with such sturdy Harry Watsonesque belief in the virtue of virtue and the absolute acceptability of ideal behavior. Lattimore assumes that we can.

The word which often suggests itself to me in these connections is *quixotic*: I have caught myself about to say that Homer's heroes, as Lattimore sees them, are quixotic. They are not. At least they are not if we insist that the quixotic hero carries on his idealistic activities in a world which is clearly real and not at all suited to such actions, so that there is explicit a conscious judgment of his error. Everyone in Lattimore's *Iliad*, from the narrator and Achilles and Hector to the Euchenors, accepts the ideal forms and values. There is no one *in* the narrative to stress an ironic awareness of the folly of human beings who cannot see themselves as trivial and silly in their heroic posturings. If we are to see any such quality—and lose nobility—we must bring it from outside; we must deny, as Rouse does, the acceptability to the modern reader of a world of "uncompromising purity and freedom."

Another word Arnold employed for this air so peculiar to Homer's great poem is *elevation*; he argued that the tone of the narrative, its subject, and its very diction were elevated, and that it was in the imitation of this elevation that so many had gone astray—he stressed some translations particularly, whose diction, while elevated, was not elevated in the Homeric manner. Efforts to achieve this kind of separateness from the affairs and representations of the world of men have been of many sorts; Arnold described most of the kinds in *On Translating Homer, I.* All the main problems seemed to turn on the kind of meter, the kind of syntax, the kind of rhetoric, and the kind of diction employed by the translator. In his famous dictum, Arnold phrased it this way:

> The translator of Homer should above all be penetrated by a sense of four qualities of his author: that he is eminently rapid; that he is eminently plain and direct both in the evolution of his thought and in the expression of it, that is, both in his syntax and in his words; that he is eminently plain and direct in the substance of his thought, that is, in his matter and ideas; and, finally that he is eminently noble . . .[7]

He then continued to illustrate how Chapman, Pope, Cowper, Newman, and other English translators of *The Iliad* had failed in one or another of these qualities. Pope's translation was "highly intellectualized" and "oratorical," and while it did all these rhetorical things well, it was not Homer; Arnold characterized Pope's *Iliad* as having an "artificial evolution of thought and a literary cast of style;" these were virtues in Pope's own verse, but they were flaws in the translation of Homer. Cowper was too Miltonic; his blank verse, like Pope's and Chapman's rime, was

[7] *Essays by Matthew Arnold*, p. 250.

out of place. The "inversion and pregnant conciseness of Milton" were "the very opposites of the directness and flowingness of Homer . . ." Cowper's blank verse and its compact syntax, like Pope's antitheses and rime, broke the flow of direct, simple thought. Chapman failed because he was given to the fantastic elaboration, the conceits, of the Elizabethans; "he cannot forbear to interpose a play of thought between his object and its expression." [8]

If we set aside the purely prosodic considerations here, except as they influence syntax and the order of the words where these reflect the order of the idea, we can see that Arnold argues essentially for a natural word order of some sort, a syntax with no consciously rhetorical rearrangement, no stress on antitheses or epigrammatic statement. The modern linguist may therefore be able to supply us with the proper term. But first observe in what respects the Lattimore and Rouse translations are syntactically similar. Here, from the Lattimore version, is the oft-repeated description of a sacrificial offering:

> And when all had made prayer and flung down the scattering barley
> first they drew back the victims' heads and slaughtered them and
>   skinned them,
> and cut away the meat from the thighs and wrapped them in fat,
> making a double fold, and laid shreds of flesh upon them.
> The old man burned these on a cleft stick and poured the gleaming
> wine over, while the young men with forks in their hands stood about
>   him.
> But when they had burned the thigh pieces and tasted the vitals,
> they cut all the remainder into pieces and spitted them
> and roasted all carefully and took off the pieces.
> Then after they had finished the work and got the feast ready
> they feasted, nor was any man's hunger denied a fair portion.
> —Lattimore, p. 71

And the same passage in Rouse's prose:

> And when they all had prayed and cast the barley-grains, they first drew back the heads, and killed, and flayed, carved out the thigh-slices and rolled them between pieces of fat, and laid more raw flesh upon them: then the old priest burnt them upon sticks of wood, and poured sparkling wine over, while the young men held their five-pronged forks ready by his side. After the thigh-pieces were burnt and the inner parts were divided, they chopped up the rest and ran spits through through the meat, roasted all properly and drew it off. This work done, they prepared their meal and enjoyed it, and no one lacked a fair share.   —Rouse, p. 19

The order of the words is almost identical. Two points of difference appear besides those of diction: (1) occasionally, as in the last sentence in the passage, Rouse compresses the longer, full introductory clause into a phrase; (2) Lattimore has a way of spelling out in full who did

---

[8] *Ibid.*, p. 263.

what and to what and how. He never omits pronouns, and he seems always to state grammatical objects in full, no matter how clearly they might be understood. Rouse, on the other hand, attempts to combine and to let series constructions permit him to omit repetition of some pronouns: compare the stated details in Lattimore's "first they drew back the *victims'* heads and slaughtered *them* and skinned *them*," etc., with Rouse's "they first drew back the heads, and killed, and flayed," etc.

From the same passage we can illustrate this syntactic difference even further. Lattimore is not at all afraid of the long string of *and*-connected verbs and clauses, but Rouse prefers to vary the pace by interrupting with a series construction. Lattimore seems always to seek the steady addition of detail, the unselfconscious repetition of a comfortable pattern, while Rouse seems to seek variety. Having established a series, he will then simplify it, omit obvious words, and generally economize. Lattimore moves methodically and calmly through the entire pattern without shortening or saving anything. I believe the differences in syntax just described are typical of these two translations.

In direct narrative, when the voice of the poem simply tells how this man struck that man with a spear—describing the course of the spear and the place of the wound and such matters—Rouse and Lattimore translate very much alike, except for the differences just mentioned. In Book VII, during the fight with Aias, Hector is hit by a spear:

All the way through the glittering shield went the heavy spearhead,
and crashed its way through the intricately worked corselet;
straight ahead by the flank the spearhead shore through his
tunic, yet he bent away to one side and avoided the dark death.
                                        —Lattimore, p. 175

Right through it went, and through corselet also. The blade cut tunic
on Hector's side, but he swerved, and saved his life.   —Rouse, p. 88

There are the same number of clauses here, and their order is essentially identical. The difference is in the detail; wherever he can, Rouse makes a single verb do the work of verb, object, and modifiers.

If the syntactic differences are least in direct narrative, they are greatest in dialogue. Here, the difference between Lattimore's syntax and Rouse's syntax is often of kind as well as degree. Consider these two speeches from Book X, where Menelaos encounters Agamemnon at night. Lattimore has the following:

It was Menelaos of the great war cry who spoke first:
"Why this arming, my brother? Is it some one of your companions
you are stirring to go and spy on the Trojans? Yet I fear sadly
there will not be any man to undertake this endeavour,
going against enemy fighters to spy on them, alone, through
the immortal night. Such a man will have to be very bold-hearted."
Then in turn powerful Agamemnon answered him:
"You and I, illustrious, O Menelaos, have need now
of crafty counsel, if any man is to defend and rescue

the Argives and their ships, since the heart of Zeus is turned from us.
For the sacrifices of Hektor have stirred his heart more than ours have.
No, for I never saw nor heard from the lips of another
of a single man in a day imagining so much evil
as Hektor, beloved of Zeus, has wrought on the sons of the Achaians,
alone, being called true son neither of a god nor a goddess.
He has done things I think the Argives will remember with sorrow
long into the future, such harm has he devised the Achaians.
But go now, running lightly beside the ships, and call to us
Idomeneus and Aias, while I shall go after Nestor
the brilliant, and waken him to rise, if he might be willing
to approach the sacred duty of the guards, or give orders to them.
Above all, these would listen to him, seeing that his own son
commands the pickets, and with him the follower of Idomeneus,
Meriones. To these above all we entrusted the duty."

—Lattimore, p. 219

The same passage in Rouse reads:

> Menelaos said: "Why are you arming, my dear fellow? Do you
> think of sending out a spy? I'm dreadfully afraid you will not find a
> man ready for that job—to go out all alone in the depth of night and
> spy in the enemy camp! He will be a plucky man!"
>
> Agamemnon answered: "We must find some plan, you and I, my
> dear Menelaos, something useful, to save our people and our ships,
> now Zeus has changed his mind. Hector's offerings, as it seems, are
> more to his mind than ours. For I never saw or heard in my life that
> one man in one day did so much mischief as Hector has done against
> us, just by himself! He's no son of a god or goddess. But he has done
> things that our nation will lament for ever and ever. What a mess he
> has made! Come along, run as fast as you can and call Aias and
> Idomeneus; I will look up Nestor, and see if he will come with us to
> the young fellows on outpost duty, and tell them what to do. They
> will listen to him more than any one, for his son is in command of the
> outposts, he and Meriones, the friend of Idomeneus. We put them in
> general charge."
>
> —Rouse, p. 116

The differences in diction leap out, but let us put them aside for the
moment and concentrate on syntax, on the order of words and its relationship to patterns with which we are familiar. The "natural order" of
the syntax which was similar in the passages of direct narrative above
has changed a good deal. Both versions may still be natural, but they are
no longer alike. Terms like *formal* and *informal, platform speech* and
informal colloquial speech come to mind as we seek to describe the
difference. Rouse's syntax is sometimes elliptical; it employs contrac-
tions; it is full of the parenthesis of conversational English; along with
the diction of the colloquial idiom comes colloquial syntax: "What a
mess he has made!" Again in the Rouse version there is economy of
syntax, but here in the dialogue there is a good deal more of it, and it
is more than simply a shortening of otherwise similar syntactic patterns
while retaining the outlines of the patterns themselves. Here the attempt
is to imitate the flow of speech itself, the varied pace of utterance, the
ellipsis, and the broken or delayed syntax of informal colloquial
English.

Lattimore's translation has none of these characteristics. There is no attempt to imitate real speech, with its syntactic false starts and its other structural uniqueness. Lattimore's language is much like that which he employed for the direct narrative discussed above. It is full, steady, and unhurried. There is none of the syntax peculiar only to informal colloquial utterance. This dialogue is unlike formal or platform speech, moreover, in that its rhetoric is not consciously studied; it does not turn periods or antitheses or do anything in the nature of formal rhetoric. Above all, it has a quality of calm. That there are no exclamation points is indicative; the same passage in the Rouse version has several. Syntax contributes to this calmness—or perhaps is dictated by it—in that patterns are meticulously filled out, without any omission, without any hurried parenthesis. If parenthesis is necessary, it receives full clausal status. It is perhaps in this respect, in the firm control of the subordination of one idea to another—such as human argument and discussion require—that Lattimore's dialogue achieves its noblest air.

Auerbach makes the distinction between *parataxis*, wherein there is little subordination and the narrative consists simply of a series of assertive statements following one another (as in *The Song of Roland*), and *hypotaxis*, wherein there is subordination in syntax as in thought. Auerbach's extremely interesting comments on this matter are surely apposite here. Perhaps nobility, if it *is* related to this quality of unselfconsciousness of which I have spoken, relies a good deal on a relatively paratactic narrative. A man certain of the soundness of his beliefs and the rightness of his actions does not feel it necessary to hedge and qualify his statements. But a man unsure—a man in a real world where "uncompromising purity and freedom" do not hold sway, or where he fears that they do not—this man must protect himself with carefully subordinated arguments and meticulously qualified statements. Hence there is a good deal of difference between the "childlike" simplicity of Roland's utterance quoted earlier, and the tormented prose of J. D. Salinger's *The Catcher in the Rye*. It is my contention, further, that the Homeric narrator, like his heroes, has this same wonderful confidence in the rightness of his values and the absolute dignity of the actions he is describing. Hence Lattimore's Homer's voice is calm; he can run rapidly, but not without dignity; his language is dressed for that occasion. When his heroes speak, they too never lose their dignity; their syntax is natural but never colloquial. It is here that Rouse's translation seems to suffer a division in itself, since, as we have said, his narrator's voice, though more economical, more brisk and efficient, is usually not widely different from that of the Lattimore narrator. But when the Rouse *heroes* talk, there is a marked change, a shift in the "world of the narrative," and what before has been pure and free is now compromised; these men are, at least in their speech, just like everybody else; they live in our impure, unfree world. Their speech reflects "the friction and resistance of real life."

THE ORPHIC VOICE*

Elizabeth Sewell

What is epic? We may well ask. It is a form of poetry which has suffered a strange fate at the hands of critics. It has been supposedly embalmed and buried, and now falls under the heading of literary archaeology. It has been classified as "oral" or "authentic" epic, arising in primitive heroic society, and as "literary"; also as "primary" and "secondary." But even literary and secondary epic is now considered to be gone for good. We are told that *Paradise Lost* is the last, that epic found there "a finality which forbade any extension of its scope." [1]

What then of Wordsworth's proposal, in those pre-*Excursion* lines, to take over from Milton? Either the poet is unaware that epic is dead, and, misled himself, misleads us, or epic is not dead at all. Funeral services for it may be well enough as an occupation for critics, but they are no concern of the poet, intoned as they are over an empty grave. For the poet epic is no more dead than lyric, or poetic drama, or any other of those tough, infinitely adaptable, and lively organs of his. It is eternally available, with its own special resources, as a method of postlogical research. Poets cannot afford to be bereft of their working instruments in this way, and neither can human thinking in general. That is why it matters so much that we should let Wordsworth reassure us, in his poetic practice if not in his theorizing, that epic is as alive and prophetic as ever it was, moving forward in our name and changing and developing as it goes.

Epic is one of the greatest of the postlogical disciplines. Just how postlogical it is we can begin to see when we look at some of its characteristics, its preoccupation with the structure of the universe and the place and course of man's life and death within it, its essential activity, its attachment to mythology. This is supremely the point where poetry

---

* Elizabeth Sewell, *The Orphic Voice* (New Haven: Yale University Press, 1960). Reprinted by permission of Yale University Press.

[1] See C. M. Bowra, *From Virgil to Milton* (London, Macmillan, 1945), p. 246, and elsewhere.

espouses time, in the form of narrative, on the grand scale. It is therefore peculiarly adapted for thinking, on that scale, about any human relationships and activities in the universe which are susceptible of development or process, up to and including history and natural history, individual or general.

But it does not merely deal with developing subject matter; it develops itself in its progress through time, in that reflexive interaction and identification of subject, instrument, and agent which is part of postlogic. When an Orphic mind selects a poetic instrument as appropriate for a special work of discovery in that day and age, that instrument will and should be changed; but the change is never a perversion, a forcible wrenching of an old tool to untried uses. Each poet who sets himself in the epic tradition is going to reinterpret that tradition. The process of reinterpretation, however, resembles a process in nature and organic growth, the drawing-out of latent possibilities, the discovery of a *Novum Organum*. These are the metamorphoses of the poetic spirit of which Coleridge spoke, by which the human race forms for itself new instruments of power according to its new needs and activities. This is the nature of living tradition.

It is beyond my competence to say much about the experiments which are made before Wordsworth's, though it seems that as early as the *Aeneid* epic is beginning to take on a more explicitly genetic character,[2] confirmed by Milton; he too conceives of epic activity as in the spiritual rather than the military field, as Dante does, who also begins to illuminate the inclusiveness of the methodology by involving the poet in his own subject matter. Now in *The Prelude* it is the reflexiveness of postlogic which comes to the forefront. The mind becomes its own subject matter.

Epic, seen from the point of view of the working poet, is a dynamic instrument concerned with heroic achievement, advance, exploration. The significance of these, in terms of man moving between earth and heaven, is inquired into in the person of the epic hero. Here, too, our critical and historical sense has not helped us. To represent epic as the high doings of one solitary figure of however superhuman proportions, a great cult of individualism, is to strike it dead, just as to represent the heroic age of such deeds and discoveries as primitive and left far behind is to strike us all dead. Unprecedented deeds and explorations, with which epic deals, are lonely courses, and necessarily so. But the important thing from the beginning has been that the hero is identified with his people. He *is* his people in some sense. What are Gilgamesh or Beowulf or Dante or Adam doing if they are not carrying us forward with them, exploring and struggling and suffering, out in advance of us

[2] *Ibid.*, pp. 15, 58.

but one with us still? [3] It is as if the deeds were consolidated only later, by after-comers, and find their ultimate justification in that; for achievement and discovery that relate solely to one individual are useless. Only the transmissible in some terms, tradition or heredity which are so closely linked together is of value. This is, so far as we know (and we do not know much about it yet) how nature and human nature make progress into newness of any kind. With this, epic is of right concerned.

[3] This is most beautifully said by an anthropologist writing on epic— G. R. Levy, *The Sword From the Rock* (London, Faber, 1953): "Thither he drove the spear, and Hector fell in the dust. *Then you and I and all of us fell down* . . . In this climax, unlike the earlier duels, the two heroes have drawn into themselves the whole fate of camp and city" (p. 191).

PART TWO

❈

❈

EXHIBITS

THE CONVENTIONS OF EPIC

Any literary form with a past is bound to be in some measure conventional. Small wonder then, that the epic with its history of some three thousand rich and eventful years should be one of the most radically conventional of literary forms. In fact, the epic is so essentially and self-evidently a matter of conventions that scholars have often defined epic by listing conventions like so many ingredients in a recipe for instant heroic poetry. Poets themselves have also relied on the same conventions, exaggerated and missapplied, to mock the bad poems which result from too slavish an allegiance to such lists of Homeric simile and catalogue, invocation and exordium, in media res and et cetera. The scholar Abrams and the poet Byron each testifies in his own way and for his own ends to the highly conventional nature of the epic form.

But simply noting that the epic is conventional or even recognizing this convention in that poem does not take one far enough. The question to be asked of epic conventions begins not what or where, but why. Virgil imitates Homer; and Dante imitates Virgil imitating Homer; and Milton, Dante; and Wordsworth, Milton; and such moderns as T. S. Eliot and David Jones, Wordsworth, all because the conventions available within the epic tradition enable a poet to see more clearly what he wants to see and to say more precisely what he must say. The epic remains conventional because its conventions have worked, and the testimony of Sewell and Jones suggests that these conventions have a future as well as a past.

DEFINITIONS

1.

Epic. The epic, or **heroic poem,** is a long narrative poem on a serious subject, related in an elevated style, and centered about an heroic figure on whose actions depends to some degree the fate of a nation or a race. The "traditional," or "primary" epics were shaped from the legends that developed in an heroic age, when a nation was on the move and engaged in military conquest and expansion. In this group belong the *Iliad* and *Odyssey* of the Greek Homer, and the Anglo-Saxon *Beowulf*. The "literary" or "secondary" epics were written by sophisticated craftsmen in deliberate imitation of the earlier form. Of this kind is Virgil's Roman poem, the *Aeneid*, which in turn served as the chief model for Milton's literary epic, *Paradise Lost*. Other poems influenced by the *Aeneid* are sometimes loosely called epic, although they depart radically from the formal qualities of the original; among these are Dante's *Divine Comedy* and Spenser's *Faerie Queene*.

The epic was ranked by Aristotle as second only to tragedy in the hierarchy of genres and by Renaissance critics as the highest form of all. It is certainly the most ambitious and most exacting of poetic types, making immense demands on a poet's knowledge, invention, and skill to sustain the scope, grandeur, and variety of a poem that tends to encompass the known world and a large portion of its learning. Despite numerous attempts over three thousand years, we possess only a half dozen or so epics of indubitable greatness. Literary epics commonly have the following features, derived from the traditional epics of Homer:

1. The hero is a figure of great national or international importance. In the *Iliad* he is the great Greek warrior Achilles; in *Paradise Lost* he is Adam, who incorporates in himself the entire race of man.

2. The setting is ample in scale, sometimes world-wide, or even larger. Odysseus wanders over the Mediterranean basin (the whole of the world known to the author), and in Book XI he descends into the underworld. The scope of *Paradise Lost* is cosmic, for it includes heaven, earth, and hell.

3. The action involves heroic deeds in battle, such as the Trojan War, or a long and arduous journey intrepidly accomplished, such as the wanderings of Odysseus on the way to his homeland. *Paradise Lost* includes the war in Heaven, the journey of Satan to discover the newly created world, and his audacious attempt to outwit God by corrupting mankind.

4. In these great actions the gods and other supernatural beings themselves take an interest and an active part—the gods of Olympus in Homer, and Jehovah, Christ, and the angels in *Paradise Lost*. These supernatural agents in an epic used to be—sometimes still are—called the **machinery.**

5. An epic poem is a ceremonial performance and is deliberately given a ceremonial style proportionate to its great subject and architecture. Hence Milton's Latinate diction and stylized syntax, his re-

sounding lists of strange and sonorous names, and his **epic similes,** that is, sustained similes in which the comparison is developed far beyond the specific points of parallel to the primary subject:

> They . . . in narrow room
> Throng numberless, like that Pygmean race
> Beyond the Indian mount; or faery elves,
> Whose midnight revels, by a forest side
> Or fountain, some belated peasant sees,
> Or dreams he sees, while overhead the Moon
> Sits arbitress, and nearer to the Earth
> Wheels her pale course.

There are also numerous minor conventions in the epic, including the following:

1. The poet begins by stating his theme, then invokes a Muse to help him in his great undertaking and addresses to the muse an **epic question,** the answer to which inaugurates the narrative proper (*Paradise Lost,* lines 1–49).

2. This narration starts **in medias res,** or in the middle of the action, and at a critical point; the events that happened before the narrative opening are introduced later on. *Paradise Lost* opens with the fallen angels in Hell, gathering their forces and determining on revenge. Not until Books V–VII does the angel Raphael relate to Adam the events in Heaven leading to this situation; and in Books XI–XII, after the Fall. Michael fortells to Adam the future of the world up to Christ's Second Coming. Thus *Paradise Lost,* although focused on the fall of man, encompasses all time, from the creation to the end of the world.

3. There are catalogues of some of the main characters, introduced to the listener in formal detail, such as the procession of fallen angels in Book I of *Paradise Lost.* These characters are later given set speeches, ceremoniously delivered, and revelatory of their diverse temperaments; an example is the great consult of the fallen angels in *Paradise Lost,* Book II.

The **mock epic,** or **mock heroic** poem, is a form of satire in which petty characters and trivial events are made ridiculous by being incongruously presented in all the pomp and ceremony of epic characterisation, narration, and style. Dryden's *MacFlecknoe* treats of the elevation of a poetaster to be Crown Prince of Dulness as though it were an episode in an epic poem. In the masterpiece of this form, *The Rape of the Lock,* Pope views through the immense proscenium of the epic a quarrel between the belles and elegants of his day over the theft of a lady's curl. The story is solemnly conducted with all the protocol of the epic, including the ceremonious opening and procedure, a grand style, supernatural "machinery," a voyage at sea, a visit to the underworld, and a heroically scaled battle between the sexes, although with metaphors, hatpins, and snuff for weapons.

2.

CC.

My poem's epic, and is meant to be
  Divided in twelve books; each book containing,
With love, and war, a heavy gale at sea,
  A list of ships, and captains, and kings reigning,
New characters; the episodes are three:
  A panoramic view of hell's in training,
After the style of Virgil and of Homer,
So that my name of Epic's no misnomer.

CCI.

All these things will be specified in time,
  With strict regard to Aristotle's rules,
The *Vade Mecum* of the true sublime,
  Which makes so many poets, and some fools:
Prose poets like blank verse, I'm fond of rhyme,
  Good workmen never quarrel with their tools;
I've got new mythological machinery,
And very handsome supernatural scenery.

CCII.

There's only one slight difference between
  Me and my epic brethren gone before,
And here the advantage is my own, I ween;
  (Not that I have not several merits more,
But this will more peculiarly be seen;)
  They so embellish, that 'tis quite a bore
Their labyrinth of fables to thread through,
Whereas this story's actually true.

From George Gordon, Lord Byron, *Don Juan*, Canto I.

SIMILE

1.

he first the Council brake;
The other sceptre-bearing States arose too, and obeyed
The people's Rector. Being abroad, the earth was overlaid
With flockers to them, that came forth, as when of frequent bees
Swarms rise out of a hollow rock, repairing the degrees
Of their egression endlessly, with ever rising new
From forth their sweet nest; as their store, still as it faded, grew,
And never would cease sending forth her clusters to the spring,
They still crowd out so; this flock here, that there, belabouring
The loaded flowers; so from the ships and tents the army's store
Trooped to these princes, and the court, along the unmeasured
    shore;
Amongst whom, Jove's ambassadress, Fame, in her virtue shined,
Exciting greediness to hear. The rabble, thus inclined,
Hurried together: uproar seized the high court; earth did groan
Beneath the settling multitude; tumult was there alone.

From Homer, *The Iliad*, Book II, lines 69–83, as translated by George Chapman (1559–1634).

2.

They who had measur'd a swift course were now
Climbing, as swift, a hill of lofty brow,
That overhangs wide compass of the Town,
And on the turrets, which it fronts, looks down.
Aeneas views the City—pile on pile
Rising—a place of sordid Huts erewhile;
And, as he looks, the gates, the stretching ways,
The stir, the din, encreasing wonder raise.
The Tyrians work—one spirit in the whole;
These stretch the walls; these labour to uproll
Stones for the Citadel, with all their might;
These, for new Structures having mark'd a site,
Intrench the circuit. Some on laws debate,
Or chuse a Senate for the infant State;
Some dig the haven out; some toil to place
A Theatre, on deep and solid base;
Some from the rock hew columns, to compose

A goodly ornament for future Shows.
—Fresh summer calls the Bees such tasks to ply
Through flowery grounds, beneath a summer sky;
When first they lead their progeny abroad,
Each fit to undertake his several load;
Or in a mass the liquid produce blend,
And with pure nectar every cell distend;
Or, fast as homeward Labourers arrive, }
Receive the freight they bring; or mustering, drive }
The Drones, a sluggard people, from the hive. }
Glows the vast work; while thyme-clad hills and plains
Scent the pure honey that rewards their pains.
"Oh fortunate!" the Chief, Aeneas, cries }
As on the aspiring Town he casts his eyes, }
"Fortunate Ye, whose walls are free to rise!" }

From Virgil, *The Aeneid*, Book I, lines 568–595, as translated by William Wordsworth (1770–1850). E. de Selincourt and Helen Darbishire, *The Poetical Works of William Wordsworth* (Oxford University Press: London, 1947). Reprinted by permission.

3.

Then thrice around his neck his arms he threw;
And thrice the fleeting shadow slipped away,
Like winds, or empty dreams, that fly the day.
Now, in a secret vale, the Trojan sees }
A separate grove, through which a gentle breeze }
Plays with a passing breath, and whispers through }
    the trees: }
And, just before the confines of the wood,
The gliding Lethe leads her silent flood.
About the boughs an airy nation flew,
Thick as the humming bees, that hunt the golden dew
In summer's heat; on tops of lilies feed,
And creep within their bells, to suck the balmy seed:
The winged army roams the field around;
The rivers and the rocks remurmur to the sound.
Aeneas wondering stood, then asked the cause,
Which to the stream the crowding people draws.
Then thus the sire:—"The souls that throng the flood
Are those, to whom, by Fate, are other bodes owed:
In Lethe's lake they long oblivion taste,
Of future life secure, forgetful of the past.

From Virgil, *The Aeneid*, Book VI, lines 971–987, as translated by John Dryden (1631–1700).

4.

                                        they anon
With hundreds and with thousands trooping came
Attended: all access was throng'd, the Gates
And Porches wide, but chief the spacious Hall
(Though like a cover'd field, where Champions bold
Wont ride in arm'd, and at the Soldans chair
Defi'd the best of *Panim* chivalry
To mortal combat or carreer with Lance)
Thick swarm'd, both on the ground and in the air,
Brusht with the hiss of russling wings. As Bees
In spring time, when the Sun with *Taurus* rides,
Poure forth thir populous youth about the Hive
In clusters; they among fresh dews and flowers
Flie to and fro, or on the smoothed Plank,
The suburb of thir Straw-built Cittadel,
New rub'd with Baum, expatiate and confer
Thir State affairs. So thick the aerie crowd
Swarm'd and were straitn'd; till the Signal giv'n,
Behold a wonder! they but now who seemd
In bigness to surpass Earths Giant Sons
Now less then smallest Dwarfs, in narrow room
Throng numberless, like that Pigmean Race
Beyond the *Indian* Mount, or Faerie Elves,
Whose midnight Revels, by a Forrest side
Or Fountain some belated Peasant sees,
Or dreams he sees, while over-head the Moon
Sits Arbitress, and neerer to the Earth
Wheels her pale course, they on thir mirth and dance
Intent, with jocond Music charm his ear;
At once with joy and fear his heart rebounds.
Thus incorporeal Spirits to smallest forms
Reduc'd thir shapes immense, and were at large,
Though without number still amidst the Hall
Of that infernal Court. But far within
And in thir own dimensions like themselves
The great Seraphic Lords and Cherubim
In close recess and secret conclave sat
A thousand Demy-Gods on golden seats,
Frequent and full. After short silence then
And summons read, the great consult began.

From John Milton, *Paradise Lost*, Book I, lines 752–798.

INVOCATION

1.

The man, for wisdom's various arts renown'd,
Long exercised in woes, oh Muse! resound.
Who, when his arms had wrought the destined fall
Of sacred Troy, and razed her heaven-built wall,
Wandering from clime to clime, observant stray'd,
Their manners noted, and their states survey'd,
On stormy seas unnumber'd toils he bore,
Safe with his friends to gain his natal shore.
Vain toils! their impious folly dared to prey
On herds devoted to the god of day;
The god, vindictive, doom'd them never more
(Ah, men unbless'd!) to touch that natal shore.
Oh, snatch some portion of these acts from fate,
Celestial Muse! and to our world relate.

From Homer, *The Odyssey*, Book I, lines 1–14, as translated by Alexander
Pope (1688–1744).

2.

Of Mans First Disobedience, and the Fruit
Of that Forbidden Tree, whose mortal tast
Brought Death into the World, and all our woe,
With loss of *Eden*, till one greater Man
Restore us, and regain the blissful Seat,
Sing Heav'nly Muse, that on the secret top
Of *Oreb*, or of *Sinai*, didst inspire
That Shepherd, who first taught the chosen Seed,
In the Beginning how the Heav'ns and Earth
Rose out of *Chaos*: or if *Sion* Hill
Delight thee more, and *Siloa's* Brook that flow'd
Fast by the Oracle of God; I thence
Invoke thy aid to my adventrous Song,
That with no middle flight intends to soar
Above th' *Aonian* Mount, while it pursues
Things unattempted yet in Prose or Rhime.
And chiefly Thou O Spirit, that dost prefer
Before all Temples th' upright heart and pure,

Instruct me, for Thou know'st; Thou from the first
Wast present, and with mighty wings outspread
Dove-like satst brooding on the vast Abyss
And mad'st it pregnant: What in me is dark
Illumin, what is low raise and support;
That to the highth of this great Argument
I may assert Eternal Providence,
And justifie the wayes of God to men.

From John Milton, *Paradise Lost*, Book I, lines 1–26.

3.

Oh there is blessing in this gentle breeze.
A visitant that while it fans my cheek
Doth seem half-conscious of the joy it brings
From the green fields, and from yon azure sky.
Whate'er its mission, the soft breeze can come
To none more grateful than to me; escaped
From the vast city, where I long had pined
A discontented sojourner: now free,
Free as a bird to setttle where I will.
What dwelling shall receive me? in what vale
Shall be my harbour? underneath what grove
Shall I take up my home? and what clear stream
Shall with its murmur lull me into rest?
The earth is all before me. With a heart
Joyous, nor scared at its own liberty,
I look about; and should the chosen guide
Be nothing better than a wandering cloud,
I cannot miss my way. I breathe again!
Trances of thought and mountings of the mind
Come fast upon me: it is shaken off,
That burthen of my own unnatural self,
The heavy weight of many a weary day
Not mine, and such as were not made for me.
Long months of peace (if such bold word accord
With any promises of human life),
Long months of ease and undisturbed delight
Are mine in prospect; whither shall I turn,
By road or pathway, or through trackless field,
Up hill or down, or shall some floating thing
Upon the river point me out my course?

Dear Liberty! Yet what would it avail
But for a gift that consecrates the joy?
For I, methought, while the sweet breath of heaven
Was blowing on my body, felt within
A correspondent breeze, that gently moved
With quickening virtue, but is now become
A tempest, a redundant energy,
Vexing its own creation. Thanks to both,
And their congenial powers, that, while they join
In breaking up a long-continued frost,
Bring with them vernal promises, the hope
Of active days urged on by flying hours,—
Days of sweet leisure, taxed with patient thought
Abstruse, nor wanting punctual service high,
Matins and vespers of harmonious verse!

Thus far, O Friend! did I, not used to make
A present joy the matter of a song,
Pour forth that day my soul in measured strains
That would not be forgotten, and are here
Recorded: to the open fields I told
A prophecy: poetic numbers came
Spontaneously to clothe in priestly robe
A renovated spirit singled out,
Such hope was mine, for holy services.
My own voice cheered me, and, far more, the mind's
Internal echo of the imperfect sound;
To both I listened, drawing from them both
A cheerful confidence in things to come.

From William Wordsworth, *The Prelude*, Book I, lines 1–58.

CATALOGUE

1.

He brought our Saviour to the western side
Of that high mountain, whence he might behold
Another plain, long but in bredth not wide;
Wash'd by the Southern Sea, and on the North
To equal length back'd with a ridge of hills
That screen'd the fruits of the earth and seats of men

From cold *Septentrion* blasts, thence in the midst
Divided by a river, of whose banks
On each side an Imperial City stood,
With Towers and Temples proudly elevate
On seven small Hills, with Palaces adorn'd,
Porches and Theatres, Baths, Aqueducts,
Statues and Trophees, and Triumphal Arcs,
Gardens and Groves presented to his eyes,
Above the highth of Mountains interpos'd.
By what strange Parallax or Optic skill
Of vision multiplyed through air, or glass
Of Telescope, were curious to enquire:
And now the Tempter thus his silence broke.
    The City which thou seest no other deem
Then great and glorious *Rome,* Queen of the Earth
So far renown'd, and with the spoils enricht
Of Nations; there the Capitol thou seest
Above the rest lifting his stately head
On the *Tarpeian* rock, her Cittadel
Impregnable, and there Mount *Palatine*
The Imperial Palace, compass huge, and high
The Structure, skill of noblest Architects,
With gilded battlements, conspicuous far,
Turrets and Terrases, and glittering Spires:
Many a fair Edifice besides, more like
Houses of Gods (so well I have dispos'd
My Aerie Microscope) thou may'st behold
Outside and inside both, pillars and roofs
Carv'd work, the hand of fam'd Artificers
In Cedar, Marble, Ivory or Gold.
Thence to the gates cast round thine eye, and see
What conflux issuing forth, or entring in,
Pretors, Proconsuls to thir Provinces
Hasting or on return, in robes of State;
Lictors and rods the ensigns of thir power,
Legions and Cohorts, turmes of horse and wings:
Or Embassies from Regions far remote
In various habits on the *Appian* road,
Or on the *Aemilian,* some from farthest South,
Syene, and where the shadow both way falls,
Meroe Nilotic Isle, and more to West,
The Realm of *Bocchus* to the Black-moor Sea;
From the *Asian* Kings and *Parthian* among these,
From *India* and the golden *Chersoness,*
And utmost *Indian* Isle *Taprobane,*

Dusk faces with white silken Turbants wreath'd;
From *Gallia, Gades,* and the *Brittish* West,
Germans and *Scythians,* and *Sarmatians* North
Beyond *Danubius* to the *Tauric* Pool.
All Nations now to *Rome* obedience pay,
To *Rome's* great Emperour, whose wide domain
In ample Territory, wealth and power,
Civility of Manners, Arts, and Arms,
And long Renown thou justly may'st prefer
Before the *Parthian;* these two Thrones except,
The rest are barbarous, and scarce worth the sight,
Shar'd among petty Kings too far remov'd;
These having shewn thee, I have shewn thee all
The Kingdoms of the world, and all thir glory.
This Emperour hath no Son, and now is old,
Old, and lascivious, and from *Rome* retir'd
To Capreae an Island small but strong
On the *Campanian* shore, with purpose there
His horrid lusts in private to enjoy,
Committing to a wicked Favourite
All publick cares, and yet of him suspicious,
Hated of all, and hating; with what ease
Indu'd with Regal Vertues as thou art,
Appearing, and beginning noble deeds,
Might'st thou expel this monster from his Throne
Now made a stye, and in his place ascending
A victor, people free from servile yoke?
And with my help thou may'st; to me the power
Is given, and by that right I give it thee.
Aaim therefore at no less then all the world,
Aim at the highest, without the highest attain'd
Will be for thee no sitting, or not long
On *David's* Throne, be propheci'd what will.

From John Milton, *Paradise Regained,* Book IV, lines 25–108.

2.

Rise up, thou monstrous ant-hill on the plain
Of a too busy world! Before me flow,
Thou endless stream of men and moving things!
Thy every-day appearance, as it strikes—
With wonder heightened, or sublimed by awe—
On strangers, of all ages; the quick dance
Of colours, lights, and forms; the deafening din;

The comers and the goers face to face,
Face after face; the string of dazzling wares,
Shop after shop, with symbols, blazoned names,
And all the tradesman's honours overhead:
Here, fronts of houses, like a title-page,
With letters huge inscribed from top to toe,
Stationed above the door, like guardian saints;
There, allegoric shapes, female or male,
Or physiognomies of real men,
Land-warriors, kings, or admirals of the sea,
Boyle, Shakspeare, Newton, or the attractive head
Of some quack-doctor, famous in his day.

    Meanwhile the roar continues, till at length,
Escaped as from an enemy, we turn
Abruptly into some sequestered nook,
Still as a sheltered place when winds blow loud!
At leisure, thence, through tracts of thin resort,
And sights and sounds that come at intervals,
We take our way. A raree-show is here,
With children gathered round; another street
Presents a company of dancing dogs,
Or dromedary, with an antic pair
Of monkeys on his back; a minstrel band
Of Savoyards; or, single and alone,
An English ballad-singer. Private courts,
Gloomy as coffins, and unsightly lanes
Thrilled by some female vendor's scream, belike
The very shrillest of all London cries,
May then entangle our impatient steps;
Conducted through those labyrinths, unawares,
To privileged regions and inviolate,
Where from their airy lodges studious lawyers
Look out on waters, walks, and gardens green.

    Thence back into the throng, until we reach,
Following the tide that slackens by degrees,
Some half-frequented scenes, where wider streets
Bring straggling breezes of suburban air.
Here files of ballads dangle from dead walls;
Advertisements, of giant-size, from high
Press forward, in all colours, on the sight;
These, bold in conscious merit, lower down;
That, fronted with a most imposing word,
Is, peradventure, one in masquerade.

As on the broadening causeway we advance,
Behold, turned upwards, a face hard and strong
In lineaments, and red with over-toil.
'T is one encountered here and everywhere;
A travelling cripple, by the trunk cut short,
And stumping on his arms. In sailor's garb
Another lies at length, beside a range
Of well-formed characters, with chalk inscribed
Upon the smooth flat stones: the Nurse is here,
The Bachelor, that loves to sun himself,
The military Idler, and the Dame,
That field-ward takes her walk with decent steps.

    Now homeward through the thickening hubbub, where
See, among less distinguishable shapes,
The begging scavenger, with hat in hand;
The Italian, as he thrids his way with care,
Steadying, far-seen, a frame of images
Upon his head; with basket at his breast
The Jew; the stately and slow-moving Turk,
With freight of slippers piled beneath his arm!

    Enough;—the mighty concourse I surveyed
With no unthinking mind, well pleased to note
Among the crowd all specimens of man,
Through all the colours which the sun bestows,
And every character of form and face:
The Swede, the Russian; from the genial south,
The Frenchman and the Spaniard; from remote
America, the Hunter-Indian; Moors,
Malays, Lascars, the Tartar, the Chinese,
And Negro Ladies in white muslin gowns.

From William Wordsworth, *The Prelude*, Book VII, lines 149–228.

3.

"REDRIFF"

Or
    did he make the estuary?
was the Cant smiling
    and the Knock smooth?
Did our Tidal Father bear him

by Lower Hope to Half Reach?
Did he berth in the Greenland or was she moored
in the Pool?
Did he tie up across the water
or did she toss at the Surrey shore?
Had he business at Dockhead?
Did he sign Tom Bowline on:
ord-in-ary-seaman
in place of the drownded Syro-Phoenician?
Did he bespeak
of Eb Bradshaw, Princes Stair:
listed replacement of sheaves to the running-blocks, new dead-eyes to
the standing shrouds, some spare hearts for the stays, a heavy repair
in the chains, some nice work up at the hound
. . . would he expedite.
It 'ld be well worth his while—for a tidy consideration could she have
preference—for she must weigh on time or the dues 'ld ruin 'em—would
he, for once, oil an elbow—would he please to hustle the job—and not
so over nice with the finish.
Not for a gratis load of the sound teak in
Breaker's Yard
and that we could well do with.
Not for a dozen cords of Norweyan, red nor yaller, paid for, carried and
stacked.
Not for a choice of the best float of Oregon in the mast-pond.
Not for as many cubic fathoms of best Indies lignum vitae as 'ld stock
us till we re-sheave the blocks for master-bargees playing the Styx.
Not for a pickin' of all the bonded stuffs passed over the quays in a full
working week between the Bridge and Battlebridge Stairs[1]
and there's a tidy jorum
to pile a mint in sterling—to rig out Ann my wife like Suky Tawdry.
Not at the price of half the freights, felled of the living wood, a lent
o' tides, brings to all the wharves, from here round to the Royal Vi't'lin',
when Prosperpine unbinds the Baltic.[2]
Not if he signed me fair a note of hand for all the gold on his fleece.
· Nor for this port's authorities
and I'm a citizen.

---

[1] That is to say on the Surrey shore between London Bridge and the
waterstairs called Battlebridge Stairs east of Hays Wharf. Warehouses set
aside for goods in bond being situated between these two points.

[2] The Rotherhithe timber-trade was particularly brisk in the spring when
the ice melted and freed the ships in the Baltic. The victualling yard is at
Deptford.

Not if the Trinity Brethren
                    and Clemens himself[3]
stood caps in hand for a month of Sundays
                    and them I must needs respect.
Not if the Holy Ghost made ready to blow on his mainsail.
Nor for a boozed Murphy's bull in curial-cursive and leaded from the
scarlet pontiff o' the West.
And, as for next Thor's Day's night tide
                    tell the Wop, to-go-to
                          Canute
if he can find him
                    down at the Galley Wall[4]
(though he's many times before *his* time).
But tell him:
                    we scamp no repairs here; no botched Riga deal nor wood
that's all American, softs nor hards, hewn or sawn, heart n'r sap, cis- or
trans- Gangem-land teak, or fair-grained *ulmus* from sylvan wester lands
or goodish East Mark oak via Fiume in British bottoms
                    let alone
heart of island-grown
                    seasoned in m'neighbour's yard
leaves this bench.
But
     tell him
tell him from me
                    if he waits his turn an' damps down his Sicily sulphur[5]
we'll spokeshave those deadeyes for him as smooth as a *peach* of a
cheek
                    we'll fay that hounding trim and proper—and of the best

---

[3] St. Clement of Alexandria is the patron saint of Trinity House—because
of the Pharos at Alexandria? I do not know, perhaps some reader may.

[4] The allusion is to the Galley Wall Road district in Rotherhithe. The
name is associated locally with an event described in *The Anglo-Saxon
Chroncile*, under the year 1016: 'Then came the ships to Greenwich and
within a little space they went to London and they dug a great ditch on the
south side and dragged their ships to the west side of the bridge. . . .' (trans.
Bohn edtn 1849). This association between Canute's galleys and this street-
name was, at all events, the popular tradition in my mother's girlhood (in the
late eighteen-seventies) and was the opinion of Canon Beck of Rotherhithe
church. 'Canute's Ditch', as it was called, was believed to run from near
where Greenland Dock now is and to join the Thames again in Walworth:
its actual siting is disputed.

[5] Apart from timber from the Baltic and elsewhere, the Rotherhithe docks
in the last century received large cargoes of sulphur from Palermo and other
Mediterranean ports.

spruce,[6] to rhyme with her mainmast, we'll square true and round to a
nicety the double piercin's o' that cap— and of keel-elm.

 If he leaves it to us
we'll fix him dandy.
But tell him—with respects from me
tell him—tell the old Jason:

 As sure as I was articled, had I the job of mortisin' the beams
to which was lashed and roved the Fault in all of us, I'ld take m' time
and set that aspen transom square to the Rootless Tree

 or dash m' buttons!

 ... he's got
till the Day o' Doom
to sail the bitter seas o' the world!

---

 [6] Cf. 'a nyew mayne mast of spruce with a nyew staye hounsyd and
skarvyd with the same wood whyche mast ys of length from the Hounse to
the step 25 yards' (1532) O.E.D., under 'hound'.

THE HEROIC IDEAL

The hero is one who is supremely gifted. Strength or beauty, intelligence or will, position or resources, any mark which sets a man apart from men may make a hero of him if he uses it properly. And there lies the rub. What is this "proper" use of the extraordinary gift? Is it to magnify one's own being and, indirectly, to celebrate that god whose special favor is so evident in the hero's person and position? Or is it to secure the well-being of a people rather than the reputation of an individual or a god? Sidney Hook puts it succinctly that the hero is one who saves us. From the other end of time the poet Homer sides with the modern historian Hook:

> Why on these shores are we with joy survey'd,
> Admired as heros, and as Gods obey'd
> Unless great acts superior merit prove,
> And vindicate the bounteous Powers above?
> Iliad, Book XII.

If Pope's eighteenth-century translation gives too Tory an accent to Homer's epic voice, listen to the recent Lattimore translation opting for the same functional aristocracy of heroes:

> Therefore it is our duty in the forefront of the Lykians
> to take our stand, and bear our part of the blazing of battle.
> Iliad, Book XII.

But the same Homer who hymns this "duty" also imagines Odysseus, the most profound embodiment in our culture of this clash between private honor and public responsibility within the heroic ideal. Attracted by Circe as well as Penelope, torn between Ithaca and adventure, Odysseus has worried his way through the centuries as the father, par excellence, who knows best—and farthest. That he has had so many lives in so many imaginations, including his own, bears certain witness to the fact that such questions as "What is a hero?" and "What is Odysseus?" are nearly synonymous. A glimpse of a few of these lives may illuminate the nature of the hero better than our abstractions can.

1.

My glory has departed now, yet I think you will still be able to see by the stubble what the harvest was like. Since then I have been overwhelmed by troubles, but in the old days Ares and Athene had endowed me generously with the daring that sweeps all before it; and when it came to planning a bold stroke against the enemy and I had picked my men for an ambush, my ardent spirits were never dashed by any foreboding of death, but I would leap out before all the rest and cut down with my spear any foeman who was slower on his feet than I. That was the kind of man I was in battle. But I did not like work, nor the domestic pursuits that make for a fine family. What I always loved was a ship with oars, and fighting, and polished javelins and arrows—terrible things, which make other people shudder. I suppose that in making such a choice I just followed my natural bent, for different men take kindly to very different ways of earning a living.

From Homer, *The Odyssey*, Book XIV, as translated by E. V. Rieu (Baltimore: Penguin Books, 1961). Reprinted by permission.

2.

After the *Returns* comes the *Odyssey* of Homer, and then the *Telegony* in two books by Eugammon of Cyrene, which contain the following matters. The suitors of Penelope are buried by their kinsmen, and Odysseus, after sacrificing to the Nymphs, sails to Elis to inspect his herds. He is entertained there by Polyxenus and receives a mixing bowl as a gift; the story of Trophonius and Agamedes and Augeas then follows. He next sails back to Ithaca and performs the sacrifices ordered by Teiresias, and then goes to Thesprotis where he marries Callidice, queen of the Thesprotians. A war then breaks out between the Thesprotians, led by Odysseus, and the Brygi. Ares routs the army of Odysseus and Athena engages with Ares, until Apollo separates them. After the death of Callidice Polypoetes, the son of Odysseus, succeeds to the kingdom, while Odysseus himself returns to Ithaca. In the meantime Telegonus, while travelling in search of his father, lands on Ithaca and ravages the island: Odysseus comes out to defend his country, but is killed by his son unwittingly. Telegonus, on learning his mistake, transports his father's body with Penelope and Telemachus to his mother's island, where Circe makes them immortal, and Telegonus marries Penelope, and Telemachus Circe.

From Proclus, *Chrestomathy* as translated by H. G. Evelyn-White, *Hesiod, the Homeric Hymns and Homerica* (Cambridge, Massachusetts: Loeb Classical Library and Harvard University Press, 1959). Reprinted by permission of the publisher.

3.

Upon the bridge I forward bent to look,
And grasp'd a flinty mass, or else had fall'n,

Though push'd not from the height. The guide, who
    mark'd
How I did gaze attentive, thus began:
"Within these ardours are the spirits, each
Swath'd in confining fire."—"Master, thy word,"
I answer'd, "hath assur'd me; yet I deem'd
Already of the truth, already wish'd
To ask thee, who is in yon fire, that comes
So parted at the summit, as it seem'd
Ascending from that funeral pile, where lay
The Theban brothers?" He replied: "Within
Ulysses there and Diomede endure
Their penal tortures, thus to vengeance now
Together hasting, as erewhile to wrath.
These in the flame with ceaseless groans deplore
The ambush of the horse, that open'd wide
A portal for that goodly seed to pass,
Which sow'd imperial Rome; nor less the guile
Lament they, whence of her Achilles 'reft
Deidamia yet in death complains.
And there is rued the stratagems, that Troy
Of her Palladium spoil'd."—"If they have power
Of utt'rance from within these sparks," said I,
"O master! think my prayer a thousand fold
In repetition urg'd, that thou vouchsafe
To pause, till here the horned flame arrive.
See, how toward it with desire I bend."
    He thus: "Thy prayer is worthy of much praise,
And I accept it therefore: but do thou
Thy tongue refrain: to question them be mine,
For I divine thy wish: and they perchance,
For they were Greeks, might shun discourse with thee."
    When there the flame had come, where time and place
Seem'd fitting to my guide, he thus began:
"O ye, who dwell two spirits in one fire!
If living I of you did merit aught,
Whate'er the measure were of that desert,
When in the world my lofty strain I pour'd,
Move ye not on, till one of you unfold
In what clime death o'ertook him self-destroy'd."
    Of the old flame forthwith the greater horn
Began to roll, murmuring, as a fire
That labours with the wind, then to and fro
Wagging the top, as a tongue uttering sounds,
Threw out its voice, and spake: "When I escap'd

From Circe, who beyond a circling year
Had held me near Caieta, by her charms,
Ere thus Aeneas yet had nam'd the shore,
Nor fondness for my son, nor reverence
Of my old father, nor return of love,
That should have crown'd Penelope with joy,
Could overcome in me the zeal I had
T' explore the world, and search the ways of life,
Man's evil and his virtue. Forth I sail'd
Into the deep illimitable main,
With but one bark, and the small faithful band
That yet cleav'd to me. As Iberia far,
Far as Morocco either shore I saw,
And the Sardinian and each isle beside
Which round that ocean bathes. Tardy with age
Were I and my companions, when we came
To the strait pass, where Hercules ordain'd
The bound'ries not to be o'erstepp'd by man.
The walls of Seville to my right I left,
On the' other hand already Ceuta past.
' O brothers!' I began, who to the west
' Through perils without number now have reach'd,
' To this the short remaining watch, that yet
' Our senses have to wake, refuse not proof
' Of the unpeopled world, following the track
' Of Phoebus. Call to mind from whence we sprang:
' Ye were not form'd to live the life of brutes,
' But virtue to pursue and knowledge high.'
With these few words I sharpen'd for the voyage
The mind of my associates, that I then
Could scarcely have withheld them. To the dawn
Our poop we turn'd, and for the witless flight
Made our oars wings, still gaining on the left.
Each star of the' other pole night now beheld,
And ours so low, that from the ocean-floor
It rose not. Five times re-illum'd, as oft
Vanish'd the light from underneath the moon
Since the deep way we enter'd, when from far
Appear'd a mountain dim, loftiest methought
Of all I e'er beheld. Joy seiz'd us straight,
But soon to mourning changed. From the new land
A whirlwind sprung, and at her foremost side
Did strike the vessel. Thrice it whirl'd her round
With all the waves, the fourth time lifted up

The poop, and sank the prow: so fate decreed:
And over us the booming billow clos'd."

From Dante, *Hell*, Canto XXVI, lines 44–135 as translated by H. F. Cary
(1772–1844).

4.

"ULYSSES"

It little profits that an idle king,
By this still hearth, among these barren crags,
Match'd with an aged wife, I mete and dole
Unequal laws unto a savage race,
That hoard, and sleep, and feed, and know not me.
I cannot rest from travel: I will drink
Life to the lees: all times I have enjoy'd
Greatly, have suffer'd greatly, both with those
That loved me, and alone; on shore, and when
Thro' scudding drifts the rainy Hyades
Vext the dim sea: I am become a name;
For always roaming with a hungry heart
Much have I seen and known; cities of men
And manners, climates, councils, governments,
Myself not least, but honor'd of them all;
And drunk delight of battle with my peers,
Far on the ringing plains of windy Troy.
I am a part of all that I have met;
Yet all experience is an arch wherethro'
Gleams that untravell'd world, whose margin fades
For ever and for ever when I move.
Now dull it is to pause, to make an end,
To rust unburnish'd not to shine in use!
As tho' to breathe were life. Life piled on life
Were all too little, and of one to me
Little remains, but every hour is saved
From that eternal silence, something more,
A bringer of new things: and vile it were
For some three suns to store and hoard myself,
And this gray spirit yearning in desire
To follow knowledge like a sinking star,
Beyond the utmost bound of human thought.
This is my son, mine own Telemachus,
To whom I leave the sceptre and the isle—

Well-loved of me, discerning to fulfil
This labor, by slow prudence to make mild
A rugged people, and thro' soft degrees
Subdue them to the useful and the good.
Most blameless is he, centred in the sphere
Of common duties, decent not to fail
In offices of tenderness, and pay
Meet adoration to my household gods,
When I am gone. He works his work, I mine.
  There lies the port; the vessel puffs her sail:
There gloom the dark broad seas. My mariners,
Souls that have toil'd, and wrought, and thought with me—
That ever with a frolic welcome took
The thunder and the sunshine, and opposed
Free hearts, free foreheads—you and I are old;
Old age hath yet his honor and his toil;
Death closes all: but something ere the end,
Some work of noble note, may yet be done,
Not unbecoming men that strove with Gods.
The lights begin to twinkle from the rocks:
The long day wanes: the slow moon climbs: the deep
Moans round with many voices. Come, my friends,
'Tis not too late to seek a newer world.
Push off, and sitting well in order smite
The sounding furrows; for my purpose holds
To sail beyond the sunset, and the baths
Of all the western stars, until I die.
It may be that the gulfs will wash us down:
It may be we shall touch the Happy Isles,
And see the great Achilles, whom we knew.
Tho' much is taken, much abides; and tho'
We are not now that strength which in old days
Moved earth and heaven; that which we are, we are;
One equal temper of heroic hearts,
Made weak by time and fate, but strong in will
To strive, to seek, to find, and not to yield.

From Alfred, Lord Tennyson, *Poems* (1842).

5.

'What gain with Odysseus,
'They that died in the whirlpool
'And after many vain labours,

'Living by stolen meat, chained to the rowingbench,
'That he should have a great fame
            'And lie by night with the goddess?
'Their names are not written in bronze
            'Nor their rowing sticks set with Elpenor's;
'Nor have they mound by sea-bord.
            'That saw never the olives under Spartha
'With the leaves green and then not green,
            'The click of light in their branches;
'That saw not the bronze hall nor the ingle
'Nor lay there with the queen's waiting maids,
'Nor had they Circle to couch-mate, Circle Titania,
'Nor had they meats of Kalüpso
'Or her silk skirts brushing their thighs.
'Give! What were they given?
                              Ear-wax.
'Poison and ear-wax,
                    and a salt grave by the bull-field,
'*neson amumona*, their heads like sea crows in the foam,
'Black splotches, sea-weed under lightning;
'Canned beef of Apollo, ten cans for a boat load.'

From *The Cantos of Ezra Pound*. Copyright 1934, 1948 by Ezra Pound. Reprinted by permission of New Direction, Publishers.

6.

"ULYSSES"

To the much-tossed Ulysses, never done
    With woman whether gowned as wife or whore,
Penelope and Circe seemed as one:
She like a whore made his lewd fancies run,
    And wifely she a hero to him bore.

Their counter-changings terrified his way:
    They were the clashing rocks, Symplegades,
Scylla and Charybdis too were they;
Now they were storms frosting the sea with spray
    And now the lotus island's drunken ease.

They multiplied into the Sirens' throng,
    Forewarned by fear of whom he stood bound fast
Hand and foot helpless to the vessel's mast,
    Yet would not stop his ears: daring their song
    He groaned and sweated till that shore was past.

One, two and many: flesh had made him blind,
  Flesh had one pleasure only in the act,
Flesh set one purpose only in the mind—
Triumph of flesh and afterwards to find
  Still those same terrors wherewith flesh was racked.

His wiles were witty and his fame far known,
Every king's daughter sought him for her own,
  Yet he was nothing to be won or lost.
  All lands to him were Ithaca: love-tossed
He loathed the fraud, yet would not bed alone.

From Robert Graves, *Collected Poems*, Copyright 1955 International Authors, N.V. (Garden City, New York: Doubleday, 1955). Reprinted by permission of International Authors, N.V.

A DIFFICULT AGE FOR EPIC

Our century has not proven conspicuously fertile ground for the epic. We moderns would not appear to be equal to its strenuous demands, or is the form not equal to our age? Is the epic the brontosaurus or, perhaps more aptly, the tyrannosaurus rex of poetry, and like these outmoded lizards too large or too violent to live? The question is not merely academic. Its implications are extensive and serious, for if we in the twentieth century have failed in our epic ambitions, we still yearn for the epic and our passion is not always either intelligent or disinterested. For example, the warrior hero, draw him as barbarously simple as you like, has proven again and again that he can attract, hold, and move the modern mind. Nazi Germany dusted off the armour of Siegfried and Gunther and arranged for the setting up of its Ordensburgen before it built the Tiger Tank. And Russia, faced with the onslaught of these unholy knights, commissioned Eisenstein to film not the heroic image of new Soviet man but of Czar Ivan and Boyar Alexander Nevsky.

If even these ghosts can live and walk again in this our modern air, then why not a new and whole epic figure conceived for our time and of it? Surprisingly, every age has asked the same question and given almost the same answer. Does this sad chorus suggest that the epic has been a long time adying—or that epic has always been both desirable and difficult? Perhaps we should listen to several of these complaints.

1.

This straunge knight that cam thus sodeynly,
Al armed sauf his heed ful richely,
Salued the kyng and queen, and lordes alle
By ordre, as they seten into halle,
With so heigh reverens and observaunce,
As wel in speche as in contynaunce,
That Gaweyn with his olde curtesys,
They he were come agein out of fayrye,
Ne couthe him nought amende with no word.

From Geoffrey Chaucer, "The Squire's Tale," lines 89–97.

Her is the revel and the jolyte,
That is not able a dul man to devyse;
He most have knowe love and his servise,
And ben a festly man, as freisch as May,
That schulde you devyse such array.
Who couthe telle you the forme of daunce
So uncouth, and so freische countinaunce,
Such subtil lokyng of dissimilynges,
For drede of jalous folk apparceyvynges?
No man but Launcolet, and he is deed.

From Geoffrey Chaucer, "The Squire's Tale," lines 278–287.

2.

And thus hit passed on frome Candylmas untyll [after] Ester, that the moneth of May was com, whan every lusty harte begynnyth to blossom and to burgyne. For, lyke as trees and erbys burgenyth and florysshyth in May, in lyke wyse every lusty harte that ys ony maner of lover spryngith, burgenyth, buddyth, and florysshyth in lusty dedis. For hit gyvyth unto all lovers corrayge, that lusty moneth of May, in somthynge to constrayne hym to som maner of thynge more than in ony other monethe, for dyverce causys: for than all erbys and treys renewyth a man and woman, and in lyke wyse lovers callyth to their mynde olde jantylnes and olde servyse, and many kynde dedes that was forgotyn by neclygence.

For, lyke as wynter rasure dothe allway arace and deface grene summer, so faryth hit by unstable love in man and woman, for in many persones there ys no stabylité: for [w]e may se all day, for a lytyll blaste of wyntres rasure, anone we shall deface and lay aparte trew love, for lytyll or nowght, that coste muche thynge. Thys ys no wysedome nother no stabylité, but hit ys fyeblenes of nature and grete disworshyp, whosomever usyth thys.

Therefore, lyke as May moneth flowryth and floryshyth in every mannes gardyne, so in lyke wyse lat every man of worshyp florysh hys herte in thys worlde: firste unto God, and nexte unto the joy of them that he promysed hys feythe unto; for there was never worshypfull man nor worshypfull woman but they loved one bettir than another; and worshyp in armys may never be foyled. But firste reserve the honoure to God, and secundely they quarell muste com of thy lady. And such love I calle vertuouse love.

But nowadayes men cannat love sevennyght but they muste have all their desyres. That love may nat endure by reson, for where they bethe sone accorded and hasty, heete sone keelyth. And ryght so faryth the love nowadayes, sone hote sone colde. Thys ys no stabylyté. But the olde love was nat so. For men and women coude love togydirs seven yerys, and no lycoures lustis was betwyxte them, and than was love, trouthe and faythefulnes. And so in lyke wyse was used such love in kynge Arthurs dayes.

Wherefore I lykken love nowadayes unto sommer and wynter: for, lyke as the tone ys colde and the othir ys hote, so faryth love nowadayes. And therefore all ye that be lovers, calle unto youre remembraunce the monethe of May, lyke as ded quene Gwenyver, for whom I make here a lytyll mencion, that whyle she lyved she was at trew lover, and therefore she had a good ende.

From *The Works of Sir Thomas Malory*, edited by Eugéne Vinaver (New York: Oxford University Press, 1954). Reprinted by permission.

3.

No more of talk where God or Angel Guest
With Man, as with his Friend, familiar us'd
To sit indulgent, and with him partake
Rural repast, permitting him the while
Venial discourse unblam'd: I now must change
Those Notes to Tragic; foul distrust, and breach
Disloyal on the part of Man, revolt,
And disobedience: On the part of Heav'n
Now alienated, distance and distaste,
Anger and just rebuke, and judgement giv'n,
That brought into this World a world of woe,
Sinne and her shadow Death, and Miserie
Deaths Harbinger: Sad task, yet argument
Not less but more Heroic than the wrauth
Of stern *Achilles* on his Foe pursu'd
Thrice Fugitive about *Troy* Wall; or rage
Of *Turnus* for *Lavinia* disespous'd,
Or *Neptun's* ire or *Juno's,* that so long
Perplex'd the *Greek* and *Cytherea's* Son;
If answerable style I can obtaine
Of my Celestial Patroness, who deignes
Her nightly visitation unimplor'd,
And dictates to me slumbering, or inspires
Easie my unpremeditated Verse:
Since first this Subject for Heroic Song
Pleas'd me long choosing, and beginning late;
Not sedulous by Nature to indite
Warrs, hitherto the onely Argument
Heroic deem'd, chief maistrie to dissect

With long and tedious havoc fabl'd Knights
In Battles feign'd; the better fortitude
Of Patience and Heroic Martyrdom
Unsung; or to describe Races and Games,
Or tilting Furniture, emblazon'd Shields,
Impresses quaint, Caparisons and Steeds;
Bases and tinsel Trappings, gorgious Knights
At Joust and Torneament; then marshal'd Feast
Serv'd up in Hall with Sewers, and Seneshals;
The skill of Artifice or Office mean,
Not that which justly gives Heroic name
To Person or to Poem: Mee of these
Nor skilld nor studious, higher Argument
Remaines, sufficient of it self to raise
That name, unless an age too late, or cold
Climat, or Years damp my intended wing
Deprest, and much they may, if all be mine,
Not Hers who brings it nightly to my Ear.

From John Milton, *Paradise Lost*, Book IX, lines 1–47.

4.

"LONDON, 1802"

Milton! thou shouldst be living at this hour:
England hath need of thee: she is a fen
Of stagnant waters: altar, sword, and pen,
Fireside, the heroic wealth of hall and bower,
Have forfeited their ancient English dower
Of inward happiness. We are selfish men;
Oh! raise us up, return to us again;
And give us manners, virtue, freedom, power.
Thy soul was like a Star, and dwelt apart;
Thou hadst a voice whose sound was like the sea:
Pure as the naked heavens, majestic, free,
So didst thou travel on life's common way,
In cheerful godliness; and yet thy heart
The lowliest duties on herself did lay.

From William Wordsworth, *Sonnets Dedicated to National Independence
and Liberty.*

5.

A poet in our times is a semi-barbarian in a civilized community. He lives in the days that are past. His ideas, thoughts, feelings, associations, are all with barbarous manners, obsolete customs, and exploded superstitions. The march of his intellect is like that of a crab, backward. The brighter the light diffused around him by the progress of reason, the thicker is the darkness of antiquated barbarism, in which he buries himself like a mole, to throw up the barren hillocks of his Cimmerian labours. The philosophic mental tranquillity which looks round with an equal eye on all external things, collects a store of ideas, discriminates their relative value, assigns to all their proper place, and from the materials of useful knowledge thus collected, appreciated, and arranged, forms new combinations that impress the stamp of their power and utility on the real business of life, is diametrically the reverse of that frame of mind which poetry inspires, or from which poetry can emanate. The highest inspirations of poetry are resolvable into three ingredients: the rant of unregulated passion, the whine of exaggerated feeling, and the cant of factitious sentiment: and can therefore serve only to ripen a splendid lunatic like Alexander, a puling driveller like Werter, or a morbid dreamer like Wordsworth. It can never make a philosopher, nor a statesman, nor in any class of life an useful or rational man. It cannot claim the slightest share in any one of the comforts and utilities of life of which we have witnessed so many and so rapid advances. But though not useful, it may be said it is highly ornamental, and deserves to be cultivated for the pleasure it yields. Even if this be granted, it does not follow that a writer of poetry in the present state of society is not a waster of his own time, and a robber of that of others. Poetry is not one of those arts which, like painting, require repetition and multiplication, in order to be diffused among society. There are more good poems already existing than are sufficient to employ that portion of life which any mere reader and recipient of poetical impressions should devote to them, and these having been produced in poetical times, are far superior in all the characteristics of poetry to the artificial reconstructions of a few morbid ascetics in unpoetical times. To read the promiscuous rubbish of the present time to the exclusion of the select treasures of the past, is to substitute the worse for the better variety of the same mode of enjoyment.

But in whatever degree poetry is cultivated, it must necessarily be to the neglect of some branch of useful study: and it is a lamentable spectacle to see minds, capable of better things, running to seed in the specious indolence of these empty aimless mockeries of intellectual exertion. Poetry was the mental rattle that awakened the attention of intellect in the infancy of civil society: but for the maturity of mind to make a serious business of the playthings of its childhood, is as absurd as for a full-grown man to rub his gums with coral, and cry to be charmed to sleep by the jingle of silver bells.

As to that small portion of our contemporary poetry, which is neither descriptive, nor narrative, nor dramatic, and which, for want of a better name, may be called ethical, the most distinguished portion of it, consisting merely of querulous, egotistical rhapsodies, to express the writer's high dissatisfaction with the world and every thing in it, serves only to conform what has been said of the semi-barbarous character of poets, who from singing dithyrambics and "Io Triumphe," while society was savage, grow rabid, and out of their element, as it becomes polished and enlightened.

Now when we consider that it is not to the thinking and studious, and scientific and philosophical part of the community, not to those whose minds are bent on the pursuit and promotion of permanently useful ends and aims, that poets must address their minstrelsy, but to that much larger portion of the reading public, whose minds are not awakened to the desire of valuable knowledge, and who are indifferent to any thing beyond being charmed, moved, excited, affected, and exalted: charmed by harmony, moved by sentiment, excited by passion, affected by pathos, and exalted by sublimity: harmony, which is language on the rack of Procrustes; sentiment, which is canting egotism in the mask of refined feeling; passion, which is the commotion of a weak and selfish mind; pathos, which is the whining of an unmanly spirit; and sublimity, which is the inflation of an empty head: when we consider that the great and permanent interests of human society become more and more the main spring of intellectual pursuit; that in proportion as they become so, the subordinacy of the ornamental to the useful will be more and more seen and asknowledged; and that therefore the progress of useful art and science, and of moral and political knowledge, will continue more and more to withdraw attention from frivolous and unconducive, to solid and conducive studies: that therefore the poetical audience will not only continually diminish in the proportion of its number to that of the rest of the reading public, but will also sink lower and lower in the comparison of intellectual acquirement: when we consider that the poet must still please his audience, and must therefore continue to sink to their level, while the rest of the community is rising above it: we may easily conceive that the day is not distant, when the degraded state of every species of poetry will be as generally recognized as that of dramatic poetry has long been: and this not from any decrease either of intellectual power, or intellectual acquisition, but because intellectual power and intellectual acquisition have turned themselves into other and better channels, and have abandoned the cultivation and the fate of poetry to the degenerate fry of modern rhymesters, and their olympic judges, the magazine critics, who continue to debate and promulgate oracles about poetry, as if it were still what it was in the Homeric age, the all-in-all of intellectual progression, and as if there were no such things in existence as mathematicians, astronomers, chemists, moralists, metaphysicians, historians, politicians, and political economists, who have built into the upper air of intelligence a pyramid, from the summit of which they see the modern Parnassus far beneath them, and, knowing how small a place it occupies in the comprehensiveness of their prospect, smile at the little ambition and the circumscribed perceptions with which the drivellers and mountebanks upon it are contending for the poetical palm and the critical chair.

From Thomas Love Peacock, "The Four Ages of Poetry," *Prose of the Romantic Period*, edited by Carl R. Woodring (Boston: Houghton Mifflin Company, 1961). Reprinted by permission.

6.

We are, in our society of today, very far removed from those culture-phases where the poet was explicitly and by profession the custodian, rememberer, embodier and voice of the mythus, etc., of some contained group of families, or of a tribe, nation, people, cult. But we can, perhaps, diagnose something that appears as a constant in poetry by the following consideration:

When rulers seek to impose a new order upon any such group belonging to one or other of those more primitive culture-phases, it is necessary for those rulers to take into account the influence of the poets as recalling something loved and as embodying an ethos inimical to the imposition of that new order. Whether the policy adopted is one of suppression or of some kind of patronage, a recognition of possible danger dictates the policy in either case. Leaving aside such political considerations as may cause such recognition under such circumstances, we may still recognize the 'dangerous' element. Poetry is to be diagnosed as 'dangerous' because it evokes and recalls, is a kind of *anamnesis* of i.e. is an effective recalling of, something loved. In that sense it is inevitably 'propaganda', in that any real formal expression propagands the reality which caused those forms and their content to be. There are also to be considered the contingent and more remote associations which those forms and their content may evoke. There is a sense in which *Barbara Allen* is many times more 'propagandist' than *Rule Britannia*. The more real the thing, the more it will confound their politics. If the dog-rose moves something in the Englishman at a deeper level than the Union Flag it is not only because of the fragile and peculiar beauty of that flower, but also because the poetry of England, drawing upon the intrinsic qualities of the familiar and common June rose, has, by the single image of a rose, managed to recall and evoke, for the English, a June-England association. The first concept being altogether and undeniably lovely, the other also must be lovely! A very satisfactory conclusion. The magic works. But it might prove most adverse magic to an opponent of the thing, idea or complex of sentiments which the word 'England' is patient of comprising.

The problems that confront the poet, as poet, in any given cultural or civilization phase, no matter what his subjective attitude toward those problems, and though they concern only such elusive matters as the validity of a word, are themselves as objective as is the development of the aero-engine, the fact that my great-uncle William served in the ranks in the Crimea, that the tree outside the window happens to be an acacia, that field-archaeology has changed some of the accents of, e.g., Biblical criticism, that an extension of state-control characterizes the period in which we now live, or that something analogous to that extension is remarked by students of the period of Valens and Valentinian, and that like effects may possibly have like causes.

The poet is born into a given historic situation and it follows that his problems—i.e. his problems as a poet—will be what might be called 'situational problems'.

If, owing to a complex of causes, sable-hair brushes, chinese white and hot-pressed water-colour paper went off the market, you would, if you were a user of such commodities, be faced with a situational problem of a very awkward but fundamentally material sort. Whatever the consolation of philosophy, no attitude of mind would bring back to your workroom the required commodities which the market no longer provided. You would willy-nilly suffer an inconvenience. The effect of that inconvenience might be most salutary, might occasion in you a most unsuspected inventiveness. Well, the situational problem which concerns us here is of an equally objective nature, but so far from affecting only the materials of one particular kind of artist, it affects man-the-artist as such, and affects him not at one peripheral point, but crucially. Nevertheless, as with the inconvenienced water-colourist, the 'inconveniences' of our situation may turn out to be, in some respects and for some, 'most salutary'. Indeed there is not wanting evidence that such is the case. And so it is that the present situation presents its own particular difficulties with regard to signs in general and the concept of sign.

The whole complex of these difficulties is primarily felt by the sign-maker, the artist, because for him it is an immediate, day by day, factual problem. He has, somehow or other, to lift up valid signs; that is his specific task.

In practice one of his main problems, one of the matters upon which his judgment is exercised ('The virture of art is to judge') concerns the validity and availability of his images. It is precisely this validity and availability that constitutes his greatest problem in the present culture-situation.

If the poet writes 'wood' what are the chances that the Wood of the Cross will be evoked? Should the answer be 'None', then it would seem that an impoverishment of some sort would have to be admitted. It would mean that that particular word could no longer be used with confidence to implement, to call up or to set in motion a whole world of content belonging in a special sense to the mythus of a particular culture and of concepts and realities belonging to mankind as such. This would be true irrespective of our beliefs or disbeliefs. It would remain true even if we were of the opinion that it was high time that the word 'wood' should be dissociated from the mythus and concepts indicated. The arts abhor any loopings off of meanings or emptyings out, any lessening of the totality of connotation, any loss of recession and thickness through.

If the painter makes visual forms, the content of which is chairs or chair-ishness, what are the chances that those who regard his painting will run to meet him with the notions 'seat', 'throne', 'session', 'cathedra', 'Scone', 'on-the-right-hand-of-the-Father', in mind? If this haphazard list is, in some of its accidents, yours and mine, it nevertheless serves, mutatis mutandis, for Peloponnesians and for Polynesians too.

It is axiomatic that the function of the artist is to make things sub specie aeternitatis.

'He said "What's Time? Leave Now for dogs and apes!
    Man has For ever".'

True, but the works of man, unless they are of 'now' and of 'this place', can have no 'for ever'.

The poet may feel something with regard to Penda the Mercian and nothing with regard to Darius the Mede. In itself that is a limitation, it might be regarded as a disproportion; no matter, there is no help—he must work within the limits of his love. There must be no mugging-up, no 'ought to know' or 'try to feel'; for only what is actually loved and known can be seen sub specie aeternitatis. The muse herself is adamant about this: she is indifferent to what the poet may wish he could feel, she cares only for what he in fact feels. In this she differs totally from her sister, the 'Queen of the Moral Virtues', who, fortunately for us, is concerned only with our will and intention.

This applies to poets, artefacturers of opera of any sort, at any period of human history. But as I see it, we are today so situated that it is pertinent to ask: What for us is patient of being 'actually loved and known', where for us is 'this place', where do we seek or find what is 'ours', what *is* available, what *is* valid as material for our effective signs?

Normally we should not have far to seek: the flowers for the muse's garland would be gathered from the ancestral burial-mound—always and inevitably fecund ground, yielding perennial and familiar blossoms, watered and, maybe, potted, perhaps 'improved', by ourselves. It becomes more difficult when the bulldozers have all but obliterated the mounds, when all that is left of the potting-sheds are the disused hypocausts, and when where was this site and were these foci there is *terra informis*.

To what degree, for instance, is it possible for the 'name' to evoke the 'local habitation' long since gone? I do not raise these questions in order to answer them, for I do not know what the answers may be, but I raise them in order to indicate some of the dilemmas which have been present with me all the time.

When I was a child there was still in vogue the Victorian catch-question 'When is a door not a door?' Today I find that question has gathered to itself unexpected meaning. It has become the keynote of a so to say auto-catechism: When is a door not a door? When is a sign not a sign? When is what was valid no longer valid?

Such questions and attempts to answer them are in part reflected in the preoccupation with the 'abstract' in the visual arts. This preoccupation, whether mistaken or rewarding, is neither whim nor accident but is determined by historic causes affecting all this whole business of sign and what is signified, now-ness and place-ness and loves and validities of many sorts and kinds.

What goes for tinker goes for tailor; and it is worth nothing, for again it is not accidental, that the man who was super-sensitive to the unique and specific possibilities and demands of his own art, should have shown in his attitude toward that art and in that art itself, how analogous are some of the problems that the muse sets for the writer and those she sets for the painter. And further that this artist, while pre-eminently 'contemporary' and indeed 'of the future', was also of all artists the most of site and place. And as for 'the past', as for 'history', it was from the ancestral mound that he fetched his best garlands and Clio ran with him a lot of the way—if under the name of Brigit. So that although most authentically the bard of the shapeless cosmopolis and of the megalopolitan diaspora, he could say

> 'Come ant daunce wyt me
> In Irelaunde'.

In taking Joyce to illustrate the problem I do so because any problem inherent in the arts today, and in particular in that of writing, is illuminated by so doing. Quite irrespective of whether we approve or deprecate his matter or his form or both, Joyce was centrally occupied with the formal problems of art, as exemplified in a particular art and in his own very particular development of that art. It is just such *kinds* of artist who alone illustrate the artistic dilemmas of any age. Hopkins, 'as one born out of due time', but before his time (yet how very much *of* his time!), was just such another. And we know how he, Manley Hopkins, stands over so many later artists, saying, in the words of another and pre-eminent living artist,

'And I Tiresias have foresuffered all'.

And Browning too might well have his say and continue the quotation,

'Enacted on this same divan or bed'.

That bed may indeed seem procrustean, for the artist may be stretched upon it

'Dead from the waist down'

and it is on such a couch that the muse exacts and interrogates, subsequent to

'The fine delight that fathers thought'.

From David Jones, "Preface," *The Anathémata; Fragments of an Attempted Writing* (New York: Chilmark Press), Copyright 1952 by David Jones. Reprinted by permission.

READINGS AND TOPICS

ANTIQUITY

Suggested Readings

1. Erich Auerbach, *Mimesis*. Garden City: Doubleday Anchor Books, 1957 (paperback reprint).
2. C. M. Bowra, *Heroic Poetry*. N.Y.: St. Martin's Press, 1961. London: Macmillan, 1952.
3. —————, *From Virgil to Milton*. N.Y.: St. Martin's, 1961. London: Macmillan, 1945.
4. Albert B. Lord, *The Singer of Tales*. Cambridge: Harvard Univ. Press, 1960.
5. Denys Page, *History and the Homeric Iliad*. Berkeley: U. of Calif. Press, 1959.

Topics for Writing and Discussion

Rhys Carpenter,
Literature Without Letters.

C. M. Bowra,
Homer.

Aristotle,
Tragedy Vs. Epic.

Edith Hamilton,
Enter the Romantic Roman: Virgil.

1. Compare primary and secondary epics.

2. Compare Homer's and Virgil's heroes.

3. Tragedy and epic are often near-allied. Discuss.

THE MIDDLE AGES

Suggested Readings

1. Erich Auerbach, *Scenes from the Drama of European Literature*. N.Y.: Meridian, 1959 (paperback reprint).
2. Arthur Brodeur, *The Art of Beowulf*. Berkeley and Los Angeles: U. of Calif. Press, 1959.
3. Ernst Curtius, *Latin Literature in the European Middle Ages*. N.Y.: Harper Torchbook, 1964 (paperback reprint).
4. Miles Dillon, *Early Irish Poetry*. Univ. of Chicago Press, 1948.
5. W. P. Ker, *Epic and Romance*. N.Y.: Dover, 1957 (paperback reprint).
6. E. M. W. Tillyard, *The English Epic and Its Background*. London: Chatto & Windus, 1954.

Topics for Writing and Discussion

Jan de Vries,
Heroic Song: Siegfried.

1. Compare and contrast pagan and Christian concepts of the epic.

Gilbert Highet,
The Dark Ages: Beowulf.

E. M. W. Tillyard,
Dante.

2. Medieval epic is sad rather than tragic. Discuss.

3. Relate the heroes of classical and Medieval epics.

THE RENAISSANCE

Suggested Readings

1. C. M. Bowra, *From Virgil to Milton.* N.Y.: St. Martin's Press, 1961. London: Macmillan, 1945.
2. C. S. Lewis, *Allegory of Love.* London: Oxford Univ. Press, 1936. N.Y.: Oxford (paperback reprint).
3. —————, *Preface to Paradise Lost.* N.Y.: Oxford Univ. Press, 1961 (paperback reprint).
4. Arnold Stein, *Heroic Knowledge.* Minneapolis: Univ. of Minn. Press, 1957.
5. E. M. W. Tillyard, *Shakespeare's History Plays.* N.Y.: Collier Books, 1962 (paperback reprint).
6. W. B. C. Watkins, *Shakespeare and Spenser.* Cambridge, Mass.: Walker-de Berry, 1961 (paperback reprint).

Topics for Writing and Discussion

Graham Hough,
The Romance Epic.

Joel E. Spingarn,
Renaissance Ideas.

Arnold Stein,
Milton.

1. Spenser learns from the Italians and the Middle Ages. Discuss.

2. Discuss Milton's hero: Satan or Christ?

3. Milton is famous for his catalogs. Discuss.

THE 18th AND 19th CENTURIES

Suggested Readings

1. A. C. Bradley, *Oxford Lectures on Poetry.* Bloomington: Midland Books, 1961 (paperback reprint).
2. D. G. James, *The Romantic Comedy.* London: Oxford, 1963 (paperback reprint).
3. D. Knight, *Pope and the Heroic Tradition.* New Haven: Yale, 1951.
4. H. T. Swedenberg, Jr., "Rules and the English Critics of the Epic," *Studies in Philology,* 35 (1938), 566–587.
5. Ian Watt, *Rise of the Novel.* Los Angeles and Berkeley: Univ. of California, 1960.

Topics for Writing and Discussion

Wimsatt and Brooks,
  Dryden.

Henry Fielding,
  Epic, Comedy, and Prose

Karl Kroeber,
  Wordsworth: The Personal Epic.

Herbert Lindenberger,
  The Possibility of a Long Poem.

1. Although the 18th century struggles to write its own epic, it succeeds in producing three distinct variations, the great translations, the mock epic, and the novel. Discuss each.

2. Discuss the Artist as Hero.

TODAY

Suggested Readings

1. W. H. Auden, The Enchafed Flood. New York: Random House, 1950.
2. Elizabeth Drew, T. S. Eliot: The Design of His Poetry. New York: Scribner's, 1949 (paperback reprint).
3. Northrop Frye, Fables of Identity. New York: Harcourt, Brace & World, 1963 (paperback reprint).
4. Sidney Hook, The Hero in History. Boston: Beacon, 1960 (paperback reprint).
5. R. Wellek and A. Warren, Theory of Literature. New York: Harcourt, Brace & World, 1956 (paperback reprint).

Topics for Writing and Discussion

Northrop Frye,
  Theory of Genres.

Paul Goodman,
  Epical Actions.

Kenneth G. Wilson,
  On Translating Homer.

Elizabeth Sewell,
  The Orphic Voice.

1. Goodman has consciously modeled his criticism on Aristotle's. Compare his treatment of epic with Aristotle's.

2. What has happened to epic?